T0296805

# Designing and Building A Security Operations Center

# Designing and Building A Security Operations Center

**David Nathans**

ELSEVIER

AMSTERDAM • BOSTON • HEIDELBERG • LONDON
NEW YORK • OXFORD • PARIS • SAN DIEGO
SAN FRANCISCO • SINGAPORE • SYDNEY • TOKYO

SYNGRESS.

Syngress is an Imprint of Elsevier

Acquiring Editor: Steve Elliot
Editorial Project Manager: Benjamin Rearick
Project Manager: Paul Prasad Chandramohan
Designer: Matthew Limbert

Syngress is an imprint of Elsevier
225 Wyman Street, Waltham, MA 02451, USA

**Notice**
Knowledge and best practice in this field are constantly changing. As new research and
experience broaden our understanding, changes in research methods, professional practices,
or medical treatment may become necessary.

Practitioners and researchers must always rely on their own experience and knowledge
in evaluating and using any information, methods, compounds, or experiments described
herein. In using such information or methods they should be mindful of their own safety
and the safety of others, including parties for whom they have a professional responsibility.

To the fullest extent of the law, neither the Publisher nor the authors, contributors, or
editors, assume any liability for any injury and/or damage to persons or property as a matter
of products liability, negligence or otherwise, or from any use or operation of any methods,
products, instructions, or ideas contained in the material herein.

**British Library Cataloguing-in-Publication Data**
A catalogue record for this book is available from the British Library

**Library of Congress Cataloging-in-Publication Data**
A catalog record for this book is available from the Library of Congress

ISBN: 978-0-12-800899-7

For information on all Syngress publications
visit our website at http://store.elsevier.com/

# Contents

**CHAPTER 3    Infrastructure.......................................................................49**

# Author Biography

David Nathans is a highly sought-after consultant on building enterprise security programs and security operation centers and as a speaker on cyber security for conferences, interest groups, and corporate events. As a former chief information security officer for a large US and international defense contractor, as well as the former global security operations center manager for one of the largest managed security services providers in the world, he has a wealth of network defense, intelligence, cybersecurity, and operations knowledge he now shares. The experiences and lessons learned also stem from his time building enterprise security programs and operations at one of the largest breached retail companies in history as well as working all over the world as a cyber-operations officer in the US Air Force. He is regularly called upon to design and build tactical cybersecurity operations for coalition and joint task force exercises. He has also written and continues to write thought-provoking and informative articles for security magazines, and contributes to industry-specific forums regarding regulations. David also maintains thesocbook.com, this book's companion website.

# Technical Editor Biography

**BRIAN KELLY,** CISSP, CISM, CEH

Chief Information Security Officer, Quinnipiac University, Hamden, Connecticut, USA

Brian Kelly joined Quinnipiac University in September 2006 as the Information Security Officer (ISO). He supports Quinnipiac University's commitment to teaching and collaborating by safeguarding information assets against unauthorized use, disclosure, modification, damage, or loss by developing, implementing, and maintaining methods to provide a secure and stable environment for institutional data and related systems throughout the university.

Brian has diverse experience in information security policy development, awareness training, computer network defense, and regulatory compliance. He provides thought leadership on information security issues across the campus and is a recognized leader in his field.

Brian holds a bachelor's degree from the University of Connecticut and a master's degree from Norwich University. He has served in various leadership roles on the local boards of the ISSA, InfraGard, and HTCIA chapters. Brian is also a retired Air Force Cyber Operations Officer.

# Foreword

The Security Operations Center (the SOC for short), for those companies who have the means to operate their own cyber security organization, is a required central nervous system – a place where all of the sensors, security devices, and personnel report back; the location from which the networks are fought during times of crisis, and the location from which routine day-to-day operations are carried out, standing vigil.

In the past twenty years, I've been involved in the building of several intelligence and analysis or security operations programs. As technical controller and communications watch officer as a young enlisted man to building the early cyber intelligence and analysis center for the Navy's Fleet Information Warfare Center, to Cisco, and as the Director of the DoD/Defense Industrial Base's Collaborative Information Sharing Environment, I watched dozens of operations mature, from intelligence consumer to intelligence producer; from immature ad hoc security operations to integrated and automated processes.

Upon the realization that a company has a security issue (…often times when they decide to build a SOC), many of the companies have one or two security people; *maybe* they have a Chief Information Security Officer. In every case, that small team – if they exist –will fight an incident manually. They'll operate as individuals with little or no coordination, and when that first incident is over, and they realize that there was more at play than a simple hacker with a simple tool, and likely the entire network has been compromised… this is when the C-Suite steps in. In many cases, this is when the company builds a security program; and in nearly every instance, they start with a security operations program.

When it comes to building security operations, there are a thousand directions one can go, and with every choice comes risk. Add to that risk the fact that the security landscape changes, seemingly minute by minute, and the need for ensuring that consistent, reliable security operations are properly configured, staffed, and trained becomes more important with every passing event.

In today's world, when breaches translate to dollars on the balance sheet and cyber claims are fought every step of the way, being prepared becomes an imperative. And one of the most important items in the Security Officers toolkit is a security operations center. This is the spinal cord at which every nerve terminates, sending signals back and forth to the brain –the CISO. If the spinal cord or any of the nerves feeding it are not operating at peak, the brain receives bad signals and makes an incorrect decision. The Security Operations Center must be able to perform three tasks to operate successfully during an intrusion: Identify those successful attacks that are currently operating in the environment, while maintaining day-to-day operations, and while creating strategy for successfully operating with now, untrusted networks into the future.

When looking for a guide, there's a ton of noise out there, and finding a cred-ible architect with in-the-trenches real-world experience can be hard. In this case, Dave's made it easy. From designing a plan to evaluating pros and cons to identi-fying sources of high-quality cyber threat intelligence, Designing and Building a Security Operations Center is the go-to blueprint for cyber-defense.

—Jeff Stutzman, CEO, Co-Founder
Red Sky Alliance and Wapack Labs

# Acknowledgments

I wish to express my thanks to the many people who have helped me create this book, to my kids for keeping me company all the late nights when I was on call while learning the lessons of this book, to my family for being supportive, to all the people I bored making them listen to paragraphs over and over again or whom I put to sleep reading the chapters multiple times, and to all the people whom I worked with in the many amazing security operations centers I have had the privilege to work in.

# Efficient operations
## Building an operations center from the ground up

1

## CHAPTER CONTENTS

## DEFINING AN OPERATIONS CENTER

Normally, the term "operations center" conjures the image of a NASA-like environment where people are sitting at desks arranged in a semi-circle with an operator at a computer facing a large wall of video monitors and projectors broadcasting critical information. That is the general conception of a standard operations center. Many types of operation centers exist, all of which have the same general purpose: a variety

1

of tasks to be performed by a group of people who interact with the data/information and with each other.

A network operations center (NOC), for example, will have someone focused on telephony or communications equipment or messaging and may even be more focused, stove-piped, on instant messaging or telephone communications. Someone else may be fully focused on web services, Internet access, and connectivity. Each will have different skill sets, but will operate in the same room because, many times, they need each other. A lot of the information each handles is interconnected with the other, so they will be focused on their own tasks day in and day out but will work together in a group operations environment. There are clear escalation paths, a clear management chain, and there is information being broadcast to them to help them do their jobs better and more efficiently, or provide them information very quickly that enables them to spot a problem or be able to resolve a problem before it becomes a larger more impacting issue.

That is a rough overview of a traditional operations center. There also might be other types of operations centers, such as a security operations center (SOC). The concept is the same and the focus is different, this time on system security. Another type may be something like an emergency operations center (EOC), which may not be stood up full time and actively providing services, it may not look like a NASA site, but rather be set up virtually or in response to a crisis. It may not have the fancy monitors nor semi-circle arranged desks, but it will have different people with different skill sets who come together to respond to a crisis, make decisions, assess damage, manage the crisis, and be able to do all of this in real time in a temporary tent. Once the crisis has ended, that particular type of operations center may just go away and its participants return to their regular jobs, only to be recalled if there is another emergency that needs to be attended to.

You can spend years and tons of money building the best security for your infrastructure, hire the best security people, and provide them with the best tools, and you still will not be able to guarantee that security breaches or compromise of your systems will not happen. When computer security issues do occur, it is critical for an organization to have an effective means of managing and responding to them. The speed with which an organization recognizes or detects, analyzes, prevents, or responds to an incident will limit damage done and lower the cost of recovery.

Having an effective and efficient SOC or incident response capability is an important part of the deployment and implementation of any technical infrastructure. With the number of breaches and amount of data loss over the past few years, organizations are beginning to realize that security is a key component to any business operation.

In direct support of the business and partnered with information technology (IT) services or operational technology services, a SOC must reduce both the duration and impact of security-related incidents exploiting, denying, degrading, disrupting, or destroying systems required for normal business operations. This needs to be done through effective monitoring—timely and alerting—and consistent tracking of incident progress. The SOC should be a vehicle where the customer or internal business partner is represented with respect to incident prevention, and is a proponent and executor of proactive remediation's and communications. A SOC needs to maintain an effective staffing level appropriate to the size of the business and the responsibilities given, with continual training and improvement, and should always able to respond effectively and efficiently.

## PURPOSE OF THE OPERATIONS CENTER

In essence, the operations center is to be whatever the goal is for the particular focus. Thus, you may choose to have an operation center running 24/7, or one that is operating only from 9 a.m. to 5 p.m. You may find it beneficial to have an operations center that is a NASA lookalike, or a center consisting individuals sitting in normal cubicles as one would see in any office situation. This latter group still works together as a "center" team. The key is a synergy among the different people, even though performing different tasks. Whatever physical format is employed, there is clear management to handle particular events, make decisions, bring situations to resolution, and provide a service to the larger business or organization.

A SOC has a key, albeit sounding simple, mission: *security*. The overall concept of having a SOC is to provide a real-time view into a network or an organization's security status, assuring that systems are not being negatively affected and has the ability to execute agreed upon protocols and processes in a consistent manner when issues arise as well as someone keeping an eye on the facilities at all times. This is similar in concept to physical security, where guards walk the premises to be certain that everything is in the right place and no thieves are about, no one is attempting to break in, and there are no other issues that threaten the security of the facility. The only, and obvious, difference is that the SOC does not monitor in the physical world so the operators cannot shine a flashlight into a corner to see if anyone is hiding there. The SOC requires a very different skill set.

Although there are varying degrees of SOCs, generally they are charged with the responsibility of monitoring and managing all aspects of the enterprise, in real time. Varying degrees of a SOC, with different facility types, depends on your organization and your objectives. The typical approach is a centralized entity in an organization or business where all necessary skill sets in the security-focused area are working together in one location, but everything in one location is not a requirement. Larger companies with a global footprint may have skill sets in Europe that are different from the skills available in the Pacific Rim that are also different from those in the United States. In such instances, you would leverage those abilities, split the work among the key areas, and establish a global SOC. Then, you would need to figure out how to build that together and make components work effectively and keep all eyes on the network to protect the company.

Size of the organization and threat to the organization can drive the size and look of the SOC. Throughout this volume, we discuss what you need to consider when designing a SOC, as well as some of the challenges you will have in making correct decisions and some of the thought processes needed in order to get to the proper result. No matter what the configuration, ultimately the SOC monitors and manages potential threats, analyzes the threats, determines risk level, and then either recommends or executes some form of remediation action to protect the company. How you go about doing all this needs to be effective, efficient, and measurable.

Somewhat of a "Nervous system" is fabricated when you build out a SOC. There is an intelligent "brain" that essentially works to gather data from all different areas. There is an automated process that attempts to prioritize events so that the more critical issues are dealt with by the trained experts and remediated in priority order. Needed are the proper tools, equipment, and people. Not unlike elsewhere in the industry, we refer to the three-legged stool of people, process, and technology. Most books on IT and security tell you that you need to focus on those three things. I tell you that is not true. You must have people and you must have processes. You do not, however, necessarily need to have technology. While it is true that you need to have all three, the reality is that it is your people who make your operation work and make it successful. The people will implement the proper processes. It is your people who will implement the technology correctly to achieve the goals. So, when building a good SOC, your focus primarily needs to be on people, and the remainder will fall into line. In subsequent chapters, we will get into very detailed presentations about how we focus on our people to be successful as the "brain" of the nervous system within the SOC.

When completed, the SOC will provide you situational awareness from a security perspective. It will give you a detailed picture of what is occurring in your enterprise from that same perspective. It will leverage the tools you have deployed specifically for security, and even other tools that were not deployed for security but have security value. A SOC does not need to be an entity of its own. I argue that a SOC cannot operate all on its own. It needs to have partners to be successful. In many larger organizations, a successful SOC is working alongside an NOC. Or, if a NOC is not present, the SOC will create partnerships with other IT units within the enterprise.

It is one thing to stay focused within a SOC and make certain nothing bad is happening on the network; but, you also must make certain when building a SOC—any type of operation center, but even more so for a SOC—that you are a partner to the business, to the IT coworkers, and you need to be certain you extend outside of your operations center to enlist support of all your users to be additional eyes and ears relative to what is going on within the network. Certainly not an empty statement, it is everyone's responsibility when it comes to security.

## EMERGENCY OPERATIONS CENTER

An EOC is the physical location where people come together during an emergency but it does not specifically have to be anything relating to IT security. This could be for almost anything such as a natural disaster, or even civil unrest. These centers alternatively may be called command centers, situation rooms, war rooms, crisis management centers, or other similar terms. This is where the coordination of information and resources takes place to respond to and perform recovery actions. As with other types of operation centers, it should be an effective and efficient facility for coordinating emergency response efforts. An EOC may be made up of a number of people from different organizations, such as state or federal emergency workers, and the users may have various types of skills and training.

## MISSION OPERATIONS CENTER

The more typical NASA environment, a mission operations center (MOC) is a place where many people of different skills and focus sets come together for a single purpose or event. A space shuttle launch is a good example. All aspects of the launch would be represented by people in the operation center who have their own sets of priorities, focus, and tools vital to the overall mission. The operation center comes together for a single planned event and then either be would disbanded or left with only core crew positions to maintain ongoing operations. Air Traffic Control centers are a type of permanent MOC and similar organizations may be seen in larger busy train stations.

## THREAT OPERATIONS CENTER

This type of operation center primarily is focused on threats, characterization, and attribution of those threats, creation, and sharing of situational awareness, and the development of mitigation strategies. Its primary focus could be in intelligence gathering and the dissemination of that information to the proper groups and teams that can do the most with it. The mission is to perform in-depth analysis using specific technology and techniques that would be proprietary to the organization. This could include identifying vulnerabilities and the potential for attacks; discovering methods of protecting global networks, computer systems, specific hardware or software; or specifically looking for threats to a business or organization. A good example of this may be the NSA's threat operations center (TOC) that has a very specific mission to discover cyber threats, characterize them and find attribution of those threats, in addition they publish information for other government organizations to use and review. Managed Security Providers may also build TOCs either as a standalone organization or within a SOC to help feed security relevant information back into the SOC for enhancing and developing rules and signature to be implemented into security infrastructure in order to better protect their customers. A larger organization or enterprise can also build a TOC specifically designed to research threats, fraud, or other potential risks to the business.

## NETWORK OPERATIONS CENTER

NOCs are responsible for monitoring IT infrastructure for alarms or certain conditions that may require special attention to avoid failure in a business system. For example, a NOC may monitor hard drive space on servers to detect when critical storage may be getting low. Or it may monitor services to ensure they are available to the user or customer; and, when they are not available, provide remediation and restoral services or contact the appropriate escalation point of contacts to institute a repair. NOCs can analyze problems, troubleshoot, communicate with site technicians, and even other NOCs such as vendor NOCs or regional NOCs, and track problems through resolution. They normally are able to escalate issues to the appropriate personnel, including contacting technicians to remedy problems not otherwise addressable.

Operation centers' core functions are:

- Can optimize communication and coordination by effective information management and presentation.
- Example process of how information flows in an operation center:
  - Event occurs
  - Detection\recognition of relevant event
  - Notification sent to front line personnel or analysts
  - Status evaluated and action begins
  - Incident log opened or initial comments made
  - Standard operating procedures implemented using checklists
  - Tasks for remediation or restoration assigned, as needed
  - Escalation performed, as required
  - Status briefings and updates to stakeholders

A successful operation is one where a team of people are working together to consistently achieve or exceed goals. In a SOC, the team's goals are to monitor and protect the organization from internal and external threats as defined by security experts, internal IT and security leaders and the business or organization who ultimately owns and funds the SOC.

## LET US BUILD A SOC!

The majority of SOCs are built out of necessity, which is the nice way of saying that SOCs are built as a "knee jerk" reactionary response to a significant security issue in an organization, such as a breach or identification of data loss. This reactionary approach is due to the fact that even today most companies do not understand the current climate and risks associated with IT, or for some reason, do not believe that they are or would be a target. It is unfortunate that these "instant SOCs" are put together more often than not. It is disastrous because companies are not secure and are having issues at an alarming rate but it is also regrettable that a lot of planning cannot be done upfront so that the effectiveness of the SOC could turn positive results faster for organizations during a time of great need.

In some cases, SOCs get "stood-up" while security issues are underway and immediately after a breach has been recognized. This gives a company very little in the way of planning or establishing an approach or following a sane methodology to building a SOC. It may not even allow the organization to hire the right people. There are times where a breach is so significant to an organization that a company would call in an outside company of experts to establish a SOC and staff it just to stop the bleeding. Or, organizations could hire a Managed Security Service Provider to take over their devices and start monitoring for problems. In all of these situations, everyone is going to have a very difficult time. Organizations assuredly will be stressed out from the issue and their heads will be spinning and not know what to do, and service providers, whether off site or onsite, will find it difficult to get the information they need to build out infrastructure to protect the organization the way they want. There are many different companies that provide this kind of service and they do a decent job, but almost every engagement begins like sticking your finger into an electrical socket. The reason for this is that the organizations in these critical situations need to rapidly work to take responsibility for security away from traditional internal IT departments and give it over to an outside organization. This hurts; people in IT usually are very passionate about what they do and treat networks they manage like their own baby and take great pride in what they do. When someone takes things away from them, it is a clear indication that they were not performing their job adequately. Additionally, further making these rapid transitions difficult is a usually large amount of knowledge transfer that must occur regarding technology configurations, such as what systems perform what function and why, organizational structure, geographical layout, and, of course, the current political climate and issues inside the organization.

Organizations do not typically include building a SOC into their growth plans unless they are going to offer security as part of their business. It almost goes without saying that there is little to no profit for a company to focus on its own security. Most, if not all, money spent on an organization's effort to secure its network is considered capital and/or operational expense and affects the bottom line. Today, as companies grow, it is typical that their IT infrastructure grows as well; and as the infrastructure grows, the potential security issues and risk to that infrastructure and its data also grows. At some point, an organization needs a SOC; but, at what point can vary greatly and depend on many different factors. Most organizations have some kind of security deployed, even if it is a simple off-the-shelf router with a built-in firewall, but they have no SOC. While other organizations can have large IT departments that manage infrastructure around the world to include many different types of security devices and still no SOC. Clearly there is a point in time when a company should be looking to build a SOC and it would be between, if not including, both of the previous examples. Security should be built from the ground up in any organization, and the concept of building or employing a SOC should all start with an organization's realization that it has something to lose, critical systems to protect that help run its organization, or regulations that it needs to comply with or else face consequences. These realizations should come with a business decision to focus on the security of its IT infrastructure, not after the fact when security is already a critical issue.

There are times when a company does not intend to build a SOC, but it just happens naturally. As stated before, when a company grows typically so does its IT infrastructure. When IT infrastructure grows, traditional IT organizations typically do a good job purchasing security tools along with that growth. I believe that the traditional IT departments in organizations are very capable and do think about security. Unfortunately, their focus is in other areas such as managing critical services like email or web. They focus on keeping the network up or performing upgrades to applications to support the business, and so on. The traditional IT department will install traditional security devices such as firewalls, Intrusion Detection Systems (IDS), and antivirus solutions. These almost always will ensure that the basics are there. But having these devices alone is not enough. There needs to be daily reviews, care, and maintenance along with regular application of vendor updates. At some point, maintaining the security devices cannot be an ad-hoc job for a generalist in the IT department because it takes too much time, and time is not the only issue. The knowledge to maintain these systems and make them work to their fullest capabilities requires specialized knowledge. Someone needs to become a security specialist and take the time to learn and then properly care for the security of an organization. If the expertise does not reside within an organization, then an additional employee may need to be hired who has some experience and can perform those responsibilities. Once an organization has a single full-time resource dedicated to security, there essentially is a SOC in place, albeit of one person.

Whether or not you are building or employing a small SOC, large SOC, instant SOC, or outsourced SOC, there typically are five phases of growth and maturity that a SOC goes through as it is being established. These phases are loosely related to the five stages of team development[1] but modified to fit what happens inside a SOC.

*Technology > Organizational > Policy > Operational > Intelligence*

## TECHNOLOGY PHASE

In the technology phase, there may not be any kind of resemblance of a SOC, although you may intentionally or unintentionally work to establish one. Instead, what you have is a bunch of security systems and tools that may or may not be deployed in an organization's environment. In this beginning or first stage, there may be one or more people in an IT organization who's responsibility is to control and manage all of the technology. The starting efforts are likely to be very rudimentary, such as just trying to figure out what tools are deployed, how many, and where. The focus in this phase is more of just trying to understand the area of responsibility. For example, maybe IDSs and antivirus management but not firewalls are part of the scope for the new security team. As you further look to see what you have protecting your organization with, this is where new equipment will begin to be installed to meet the needs of the organization. This is not the only phase for new installations of security technology, but this is where it will begin. In the case of instant SOCs, it is typical

---

[1]Abudi, Gina. The Five Stages of Project Team Development.—*PM Hut*. 8 May 2010. Web; 25 Mar. 2012. <http://www.pmhut.com/the-five-stages-of-project-team-development>

that new technology will be installed specifically to address any issues or vulner-abilities that were detected as being the cause or significant contributor to a breach or data loss.

## ORGANIZATIONAL PHASE

In this phase, most if not all of the basic security equipment under management and utilized by the organization is already known to the security organization. Respon-sibility for the security equipment is handed over or in the process of being handed over to one or more people heading up the security operations team. At this point, security operations personnel start to make sure that systems are in good health. This is also the phase where initial training on the security tools should take place if individuals are not fully qualified or experienced enough to manage the systems. It is really important during this phase that processes begin to be developed to manage and maintain systems to keep them up to date. Also, processes to modify and change the systems need to be established into some form of documented change manage-ment approach. The organizational phase could be a very troubling thing for an or-ganization to go through. There can typically be a lot of struggles for a new security organization to gain control over equipment typically maintain by a traditional IT department such as firewalls or corporate web proxies. These types of changes can bring out a lot of emotion in people as sometimes people feel as though they are los-ing responsibility and giving it up to a new emerging empire in the organization. In-stead I urge anyone building a new security organization to ensure they partner with all aspects of the IT department and gain strength and support from within the overall organization. Organizing a SOC should be a positive event in an organization and everyone should feel as they are part of the solution. When organizing your SOC, it is not always good to bring everything in new, make sure you work with, engage and include resources from other departments inside your organization.

## POLICY PHASE

Policy in this section is really two different things. First is a review of existing policy related to IT security of the organization that is standing up the SOC. Most organi-zations have at least some policies that govern the control and acceptable use of IT systems such as computer use and the use of the Internet. If complete IT security policies have not been created, then this is a good time not only to create the policies but get them approved by senior management and then communicated around the company. There are many examples of polices available for view that you can use as examples, and many companies even in your industry may be willing to share their policies with you so you can draft ones that are the best for your organization. I do not want to get into published standards and guidelines too much, but if you need to start from scratch, ISO/IEC 27002 is a good beginning point from which to establish basic guidelines and general principles for initiating, implementing, maintaining, and improving information security management in your organization. The standard provides general guidance on the commonly accepted goals of information security management and contains best practices. It is intended as a functional guideline for developing organizational security standards and effective security management practices. The SOC should not perform this task alone, but could be a great help in developing these policies. The policies should be reviewed carefully and then all the deployed security tools and future security purchases need to be evaluated to ensure that they are enforcing those policies as best as possible. Second, this is when the SOC really starts to develop internal policy as how it controls and governs the configurations of the devices it is now managing. Modifications are made to ensure the devices are in alignment with policy and doing the job expected of them.

One of the primary policies and procedures that need to be developed in this phase is communication. A SOC needs to make sure that information system security incidents are promptly reported, system security events and weaknesses are promptly communicated to the appropriate system administrators, and timely corrective actions are taken. Additionally, the SOC must establish a formal information security event reporting procedure with proper points of contact so it can perform incident response effectively.

## OPERATIONAL PHASE

This is where it all starts to come together and the SOC begins to operate, systems are configured properly and tested to be working well. Regular monitoring of the security systems is occurring and investigations are taking place to understand activity that is out of the ordinary or in violation of established policies. IDSs signatures are updated regularly, systems are properly maintained, and any vendor updates are applied within internally accepted change management procedures. During the operational phase, there is also ongoing activity to integrate tools and products. This could take the form of integrating tools, ticket systems, or processes that make the whole operation easier. So how do you know when your operation center is fully operational? This means different things for different organizations but for me typically when things are up and running if I can sit back and know for a fact that there is paper in the printer and I know exactly where the stapler is, then we are good to go! Ultimately you are in the operational phase if you are getting expected results and are following the established processes.

## INTELLIGENCE PHASE

Although there are a lot of attributes that a SOC shares with other types of operation centers, the use of intelligence is a clear differentiator between a SOC and others. The utilization and application of intelligence is also what can set apart different

SOCs from each other. Intelligence gathering and usage is also how a SOC can begin to become proactive in the IT security fight. In this phase, SOCs take information from various sources and use the data as input into security tools. It is the hope that this intelligence data will help to spot issues or potential problem areas. In Chapter 9, we will cover this in great detail and review where and how to get the information you need, as well as how to use it. But ultimately in this phase, a SOC has the ability to take information from external sources, apply it internally, and utilize the information appropriately. Additionally, a SOC in this phase will seek out new sources of intelligence, create their own or have a natural desire or thirst for more and more information that will help to tune their tools to provide more qualified information or precursors that would indicate a negative event.

## PLAN YOUR SOC

As you can see, before building a SOC, there are a huge amount of things we need to consider. The planning should not happen at a single level in the organization; there are too many issues and questions that need to be answered. Several areas from across the organization should be involved, such as finance, human resources, legal, and any critical lines of business you may have, not just IT. Getting people involved from the beginning as part of the project and its planning will go far down the road for you when your SOC starts performing its mission. By getting other groups involved, the mission and overall business issues the SOC will resolve need to be socialized into these groups so that there are no surprises later. More often than not, when planning a SOC, people focus on the technology, staffing, training, and other technical aspects; but you cannot forget the business reasons why you are doing this in the first place. Communication is a key to moving your SOC forward with as little friction as possible. Sometimes the SOC is not a welcomed addition to an organization. By being transparent in your mission, giving outside groups and even the general IT organization the ability to help develop processes, makes the SOC something that everyone understands, welcomes, and can be a part of.

Now that we have gone through some of the basics of what an operation center is, let us discuss terminology. Because there will be many people involved in the planning and building the SOC, one of the keys to making the process smooth and successful is building a lexicon as early as possible. Organizations typically have an internal language that takes a while to understand. Add to that organizational language the complex terms of IT security and you will have a lot of people who do not know what each other is talking about. For example, imagine your company has a business unit called IDS, if you are a security person, you can already see how that can be confusing because conversations about IDS could mean the security tool IDS or it could be a business unit inside the organization. The formal lexicon is a great tool not only to build for your SOC, but also for other people outside the SOC. Some information will be nonsense for people but other information will be helpful. The lexicon is a tool that should be shared freely. As contractors or new employees come in and out of the SOC, share this with them to help them understand who you are and use the same language. For the SOC, IT security can be a language of its own that people who are not in the security business will find hard to understand and use to talk knowledgably about security topics and issues. Additionally, there is a lot of debate among security people on the meaning of some things and it is important to have a common set of definitions from the beginning.

**What is an "event"; what is an "alert"; what is an "incident"?**

It is all right if you disagree with some of the definitions I present here because there always seems to be some confusion and arguments around the words, "event," "incident," and "alert." We also cannot forget about what a "log" is. Everything starts out with a log so it will need to be addressed and defined along with the others key terms. It is important to figure out what these mean to you because your SOC will be working with these terms every single day. The SOC will analyze them, report on them, correlate them, create metrics on them, and pull their hair out over them. Particularly during stressful periods, such as anything that would cause an operations center to be called into action for incident response, it is critical that all personnel involved use and understand key terms effectively. Even if you use those terms incorrectly according to someone else outside of your organization, as long as there is an acceptable understanding of the use in your organization, you will be fine. For example, if someone said, "we receive 1,000 <u>logs</u> a day" I may think that is a bit low, but on the other hand if someone said "we receive 1,000 <u>events</u> a day," I may be a bit worried.

The Information Technology Infrastructure Library (ITIL) V3 provides some clarity and uniformity in the definitions. ITIL defines an event as a change of state that is significant to service management, but possibly could be a normal change of state opposed to a negative change such hard drive error. An incident is unplanned interruption of an IT service, reduction in quality of service, or a failure of a configuration item. Thus, an incident characterizes a negative impact on the service or service quality.

Every incident needs to be recorded and needs to be tracked as well as documented to make sure that everyone is doing what they are supposed to be doing and following the correct procedures; a system like this that automatically numbers the incidents recorded is called ticket system. There are many ticketing systems out there and we will cover some of the features later on. But, it is important to note that each ticket system may have its own way of viewing and defining these terms as well. There are additional terms that ticket systems understand, such as "problem," "exception," or "change," but we will not get into those right now. Instead, be advised that if you already have a ticket system in your organization, you may want to review how it handles these terms and adopt the terms used by the ticketing system because it will make your life much easier. Otherwise, you will have to go out and find a new ticketing system that agrees with *your* definitions and that could be expensive and time consuming.

*Logs > Events > Alerts > Incidents*
*Lots of things > Some things > Few things > Few very important things*

# LOGS

Logs are the most basic form of information a system can generate. An operating system, application, service, or almost anything can generate a log that records basic information about something that just happened. Typically logs are produced by systems as a form of audit trail. This would give a system administrator, or in our case the SOC, an indication of something that may have gone wrong and would provide hints on how to diagnose a problem. Transaction logs are similar but do not typically depict a fault. Instead, it is a recording of something that happened, such as an entry or record deletion from a database. Correlation is where you can combine logs from different systems and apply analysis to those logs. This is where most modern Security Incident and Event Management (SIEM) systems really prove their value. By taking logs from different systems that appear unrelated and correlating them together to generate something new can be a very influential and useful system. For example, by taking a database transaction log that shows a record entry by a user and then a firewall log showing network activity from an IP address registered to the same user who made the record entry, we can validate that if the user is who he says he is and has authorization to make that entry, then all is well. This is a very simple example and there are hundreds more, how you correlate logs is up to you and your objectives. In Chapter 3, we will spend much more time on SIEM tools, correlation, and the value of the log as well as log collection. For now, it is important to define what a log is, how it can be used, and then build on that.

System logs have many good uses and have more purposes than you may realize. For example, one great use for logs is forensics. There are many organizations that archive log data for long periods of time for potential future reference. These types of logs usually are protected by an organization's log repository or storage system and kept according to an organizations retention policy. The usefulness of keeping logs can come from any situation where a system problem is discovered to when a possible fraud has been detected and historical logs need to be reviewed to see how long this issue has been happening and possibly when or how it started. In criminal or legal cases, logs can help prove an action and are typically allowed as evidence in court. Because logs can be used as evidence, it is important that your logs are protected forensically. This means that once a log is written, if you can prove that controls are in place so that no one can alter, or delete that log, they are considered protected. Typically, to protect the logs, you would send the logs from the system that generated it to another system designed to receive those logs and store it securely.

As we began to discuss above, logs can help you triage and diagnose system problems or even tell you when everything is working correctly. Problems could consist of services not starting properly, users failing to present their username or password correctly, or a record of tasks an administrator is performing. Additionally, logs can be generated showing errors on a hard drive or other hardware-related issues. Logs can provide information such as which accounts were accessed and what actions were performed.

Unfortunately, in a lot of situations within organizations where SOCs do not exist, an "Instant SOC" or an incident response team will find during an incident that logs contain no information or evidence because logging was either completely disabled on a system or configured improperly. Organizations should baseline all their systems to ensure a level of logging appropriate for each system, and look to enable a higher level of logging on more critical systems. All systems should have file auditing activated and should log audit those events, particularly administrative-level activity. If you are running a central logging system, you should have a log health monitoring system to verify that logging is functioning properly and you are receiving events properly. In addition, you should audit your logs on a regular basis to ensure that the logs contain the proper information that you need. Do not just log everything, make sure you make conscience decisions on what to log as it can get very expensive to store all that information and you will need an ever increasing high-powered system to use large log storage systems for anything meaningful.

Logs always should contain some basic information and include the required information you need to make it valuable enough to keep it. One of the primary items you need in a log is a time and date stamp. It is very important that you have all your systems configured to have their time updated from a central authoritative time source. Thus, when you are reviewing logs from several systems you can be relatively certain that logs were generated at or near the same time and would be likely generated by the same action or user. Additionally, the time stamp is vital to be able to correlate events among different systems and piece together a real picture of an event. Next you need some kind of description as to what the log represents or why the log is being generated. For a network-based event, you also may want the log to contain IP address information such as the source IP of the system that took an action and/or the DNS name; you also may want the authenticated user information. The items that can go into a log are almost endless and depend greatly on the capability of the system or application that generates the log. Logging mechanisms and the ability to track user activities are critical. The presence of logs in all environments allows thorough tracking and analysis if something does go wrong. From a log, you should be able to answer the basic questions of, who, what, when, where, and why? Additional information that you may find in a log or events that may be required by regulations to ensure they are logged could be:

- User identification information
- Type of event
- Success or failure indication
- Event origination point
- Description
- Severity
- Time
- Service name
- Protocol
- User

There are also a bunch of things that you have to be careful of when setting up your logs. You want to ensure that private or protected data are not going to be sent to the log files or transmitted from system to system. This is a vital concern for a SOC as it is one of the things a SOC is looking to protect against. A quick list of things that you do not want to see in a log:

- Source code
- Passwords
- Encryption keys
- Bank information
- Credit card information
- Personal identifiable information (PII)
- Personal health information (PHI)
- Information that is illegal to collect

The type of information for which you may want to consider ensuring there is a log may include:

- All actions taken by any individual with root or administrative privileges
- All administrative access and action taken by administrators
- Access to the logs
- Use of identification and authentication mechanisms, success, and failure
- Initialization/clearing of the audit logs
- Creation and deletion of system-level objects

Systems typically give you the ability to set different logging levels and you sometimes can find documentation on how configure the levels and what information you get at those various levels. You also may find that some systems will even give you a severity level in the log, where each individual log entry is marked at a level such as "Warning," "Error," or "Information." This is very helpful because you may decide to filter for all events at a Warning level that could help you reduce the amount of noise you need to review or collect. If you are filtering logs such as this, it also could be very helpful to reduce the amount of hard drive space you require to store all the necessary information.

In looking at the different logging levels, you may decide that one level will work on one system and another is needed somewhere else. Logging levels are a good way to squelch the noise and tune the log information to just the right level for what you need. Most systems will follow some kind of escalating scale of verbosity in their level of logging. Typically you will see Debug, Information, Warn, Error, and Fatal. Different systems may call them by different names, but those are the basic levels you typically will see. Ideally, you will want to tune your logs to get just the right information you need.

The *Debug* level is the most verbose logging level. Because debug will produce a large amount of logs, you have to be very careful when enabling this setting on production systems because it could cause latency or performance impact to the individual system required to produce the logs. Also, be warned that in some cases the debug level of logging in application can write personal identifiable information, financial, or other types of data that you may not want to be exposed inside a log.

The *Informational* level, which is one step below debug, typically is used to output information that is useful to the running and management of a system.

The *Warning* level often is used for handled "exceptions" or other important log events. For example, if an application requires a configuration setting but has a default in case the setting is missing, the Warning level should be used to log the missing configuration setting.

*Error* is used to log all unhandled exceptions. Some error logs list every single error that may occur. Others may be configured to save information about errors selectively, listing only certain error codes. However, the system may work, each error log entry should include an error code, a time, and may add other information such as an action someone was trying to complete, someone's location, and whether or not the error was resolved. Error logs can be searched to identify specific patterns or errors encountered by a particular user or application.

*Fatal* is reserved for special exceptions/conditions where it is imperative that you can quickly pick out these events.

Auditing is another important area for logs, and at some organization, this is where logs are used the most. Reports from system logs for audit and compliance may satisfy requirements in regulations such as PCI, SOX, or HIPAA. Log auditing should be automated, and logs can be used to reconstruct events.

An example requirement from PCI pertaining to logs:

- 10.3 Record at least the following audit trail entries for all system components for each event:
    - 10.3.1 User identification
    - 10.3.2 Type of event
    - 10.3.3 Date and time
    - 10.3.4 Success or failure indication
    - 10.3.5 Origination of event
    - 10.3.6 Identity or name of affected data, system component, or resource

## EVENT

An event can still be a log, but it is a log that has specific context for you. Events can come from multiple sources, not just logs. For example, a user calling to complain about too many spam messages in his email is an event. Additional examples are provided below. In all cases, an event is an input to the SOC that needs to be filtered and reviewed to determine if it warrants further investigation or analysis. It is typically a log of significance that someone wished to record about what is happening but mostly will not require a user's attention or intervention. It really has or should not have any level of importance, but typically can include the notation of Information, Warning, or Exception.

Examples:

- Disk space has exceeded a certain threshold, such as 95%
- CPU utilization exceeded 99%
- A user logged into the system
- Starting a print job
- Updating a database

Not all logs that you collect will be worthy enough to be an event that someone may have to review. For example, you may log CPU performance over time so you can graph it later; this would not constitute an event. Many events are not necessarily bad things and could even be an expected outcome. It is important to think about what events are relevant to your SOC and what other types of events you receive that may be relevant to other parts of the organization, such as an application support group, a NOC, or help desk.

## ALERTS

Alerts are a graduated event, an event of interest that typically sets off a preconfigured notification or alarm because something has reached a specified threshold and requires attention by a responsible person with the appropriate tools and authority to investigate. It does not have to stem from a log, but typically alerts begin as events that are critical enough to require some level of attention. In the previous section, we gave an example of a user calling about too much spam, but in the case of an alert, it would be a user calling to report a suspicious email with a potentially malicious attachment. It could also be a notification from an external organization or government agency telling you that something is wrong. An alert is an event that is of special note because someone or something has indicated an interest in that event and wants to be alerted to it. It is also very important to note that alerts are indicators of Incidents and/or Problems, as we will discuss later.

There are many different types of monitoring tools, but they typically do the same thing: monitor logs or system changes on devices and then somehow notify an operator or system administrator that there is a problem underway. In our case, it raises the awareness on a potential security issue that needs further investigation by the SOC.

Not all events are worthy enough to be considered an alert. Years ago, if a CPU spiked on a server or a user's workstation it caused an alert, one of the main things you may think of in the realm of security is that the system may have contracted a virus, but that is not necessarily the case with most modern malware. So, for security considerations, a short burst of a CPU spike most likely will be noise and not important. If there is a CPU spike on a web server once every day and a NOC is monitoring the server, then the NOC could use something like a problem management system or a ticket system and by using reports on these types of events can see this as an ongoing pattern of a potential problem and investigate. Other examples like this could be the failure of a print job or an unsuccessful attempt to update a database. All alerts should create incidents and/or problem tickets indicating that something is amiss or is soon to be, requiring immediate or near immediate action/work.

*Key Points*: The more alerts your SOC receives, the more work your SOC needs to perform. As your tools tell you something is wrong, the SOC needs to analyze these alerts to ensure that SOC staff understands why the alert was triggered and to remediate any issues related to that alert. So, the more alerts you have, the more resources you need to address those alerts. Efficiencies can be created to reduce alerts, and make alerts easier and quicker to respond to or remediate. This is called tuning, just as we discussed with logs and events but now we are doing it with security tools to reduce the number of alerts to something meaningful, actionable, and important that the organization can handle. Keep in mind that tuning is a bit of an art and should be handled by skilled individuals only and in some cases, depending on the sensitivity of the network the tools are protecting and the type of tools being tuned, they should also conform to a security review board or some form of change management process. In some cases, an organization can become overtuned and therefore essentially blind to real security activity.

Typically, security tools not only will produce alerts to tell you that there is a potential security issue, but they almost always produce too many alerts that do not really have meaning. When you plug a security tool into your network, you will see tons of alerts, as every vendor wants to show you the "value" of its system as quickly as possible. Unfortunately, these devices always need initial tuning as well as essential ongoing tuning that will be a critical function of your SOC. There are different types of alerts that the tools will produce; it is up to your SOC to determine the validity, criticality, and importance of these alerts and then do something about them. Understanding the various categories of alerts the system can produce is important to your operation. It will help your SOC follow key processes that we will discuss later and also will help you with key metrics that we also will review later.

There are four primary categories of alerts that you may see:

- False positive
- True positive
- False negative
- True negative

## FALSE POSITIVE

A false positive alert, as it relates to our world of IT security, occurs when an action or transaction occurs and a tool is configured to detect that action and then fires off an alert, although the action or transaction is actually legitimate traffic or not the right situation it was supposed to be a trigger This can occur when you create a rule to catch something seemingly bad but find out that some applications in your environment do that "bad thing" you are seeking to detect as one of its normal functions. Because the application performs this action that triggers the alert does not make it something worrisome, but rule you created will cause a false positive alert. In that case, you should attempt to filter out that known normal behavior to reduce the number of false positive alerts. Another way a false positive can be generated is when the SOC creates an incorrect or too-broad of a rule in the security system, causing the tool to find too many things that match the conditions of the rule. There are many other ways a false positive result can be generated from your tools, and these were just quick examples of why this would happen. It is also important to understand that a false positive alert can have two different outcomes. First, the false positive can be determined to be a false alarm; it is a false alarm when it requires an unnecessary intervention to analyze and diagnose the alert because there is nothing wrong. False positives also can be a true alert, this happens sometimes when a rule is created to detect a specific kind of traffic and when an alert is triggered the information that triggered the alert is not the same information or reason the alert was established but is still bad in nature and needs to be investigated further or even remediated. A simple analogy for this would be that your fire alarm sounds indicating a fire, but in reality there is a flood.

## TRUE POSITIVE

True positive alerts are those that you really never want to see because it means something bad happened from a security perspective. These are alerts that are configured correctly and are triggered properly to notify the right people that a security issue exists and further analysis or remediation is needed. Depending on your view, obviously true positive alerts are what you want to have and the closer to 100% of all your alerts are true, the closer you are to maximum efficiency. An intrusion detection signature is a pattern created by your IDS detection vendor, by you or by your company to match known traffic against unknown traffic and is applied to currently traversing data on a network. A pattern or signature that matches an installed signature for the exact reason you want it to match, whether good or bad, is considered a true positive. The accuracy of your rules, signatures, and configurations will determine the percentage of how true your alerts are. Therefore, with an IDS system, a signature may fire 10 times and only one is a true positive event. This will need to be reviewed to see if the signature could be fixed to make it more true or accurate.

## FALSE NEGATIVE

A false negative occurs when the security system fails to detect the specific transaction or event it was designed to find. It can also be a security tool's inability to detect true actions under certain conditions. A false negative is very serious because it is the failure of the tools, your operations, and your SOC to detect and respond to a real event that could harm or damage your organization. When we discuss moving your SOC into the intelligence phase or maturity, this is where we get your SOC to close the gap on false negatives. Additionally, when a SOC focuses on tuning the tools and trying to reduce what is perceived as noisy signatures or events, a condition known as being "overtuned" can begin to become a problem. As in the true positive example where only 1 out of 10 times an IDS signature fires is true and the other nine are false, we then have to ask the question, do you turn this signature off until it can be fixed? In tuning, this may be the question you face. In other words, is it better to not have nine false positive alerts and risk missing the one true alert? Being overtuned means that the squelching and turning off of rules, signatures, or events was too aggressive and you are now missing relevant information. This is a very difficult thing to measure, but you can test for it using vulnerability scanners and exploit testing tools to ensure you have some good level of fidelity. These tools will generate or simulate a desired attack against a system or network of you are choosing and will allow you to test your systems to help ensure you are not overtuned.

## TRUE NEGATIVE

When no attack has taken place and no alarm is raised, you have a true negative condition. Another way of describing a true negative is that all your rules, tools, and signatures have evaluated a packet of data or log and there were no matches to indicate a condition that would trigger an alert. When tuning, you must be mindful of true negatives because as you tune you will change the sensitivity of your security systems and may turn true negatives into false positives. The true negative also can be considered an event that promoted to an alert. These are all important things to view; it will help you ask questions such as why are you collecting that information? Can you eliminate the generation of that event to help save on resources? Or, what can you do with that information to make it more relevant. In many cases, you can take several events that are truly negative events and correlate them together to make alert of significance.

## INCIDENTS

Now that we have some good definitions to work from, we can start to assemble our SOC and provide the security services that our organization needs. But, in order to do this, we need something to happen!

We need an incident, well actually we really do not want an incident because that means something bad has happened … but that is why we are here. As National Institute of Standards and Technology defines an incident, it is a violation or imminent threat of violation of computer security policies, acceptable use policies, or standard security practices.[2] Although that is a very good raw definition of an incident, I believe that we need to break that down a bit further. An incident can be very detailed or contain very limited information. After investigation, it could turn out to be a false positive or a very serious breach, but in all cases, an incident is something that needs to be dealt with quickly and effectively. The reason we need to break this down is

[2]United States. National Institute of Standards and Technology. Computer Security Division Information Technology Laboratory. Computer Security Incident Handling Guide. SP800-61rev1-1. Gaithersburg: NIST, 2008. Print.

because when we talk about incidents, people automatically will start talking about incident response. Although it is true that the generation of an incident means that you need incident response, the SOC will handle incident response all day long and it may never go beyond a single analyst's review and closure where other incidents will require the involvement of senior leaders, legal teams, line of business representation, outside vendor support, and so on.

It is all right to interchange the terms alert and incident, the classification of the two are so loose that it would not be wrong to speak in terms of alerts opposed to incidents or vice versa. In some businesses, it is better to not use the word incident because of how it is perceived or understood culturally. As you build your SOC, these terms will settle in with your organization and will start to mean things to you unlike it means outside your organization. In some places, alerts may not become incidents until they involve resources outside the SOC. In other places, alerts do not become an incident unless there is a negative impact of some degree. We will discuss incident response, communications, and thresholds later in the book. For now, it is important to know that just because your tools generated alert or incident notices does not mean you should overreact … there are many more items to consider.

An incident could be a virus that infected a single computer and could not be cleaned by the antivirus tools. It could also be the correlation of 500 logs showing a rapid failure of a user logon occurring all within three seconds of each other and for a user account of an employee who was previously terminated. Another example could be a single event showing a successful administrative login from a known bad IP address. Other examples of potential incidents could include:

- Denial of service
- Inappropriate or unauthorized use or access
- Vulnerability identification
- Hacker activity
- Data loss
- Lost or stolen devices

See appendix A for more.

All of these examples require very separate responses. Some can be and should be handled inside the SOC, where others require more involvement and the enactment of a full incident-response plan.

For a SOC to function correctly and to be able to produce meaningful metrics, there must be a record of the incident. Therefore, all incidents must be ticketed and tracked in some form of ticket system. Later we will discuss ticket systems and the ways they can help or hurt an organization. For now, it is important to know that all these incidents need to have a place to be recorded and tracked. If for nothing else, there needs to be a clear record of what happened, what was done, and what the results were regarding the specific incident. In all cases, an incident requires some kind of after-action review or root-cause analysis. This practice will help spot problem areas, help define never repeat action items an organization needs to implement, or what failures need to be avoided in the future to prevent these types of incidents from occurring again.

## PROBLEMS

I do not want to step on any toes when it comes to ITIL definitions or practices and I certainly do not want to start any wars over incident management and problem management, but it is worthwhile to understand "problems" as they relates to security incidents and ticketing systems. There are several ways that a problem can be generated. In some cases, hopefully rare, there will be an incident generated that when investigated, a root cause is found right away and restoration or a fix action can take place right away. For example, an incident can be generated into the SOC that a critical server failed to update its antivirus definitions. After a quick look, it appears that the hard drive on which the antivirus application is installed does not have enough space to handle the update. A quick bit of housekeeping may resolve this incident. This is an important classification change because it would not be right to include this in any kind of incident or alert metrics. Instead, it is a problem and once the root cause of the problem is resolved, the problem is resolved and there is no adverse impact. It would not be fair to call this an incident; similarly an incident that turns out to be a false positive should be recycled back into the system as a problem needing further investigation and the determining of root cause so that future false positives can be avoided. A problem can also be created if after reviewing several incidents, a pattern emerges and a root cause is found for why these incidents were generated. Then a problem can be created to resolve those issues maybe from a tuning perspective. A problem would be generated and escalated as needed for a request of some kind of work to be performed in order to resolve or solve an issue.

An entire chapter is dedicated to metrics, but it is good at this point to introduce some elementary metrics. Below is a typical funnel chart that you eventually will want to generate for your SOC. This shows that you have collected some number of total events, in our case, it is 9 billion events over the course of whatever time frame you are observing. Out of those 9 billion events, there were 645 alerts/incidents that the rules, tools, and signatures generated that the SOC investigated. After all the hard work, your SOC performed in investigating all those incidents, you very successfully had responded to 85% security issues, where the remaining 15% was probably recycled back for tuning or further review.

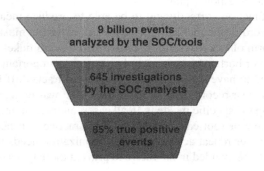

## DEFINE YOUR REQUIREMENTS

With the basic understanding of what we will be dealing with in the SOC and that we have now established a bit of common language, we can begin to think about what we need the SOC to do and start to build requirements. Every SOC is different and every organization is different that employs a SOC. You have to define what is important and focus on operationalizing that aspect to make it successful. The SOC can provide many, many different functions based on your organization's requirements. For example, the SOC could be focused on unauthorized data access and closely monitor file servers, or the proper handling of virus and IDS events. Maybe the SOC does IDS monitoring and handles incident response as a computer emergency response team. A SOC can handle all aspects of IT security from the monitoring and management of antivirus, web proxies, log management, firewall policy approvals, and all the way to defining configuration standards of technology deployed at the organization and penetration testing the environment. This was not presented to be an all-inclusive list of functions a SOC typically can perform, more it is to give you an idea and help start you on a path of defining the required functions you need from a SOC. A larger list is available in Appendix C. If you are reading this book, you probably already have a few key requirements, but that does not mean they are your only requirements.

As you define and then subsequently build your SOC, you should always consider how to build it efficiently and cost effectively. You need to make sure you can scale and grow with as little impact to the overall organization as possible. This will help the SOC become or continue to be a vital asset to your organization, as opposed to a drain on funds and resources. As you build or redefine and understand your requirements for the SOC, the next chapters will help you scope, size, and better address all the items you will need to consider for you to be able to run and maintain a successful SOC organization.

## SUMMARY

You have taken on the task of building a SOC and after reading this chapter, you have a good understanding of the fundamentals. I believe this is a lot of information for defining an operation center and although some does not seem to directly pertain to the center itself, without doing some up front fundamental definitions, we cannot all be singing from the same sheet of music. As stated before, I strongly recommend that as you build your SOC, you also build an internal lexicon document: a document that defines terms that mean something to you, which outsiders may not necessarily know, or what is commonly referred to as internal knowledge. This will go a long way when you have both new employees and external auditors.

We have discussed the different types of operation centers and when you may use one opposed to the other, and the purpose of the SOC. Your SOC is going to go through phases of development and maturity. Because every organization is different, the path you go with your SOC will be different. There are things that are important to you that may not be important to other organizations. Because of this, you need to make sure you measure yourself against the needs of the organization you are protecting, as well as external security organizations, to see where you need to improve and find your areas of focus. It is all right to not be in the intelligence phase on Day 1, you will get there if you employ continual improvement programs and focus on your team. The business of logs, events, alerts, and incidents can be very confusing. In the end, all that really matters is that when you receive something from a tool, you investigate it, and if needed, resolve it properly and with minimal negative impact to your organization as possible.

In today's cyber security environment, it is not a matter of whether an organization will be compromised, but when and how badly. It is your SOC's responsibility to find the indications that something is wrong and put a stop to it as quickly as possible and before any real damage is done. More now than ever, it is vital for operations to be efficient, capable of proper reaction, and knowledgeable enough to guide remediation efforts when needed. The SOC needs to understand organizational policy and be able to configure the security tools to find violations. But it is also more important for the SOC to understand the organization or business it protects so that when rules, tools, or signatures fire, the SOC can put the information into the proper context of those policies and the operation of the organization or business. This will help to level-set the severity of an incident and ensure that proper attention is paid to the right things.

# Identify your customers

## CHAPTER CONTENTS

If you are building a SOC you should already have some kind of idea of who your customers are or why you are doing this whole SOC thing in the first place. The SOC may have been kick started because of a recent event or as a precaution to a potential event that could bring great risk to an organization. The charter for a SOC may just be simply to ensure a repeat event does not happen or that your organization does not get into as big trouble as some other organizations in your industry. It could also be that your organization has a lot to protect and needs the right monitoring and safeguards put in place. For whatever the reasons are that you want to build a SOC, you will quickly find out that the initial reasons that you wanted to build it will be greatly increased as soon as you start to build it. The scope of your project to build a SOC could become very large; therefore, it is important that you identify all the potential customers for the SOC prior to or during the initial phases of building the SOC. Once you identify who the potential customers are for the SOC, you can then start to design services and objectives to meet the needs of those customers. The various types of customers you may have will help dictate the types of services you will provide, the service level agreements you will need to maintain, and the key success metrics or key performance indicators that you will need to provide on an ongoing basis. Once you have a good idea as to who your customers are, you need to sit down with each of them and discuss what their goals and objectives are so that you can build out use cases that document what the specifics are that you are going to be providing and the reasonable expectations for the outcomes of those use cases.

In this chapter, we are going to explore the various types of customers that your SOC may be providing services for. We will also take a look at how different customers may have different objectives, but if you build efficient operations you will find easy ways to service almost any type of request. Documenting use cases for your customers will not only help your operations understand their performance requirements but will also help customers understand what they will be getting from you. We are also going to discuss several different types of use cases for the SOC to give you a broad-spectrum understanding and a basic list of what a SOC could do for the organization. No two SOCs are alike. Your customers may be very different from the customers of other SOCs. The objectives and tasks may be similar, but the processes, risk tolerances, and reporting requirements along with the culture inside your SOC would almost always be different from any other SOC. This does not mean that you cannot share ideas and learn from other SOCs, as each SOC should strive toward being better and better with every ticket for every incident they face. As we discussed prior, a SOC is typically built out of necessity. There is a very specific and direct need to build an operation center that is responsible for the management and monitoring of the security infrastructure. The SOC needs to ensure that alerts and events are addressed in a timely manner and that all incidents are handled appropriately and escalated effectively. Once we have a clear understanding of what the expectations are, we then need to address the customers' concerns and ensure that the tools and processes in the SOC are going to appropriately meet those expectations.

## INTERNAL VERSUS EXTERNAL CUSTOMERS

A general understanding of who the customer is, is a vital step when looking to build a SOC for the first time. Initially you may think that the customer is just internal, that it is the IT department or the entire organization or company the SOC is working for. You may also think that if you are a Managed Security Service Provider (MSSP), it is easy to see who your customers are because they are whoever is paying you for your services. These would all be dangerous assumptions, and the SOC leadership needs to dig deeper and make sure that not only do they understand who the customer is but also that everyone working in the SOC understands. All too often working in a SOC I hear people complain about users who constantly get viruses or try to access blocked sites. The analysts get frustrated because the users never learn and just make more work for the analysts because all the tickets need to be addressed no matter how many times the user gets a virus or accesses something bad on the Internet. These types of events can happen often, but when you realize that it is the user in this case that you are working for then it should be easier to deal with. In other words, when a SOC analyst understands that their responsibility is to protect the users and ensure that they do not lose their identity or that malware does not access or transfer protected data off of a user's computer, then their attitude may change. In the above example it is the user the SOC is working for, but users can be a part of many different internal organizations and may have different needs other than just having someone make sure their endpoints are safe and clean of malware. A data breach is a good reason to set up a SOC but what data do you protect, where is the data to protect? Typically, organizations that have had an issue start off looking in one direction for their security requirements but soon realize that there are a ton more areas that need to be protected. From an organization's standpoint, a SOC is a great way to get experts focusing on a problem. From a security or SOC's perspective, there are many different things to focus on. Building an efficient Security Operations Center is a corner stone of execution to any organization's security program and is an essential element in achieving the overall organizational goals.

Let us take a look at who the customers are and how the SOC can help each one. Keep in mind that the security infrastructure and tools may be the same but how the systems are configured, designed, licensed, or used may be different in different organizations.

## HUMAN RESOURCES

The human resources (HR) department is typically a very important customer of a SOC. The ethical behavior of the people inside an organization is a great concern to the HR department. For many years organizations have authored codes of conducts, ethical behavior policy, harassment policies, acceptable use policies, and more. But until recently an HR department was at the whim of the people in an organization to report issues or bubble up real problems to be addressed or investigated. But now with the availability of the types of tools being installed to protect an organization's infrastructure, HR can become a valuable customer and partner of the SOC and get regular services to help them evaluate what is going on inside an organization.

In many organizations. the policy applied to a web proxy that allows or disallows access to certain types of websites has been contested. In a lot of cases, it is the IT or security department that owns the web proxy devices, so consequently they own the policy. In a mature organization, it would be the HR department that owns the proxy policy and collaborates with the SOC. HR should be the organization that directs and controls who is allowed to access what, as this is a personnel and organizational policy issue. As a customer of the SOC, HR would be given the opportunity to set policy and the SOC would configure that policy and monitor against that policy. When issues arise or requests come in to open websites previously blocked to users, the SOC can either grant that access if it falls within a specified or previously agreed parameter or if in question they can engage HR for a ruling. This is a simple example of how HR can be a vital customer of the SOC. Additionally, the protection of users' computers from malware or the management and control of lost mobile devices are also elements of services that can be provided via the HR department. As a further example, it may be the IT department that issues mobile devices to employees, but who enforces policy on lost devices or the repeat offender who keeps loosing devices? Eventually these types of things go to HR but what about the data on the mobile device, who manages the risks associated with that? If the SOC is effectively working with HR from the beginning, then tight controls, processes and expectations can all be worked out from the start. Once you start effectively working with an internal HR department, there will be many things a SOC can provide as a service, such as disciplinary review of web accesses habits or other employee system reviews that are legally allowed such as in the case of harassment. Ultimately it comes down to a violation of policy by a member of an organization that the SOC would need to aid HR in investigating or vice versa. People will always find ways to circumvent security and violate the rules. Sometimes it is in an effort to get their jobs done in a perceived easier way or because they are dishonest and want to steal or defraud the organization. As a customer of the SOC, HR can consistently enforce organizational policy and avoid discriminatory or unfair issues in a way that they never could have done before.

## LEGAL

The relationship the SOC has with legal is very symbiotic in that the SOC needs the legal department while the legal department needs the SOC all for different reasons. The fact that the SOC may be in existence in the first place could be because of the legal department. It may have been a mandate that due to a breach of the organization's computing systems or a loss of data, the legal ramifications were so great that very specific steps needed to be taken to ensure that the issues were either contained or prevented from happening again and the answer was to set up a SOC. In some cases this could have been the legal department or as an action of an organization's board of directors at the discretion of the legal department. Services that a SOC provides directly to a legal department can vary depending on the organization's goals or industry. One of the very important services that could be provided to legal is that of e-discovery. The SOC has tools it uses that perform e-discovery, and the SOC will typically have a much larger headcount than the legal department that it can utilize for these operation of those tools. Because of specific industries becoming more and more regulated, various types of court case are requesting reviews of electronically stored information. This could be data stored in email, on file servers, or even backup systems. Legal needs experts that not only know the tools but also know the organization's infrastructure and where all the data are stored and if encrypted, the mechanisms to access that information. The legal department also needs the SOC to be the watcher of data and to not only protect the organizations data or monitor access to data but also quickly notify the legal department of any loss of protected data. Many data protection laws have been created around the world and the legal department is required to make determinations on the organization's legal requirements surrounding the loss of specific types of data. Additionally, the legal department needs to determine what the requirements are to notify regulatory bodies or publicly announce if there was any loss of that protected data, and they need to do this in a timely manner.

## AUDIT

Nobody really likes being tested and when auditors come around, it can often seem like a bad day is about to happen. Spending time documenting and making someone believe you do what you say you do instead of actually doing it can be a drag when there are "real" tasks that need to be completed. But it does not have to be that way, especially for a SOC. The SOC should see auditors as a customer and should look for opportunities to help the overall organization not only perform audits easier but more efficiently and effectively. The SOC should be a high quality, well defined, and repeatable processes-driven organization, which must have fully documented procedures and reports that support the actions of the SOC. This aligns perfectly with what audit groups are looking for and as such, the SOC should be able to leverage the tools they already have to build additional services for audit that can help cover the IT department or other departments that have reporting requirements. Additionally, by producing specific reports designed for internal or external auditors, the overall process to complete an annual audit can be done in just a matter of a few days instead of weeks. The SOC should be ready to contribute to, and perform, an audit every day, as long as the SOC documentation is prepared, put it all in a single or series of binders for easy access and also store it logically on a common file share. This way the SOC already has it ready to go. Lastly, the SOC should sit-down and work with the auditing department to help define additional audits or controls that should be measured. Auditors are not going to be as savvy security experts as the people in a SOC or sometimes they will be smarter depending on who they are. The SOC needs to look at the auditing department as a customer that needs to be provided metrics, documentation and training so that what is going on in security or other departments inside an organization can be well understood and everyone can agree that the outcomes are proper and appropriate but if not, then the right corrections and recommendations can be made.

## ENGINEERING/R&D

Not all organizations have a large security department, and as we will discuss in later chapters the SOC may be run by a Chief Information Security Officer or could even only consist of a single person. Organizations that are producing products and services for customers or for internal purposes such as governments or military need to be more and more focused on security. This is not only the security of the products and services they are providing, but organizations also need to be aware of the how what they do affects the overall security of their customers. Whether it be information security of IT systems or operational security of automation systems, the entire enclave needs to have security considerations consistent with the customer's goals. When designing and building products and services, developers typically do not worry about security. They are focused more on the functions or components they are given to build. The requirements for building come from design requirements, feature requests and validated bugs of previous versions. The requirements in building, designing and upgrading products and services have also come from security especially when security flaws and issues have been discovered or are publicly disclosed. The SOC can work with engineering departments to help apply security best practices into their products. From a customer standpoint, the SOC is a great resource as a consultant to engineering or R&D. Since the SOC understands industry best practices and sees all kinds of threats every day, they are well suited to work with the Research and Development teams to guide and make recommendations as to how best to secure new products, enhance old ones, or install compensating countermeasures around others. The SOC's understanding of the System Development Life Cycle and its ability to use tools such as application fuzzers, packet captures, and vulnerability scanners make them a great resource to engineers. In addition to engineering working with the SOC as a consulting customer, engineering and development organizations may also get the SOC to send them advanced vulnerability information on third party software and also have the SOC scan and interpret penetration tests and vulnerability scans as needed on new projects.

## IT

Having the IT department as a customer is going to be a hard concept for a lot of existing SOCs to comprehend. Most of the time the SOC is born out of IT or people are taken out of IT to be a part of the SOC or a larger security department. As such, sometimes people think that this is a step up and that the IT department is filled with people that are beneath them or not worthy or smart enough to be in security. In some organizations I have seen there being an outright adversarial relationship between the SOC and the larger IT organization. This relationship could be because of a breach and IT was not given an opportunity to clean up the mess, as they were perceived to be the cause. It could also be because as a SOC finds vulnerabilities, gaps in security, and other issues they dump it all on to IT and point fingers. IT departments are having a very hard time these days and it is very difficult for them to keep up. Technology has outpaced most IT departments, and users in an organization constantly want the latest and greatest gadgets and gizmos but traditional IT departments cannot successfully support one off toys for everyone. Instead they have to figure out how to manage the needs of the organization as best possible. The last thing they need sometimes is a security operations group breathing down their neck pointing to and reporting on everything they are doing wrong. This type of attitude and environment plays heavily when we discuss organizational structure and where a SOC reports into. The bottom line is the SOC needs to view IT as a customer if not their most important customer. The majority of what the SOC needs to protect the organization will come from IT, but what will IT get out of it? The SOC needs to spend time up front and understand what the best services are that it can provide for IT. It needs to be customer driven and services provided in a way that can best be consumed by IT. So for a SOC, sending over a thousand pages of vulnerabilities from the last scan is not going to help, but maybe there is a benefit for a SOC to send over a simple report of the top ten must critical vulnerabilities affecting the most number of systems. This way IT can take care of critical issues that will have the most impact first. There are a ton of different ways that a SOC can be a great provider of services to IT, such as infrastructure troubleshooting, anomaly investigations, bandwidth issues and more. By sitting down with IT as a customer, the SOC can find great ways to provide value to not only IT but the overall organization.

## EXTERNAL CUSTOMERS

If your SOC is looking to provide services externally, then your customers are not going to be as obvious as the finance department or HR. As an individual organization that is not looking to manage security as a service and make money, external customers could just be interested third parties. They could be other organizations that use your organization's services and as such are connected to your network in some way. It could be external engineering companies, or contractors that you need to provide protection for. Your organization could have wholly owned subsidiaries, partnerships with other organizations, or sister services and departments that need to leverage your SOC's capabilities. The security services your SOC would provide to these customers may be limited to what equipment and visibility they have into those other organizations but may also be dictated by organizational requirements, regulatory restrictions, policy, or even international privacy laws. It could be that your organization provides IT services to third parties or they provide IT infrastructure to contractors who need to support your organization. Either way, the SOC may have deep responsibilities in protecting the two organizations through virtual environments, Virtual Private Networks (VPNs) or shared infrastructure. Sitting down with these types of customers may uncover many different ways that the SOC can provide value.

On the other hand if you are a Managed Security Service vendor, you instead need to find companies that want to pay for your security services. Your specific skills or expertise in the SOC will determine who you get as customers and how you acquire them when you first start up. An MSSP will focus on a vertical market and try to specialize in security services for that market. But once the MSSP, especially a small start-up, starts to gain customers it needs to work hard to keep those customers. The service it provides has to be good, it has to show value, and it needs to work hard to stay salient to its customers. One way to do that is to work with the customers and see how it can better serve the needs of its entire customer's organization. An MSSP may have only been hired to monitor IDS logs, but if it can work with departments internal to the customer such as HR and gain support to monitor proxy logs or perform Acceptable Use Policy violations, then it can increase its value to the customer. For an MSSP, it's not just about providing service but also about providing a valuable and expandable service that is scalable and that a customer can trust and rely on.

## CUSTOMER OBJECTIVES

Regardless of who your customer is or where they are located, you need to make sure that you understand their needs completely. Additionally, a SOC needs to make sure that the services they provide are going to meet their requirements and expectations. In order to ensure that both the SOC and the customer are speaking the same language, service level agreements (SLAs) need to be documented but also the SOC needs to produce use cases for the individual elements of security services they will be providing. These documents are a critical step in establishing the parameters of how a SOC will operate and what are the elements for success.

## SERVICE LEVEL AGREEMENTS

SLAs are documents that are drafted and agreed upon between the SOC and the customer (internal or external) needing security services. You would typically see an SLA document drafted as part of an overall contract between an outsourced provider and the customer, but internally a SOC can build an SLA as well. These could be traditional SLAs or even Service Level Objective (SLO) more common in inter-organizational relationships. Regardless of what it's called, most organizations that operate internal to an organization will not fully engage in this type of activity and will instead just focus on operations. In order to be a world class or best in class, the SOC needs to invest the time it takes to build these documents. The SOCs that I have been a part of that have been the best will spend the time documenting their services as best possible. Having a service catalog of capabilities, communicating those services, and then documenting expectations go a long way in helping ensure that everyone is on the same page and that the SOC is meeting its goals. There are several types of SLA documents that can be written. Depending on your SOC and who you are focused on protecting, one or the other will suit you best. First you can have a customer SLA. This is a document that details your SOC's services that will be provided to a specific customer. This would be a custom document that would be discussed, negotiated, and agreed upon as a collaboration between the SOC and the customer. Next you may want a specific service SLA. This is a document that details an agreement specific to an individual service that your SOC may provide. The service specific SLA is nice as it would be the same for every customer and would just detail all the relevant information regarding how the service was going to be delivered and executed. Lastly there is a multi-level or tiered SLA that can be written. This tiered SLA document can detail the level of services you may provide if you give customers the option to pay for different levels of service delivery such as 24/7 versus 9 a.m. to 5 p.m.

The SLA document should include some basic sections with as detailed information as possible. To start off, a summary and overview of the agreement should be created. This would detail key dates and a basic mission overview. Next there should be a section outlining the specific goals and objectives of the services to be provided. This is where a service catalog comes in handy. Items from the SOC service catalog can easily be listed. By listing from the catalog, it ensures that services being provided to multiple groups are consistently named and that there is no ambiguity in what people think the services are. For example, security intelligence services may be the same as threat intelligence service, or they may be different, who knows? But if you have documented use cases, as we will discuss, and each use case is part of your service catalog that gets called out in the SLA document, then you have consistency. Consistency in your documentation will help reduce errors and misconceptions.

Use cases <> SOC service catalog <> SLAs

Next you will want to document how the SOC is going to be measured against their execution of the services to be provided. This could be specific metrics that the SOC will produce on an agreed upon frequency of periodic reviews or in an annual customer review. This measurement may not just be about how well the SOC did but it could also be about how the services were utilized and how the customer could improve its security posture. It may also allow a customer and the SOC a predefined time that allows each group to review the services together and see if they are still in line with expectations or if adjustments need to occur. Making adjustments to services is a good thing and should be welcomed by an operations group. It is an opportunity to better align the team's efforts with customer expectations or to reset those expectations if needed. If a SOC is inflexible and unable to adapt or change, then the SOC may soon find itself not only at odds with its customers but it may also find itself in a losing battle with malicious adversaries.

The stakeholders and members of the team should also be documented in the SLA. It should clearly state who is responsible for what. There are many different stakeholders that can be identified in this section of the SLA. First you may want to detail who are the primary individuals responsible and accountable for the relationship between the SOC and the customer. These individuals would be considered the primary stakeholders of the agreement and would have ultimate power to change or modify the SLA. The primary stakeholders or their designees should be the individuals responsible to review metrics and service expectations. Next, the SLA document should detail any individuals who are required to be a part of any escalations. Additionally it may be good to also detail under what circumstances or how escalations are to be made. Sometimes SOC's will have an additional document detailing escalation conditions, contacts, rotations, and their contact methods, so in the SLA you could just refer to that additional document and then ensure it gets filled out when the service starts for that customer. You should also make sure that not only are there named people who are the primary contacts for escalations but also backup personnel that should be notified by the SOC in case of any incidents.

Service scope is a big meat and potatoes section of an SLA. This is where you will detail some of the finer points around how your services are going to be delivered and what is covered. The SOC level of service and methods would be stated in this section to start with. Depending on if your SOC has a tiered level of service, you may want to state all the levels and then specifically call out the level of service that the customer has agreed to. This is typically something that you may see more in an outsourced relationship with an MSSP, but if you are building an internal SOC for your organization you may want to list your level of service as well. In some cases, larger enterprise organizations will have different levels of service in the SOC, especially for internal customers or business units that are allowed to operate independently, but may use shared enterprise-based services. The business units would sign up for a level of service just the same way an external customer would and internal transfer of charges would reflect that level of service.

For example, the SOC can divide its service into multiple tiers. It may start off with a trial service that is 24/7/365 but has no cost during the trial period. Next it could feature three levels of service options that include silver, gold and platinum. All three may include a virtual helpdesk system through a web based or mobile portal system and troubleshooting information through a chat function online. Additionally it may include software and signature updates for specific devices, and professional help for managing security incidents. The biggest differences in the services could be in the hours of operation; for example, platinum would provide 24/7/365 live phone support, and if an incident occurred, the SOC would phone the primary and secondary contacts to notify and engage on the problem. Next, gold would provide 9 a.m. to 6 p.m. live telephone support, seven days a week and email notifications of incidents after hours. Finally, silver service would provide 9 a.m. to 6 p.m. live telephone support, Monday to Friday, and email support for escalations after hours. There are many ways to tier the services a SOC offers. They could limit the number of incidents per month and charge additional fees for excess. They can also charge for different types of services or even the number of devices, such as for the management of different types of devices like IDS, Firewall, web proxy, antivirus, and so on. There can also be additional charges for enhanced services, such as threat intelligence, forensics, log storage charges or incident response. However the SOC slices and dices the service they are going to provide. The service scope section of the SLA should detail what the customer has available to them and what they are signing up for. Additionally the service scope section should detail what the customer has that is coming under the SOC for service. It should detail for each capability what devices or assets are going to be managed. If the SOC is going to manage antivirus, then the number of servers, desktops and antivirus server systems being managed should be listed. If it is IDS/IPS devices that will be managed and monitored by the SOC, then the device count should also be listed. Similar to how the customer contact and escalations document can be separately documented, the listings of devices and equipment that are going to be monitored and managed by the SOC can also be separately listed. You will want some indication of what is covered as far as devices per service in this section, but the larger details could be acknowledged as an additional document. Service scope could also include items such as the SOC's planned maintenance schedules, shift schedules and holiday schedule. You may want to consider listing any additional items that are available that a customer may want to take advantage of but would incur additional costs. Those could be professional services, consulting, or even staff augmentation for specific security-related projects or issues that are performed at the customer's site.

Customers should also have their own section in an SLA that captures any specifics or custom requirements that they may have imposed on them. It should detail what their responsibilities are to the SOC for ensuring the SOC can provide adequate services. It could include items such as payments or frequency of payments. You may decide that it should include what would happen if payments were not made. You will also want to include the responsibilities of the people that were named as primary contacts for the customer. If the SOC analyzes an incident and reaches out to one or all of the customer's contacts with no reply, then the customer's requirements to engage with the SOC service are not met and the SOC should not be held responsible for any damage. The customer may also be responsible for keeping maintenance plans on all hardware being monitored and would also be responsible for managing the process of device replacement if needed. Sometimes the SOC can handle these types of things for a customer but those responsibilities should be carefully spelled out to ensure both parties understand the expectations. Additionally, even though the SOC may manage devices for the customer, it may be the customer's responsibility to ensure the SOC has access to those devices. So if the network goes down or the SOC loses access for some reason, the escalations go to the customer and it would be the expectation that the customer will work to resolve the issues for the SOC. A lot of times you will see the same type of device health and connectivity expectations between an internal SOC and an internal IT group as the SOC does not control the network but would need IT to help manage and maintain connectivity. If this is the case in your organization, then an SLA would help set the expectations between the two groups as an outage of security devices may not carry the same priority to IT as it does to the SOC. But if it is documented and agreed upon, then the expectations are there for everyone to see and for each team to execute on.

Just as we have a section on customer expectations and requirements, there should also be a section of the SLA that details some requirements for the SOC. This could include the number of dedicated hours a customer will get from a service representative or engineer in working with the customer on evaluating the effectiveness of the service, fine tuning the service, or building custom rules and signatures. It could also detail any required notifications to customers for planned or unplanned service outages. It should also detail the expectation of how long it will take the SOC to address newly created tickets, emails and phone calls placed into the SOC. As mentioned before under customer expectation, when there is a critical incident that needs to get escalated the SOC requirements section should detail the level of effort that is going to be made to make positive contact with the customer to escalate and inform them of the situation.

The recipe of how you build your SLA documentation will be up to you, and if you are providing external services for a fee it may also be up to your legal department. Regardless, the documentation surrounding what services you will provide, how you will provide them, and the expectations for your SOC and the customer is an invaluable tool especially for SOCs that are responsible for protecting a single organization that may have multiple departments. The SLA documentation may be a luxury for new SOCs that are just starting up especially if it is in response to a breach or compromise, but do not neglect it forever. The full and complete understanding of what the SOC does for an organization is critical and once documented, the SOC needs to execute and strive to always exceed expectations.

## BUILD AND DOCUMENT YOUR USE CASES

Now that we understand the circumstance of how we are going to provide our service and who we are going to provide it to, we need to start to understand what we are going to provide in the SOC. There are so many different types of service that a SOC can provide to an organization and the core function of a SOC in the beginning may be to stop another breach from happening, but a SOC needs to understand what it is doing. Understanding what to do is best achieved through the documentation of use cases. I have spent many hours in front of a SIEM tool developing rules or an IDS building signatures and although I have solved the world's security problems only to find out the next day that I can remember what I did. Even worse, I have created very complex series of rules and chains that seemed to work great but because I did not document them, I could not troubleshoot them and had to reinvent them all from the beginning. I have also created so many rules that when they started triggering alerts and were ticketed into the SOC, they were all true positive events but I could not, for the life of me, remember why I wanted the event or what the event meant. I know this sounds silly but when you create hundreds of rules and signatures and if your documentation is lacking, there is no way you will remember what you did or why and it will be next to impossible to tell an analyst what to do with the ticket once it gets created. The better your documented use cases are, the less trouble you are going to get into. I started to document every rule, no matter how simple or how complex. Once I got into the habit of documenting my rules and building use cases, the world seemed so easy to navigate, and as an additional bonus when auditors came around and asked what the SOC does, I could just hand them my use case book, perfect!

I hope that short rant gave you enough of a kick to believe me that documenting use cases is a good thing to do. It will also help you when you sit down with customers and try to explain what you do or how you do it and the value of why they need you to do it. Keep in mind that your use cases should be a guarded secret, it is your internal play book and needs to be confidential. This is because you are building use cases that are important to your organization or customer's organizations. It could detail vulnerabilities, gaps, or risks that you would not want to let outside entities get a hold of. Let us go through a few use cases but first let us describe some of the key elements you should think about documenting for each.

First you will want a use case name and identification number. You could have many if not hundreds of use cases that you will use. These use cases could be active, inactive, or in development and you need an effective way to track them. Trying to find some simple naming convention will help you. You could even use your ticketing system to help, by creating a ticket and then giving your use case the ticket number and common name, you can easily track not only the use case information but also comments, suggestion, issues, or known issues with the use case. Additionally by tracking the use case in a separate queue in your ticket system, it would give analysts easy access to the use cases and any needed reference documentation all inside the ticket. You may also want to name your rules in your SIEM tool by the ticket number and simple name so that when the system does generate an alert that gets ticketed you will have an easy reference. For example "Virus found – 1337", this would be an alert for a virus found but the use case ID leads you to find the ticket number 1337. Just a suggestion but having an easy-to-use reference system that ties your tickets back to each use case its generated from is an invaluable reference for the SOC (and for auditors) to have.

Next you will want to describe your use case; this should be a detailed description of not only what the use case is but how it is going to work and why you need it. You want to start with a justification or a short statement as to what the problem is that you are trying to solve. For example, if you have a use case that is designed to detect brute force attacks against your users passwords in active directory, you might state that since password cracking tools have become so efficient and that computers have become extremely fast that the detection of brute force password guessing or the rapid creation of invalid logon attempts need to be detected quickly to interrupt any unauthorized attempts to gain access to the organizations systems. Your organization may have a policy that locks accounts out after three failed password attempts but this does not stop the usage of a use case like this since an attacker may not know that policy is in place. The description does not have to be very long; it just needs to state the facts.

You will also want to detail any specific stakeholders or any interested parties that the use case would affect. For example, in the case of a virus, it may affect an end user or a server system. In those cases, there are two separate groups that may need to get involved and need to be notified. If the virus infects a desktop then there may be a desktop or helpdesk support system that needs to get an alert from the SOC so that they can resolve the issue. On the other hand, if it is a virus on a server it may be a specific server team that needs that information and may even need some incident response or remediation support from the SOC to perform containment and cleanup. Either way, it is good to detail who would be the primary stakeholder groups or teams in these cases. It will help coordinate escalations when needed and can lead analysis and incident response managers in the right direction when they reference other SOC documentation like escalations trees or incident response communication plans that we will talk about later.

Lastly, a SOC will want to detail any rules, tools, or processes used in the detection and creation of a ticket for the specific event. As a best practice policy, it is always good to directly copy or make a screen shot of the actual rules or signatures that are configured in the security devices. This way not only do you have a complete use case documented but also that use case can become a nice reference document. Each and every time you need to update the rule or signature you can document that update by updating the use case documentation and the ticket. This is a great change control process and can also save you in a pinch when something goes terribly wrong, as it is also a kind of off line backup to your rules.

Here are a few examples of some simple use cases that the SOC can use to help monitor and manage the security of an organization. This is not intended to be a complete list, instead it is just a few basic services that the SOC can provide detailed in a simple format. Your organization may need something more robust as far as the format is concerned but if you are just getting started then this should be a great list to get you going in the right direction.

## USE CASE: UNAUTHORIZED MODIFICATION OF USER ACCOUNTS

*Description*: In our environment, we do not have a good way to track which administrative account is authorized to add, delete, or modify user accounts. According to our regulatory requirements, we need to ensure that all user modifications are appropriate and have the correct approvals in place. This rule is designed to capture evidence of user modifications that take place by administrators that are not authorized to make those changes. There is no need to escalate these events, all violations will be documented in a report sent to the primary stakeholders and interested parties listed below monthly.

## STAKEHOLDERS: COMPLIANCE AND AUDIT DEPARTMENTS

*Detect condition*: The servers that maintain all the primary user accounts for the organization have been configured and validated to generate appropriate logs to signify an addition, deletion, or modification to any and all user accounts. Lists of these log types and codes have been placed inside a rule for the SIEM tool to monitor for. A list of administrative accounts will be maintained who are the authorized individuals that are allowed to make user changes and modifications. These admins will be put on a list in the SIEM tool so that any account modification they make will not result in an alert. The SOC will still be able to run reports from the operating systems logs collected for all administrative account actions but no alerts will be generated for any admins on the authorized list.

> *Rule*: Unauthorized modification of user accounts
> > If administrative account is not in "authorized administrators" list
> > & (Windows event or *nix event list)
> > Then create ticket

## USE CASE: DISABLED USER ACCOUNT REACTIVATED

*Description*: It is organizational policy that user accounts are retained for 90 days after an individual leaves. This is due to management issues or legal issues and IT has been instructed to retain these accounts. As such, the organization may have many accounts that are disabled, which present a risk to the organization. In order to ensure that insider threats or attackers are not able to take advantage of these disabled accounts the SOC will be monitoring the accounts for unusual activity.

## STAKEHOLDERS: HR AND IT

*Detect condition*: The servers that maintain all the primary user accounts for the organization have been configured and validated to generate appropriate logs to signify an when an account is disabled and when an account is re-enabled. Lists of these log types and codes have been placed inside a rule for the SIEM tool to monitor for. Any account that gets disabled will automatically be placed on a "Temporary disabled user list." The temporary list will place the account on a 24-h hold to prevent false positives as sometime people lock out their accounts with excessive incorrect password attempts. After 24 h,, the account information will come off the hold list and get placed on a disabled account list. When an account is re-enabled the SIEM rule will look at the temporary list first, if the account is there then it will not do anything, if not on that list, it will look on the disabled user list. If the account is found on the disabled list then an alert will be generated and a ticket created for the SOC to investigate.

Rule #1: User disabled
    If user account is disabled (Windows event)
    Then place account name in SIEM "Temporary disabled account list"
Rule #2: Disabled temporary hold
    If user account has been on "temporary disabled account list" > 24 h
    Then delete account from "temporary disabled account list" and add to
    "disabled account list"
Rule #3: Disabled user account re-activated
    If user account is enabled (Windows event)
    & Account is not the "Temporary disabled account list"
    & Account is on the "disabled account list"
    Then create ticket

## USE CASE: ANY IDS EVENT THAT SCORES OVER A SEVERITY OF 7

*Description*: IDS/IPS events happen on a regular basis, as such every effort has been made to tune the IDS/IPS system directly to provide the best threat information as possible. Additionally each event in the IDS/IPS systems has been configured with a reasonable priority or severity level. These severities have been assigned by engineering to ensure that signatures that are triggered have the correct value assigned to them as related to the devices they are configured to protect as well as according to the organizational and business risks. This rule will detect any event with a severity rating of 7 or greater and will trigger and event for the SOC to analyze and respond to.
    Stakeholders: IT System owners
    Detect condition: IDS/IPS events with a severity rating greater than 7
    Rule: IDS alert
    (IDS/IPS Signature) > = 7

## USE CASE: AV FAILURE

*Description*: Malware remains a reliable tool for attackers and the primary way attackers are able to breach inside network boundaries. As such, the direct installation of malware by an attacker remains to be the single common risk vector for an organization. Successfully finding, containing, and removing malware not detected by antivirus software from our network involves a series of steps and must be addressed properly. There are several rules in this use case that will be used to alert the SOC to perform an investigation. Antivirus is not enough to combat this issue, so several open source and close source intelligence feeds will also be used to help detect malicious activity.

## STAKEHOLDERS: DESKTOP SUPPORT TEAM, IT SERVER MANAGEMENT TEAMS

*Detect condition*: The first way that we will detect malware is by identifying traffic from one of our internal address going to a known malicious destination. This will be accomplished by regular downloads of malicious IP address and domain names from our reliable sources, both free and subscription based. The SIEM will be configured to evaluate all external firewall traffic against these lists. If any internal system communicates with an IP address or domain name on that list then an alert will be generated and a ticket created for the SOC to analyze.

The organization's antivirus system also generates a number of different alerts based off the policies set by security engineering. The system will alert on the detection of malware, but in some cases, the malware is automatically cleaned. In other cases, the malware is detected but cannot be cleaned for various reasons. It is imperative that every system be cleaned of malware and before it spreads beyond a set number of hosts. The rules below detail how we are going to detect a system internal to our organization communicating with a malicious host as well as when a system gets a virus that is not cleaned or when we have a potential outbreak of the same virus on five or more systems.

Rule:

Rule #1: Load and fire, lists of bad IP address and domains
    Add Malicious IP and domains to list "Bad list"
    If (from firewall log) Any internal IP communicates with "Bad list"
    Then create ticket
Rule #2: Virus found
    If alert = "virus found" & Status = "not cleaned" or "left alone"
    Then create ticket
Rule #3: Potential virus outbreak
    If alert = "virus found" & Status = "not cleaned" or "left alone"
    Add to list "Virus infection"
    If "Virus infection" list contains $> = 5$ count of same virus
    Then create ticket

## USE CASE: SECURITY DEVICE OUTAGE

*Description*: Monitoring the health of all the logs and events that feed a SIEM or that are received into a SOC ticketing system is vital to the success of the operation. Without logs and events, the SOC is blind and will not be able to detect any significant events. Systems can stop sending logs for a number of reasons. One of the worst reasons is that after an attacker gains access and control over a system, one of the very first things they will try and do is cover their tracks and they want to hide their actions so they will accomplish this by turning off logging. Other reasons could be that the system stopped responding, crashed, or that there is a network outage causing the problem. Either way, rules are created so that when logs stop after a preset time limit an alert will be generated. Systems are configured into three different groups, high, medium, and low. Devices in the high group are expected to constantly log so any loss of logs greater than 5 min will trigger an alert, whereas a medium is one day and a low will be 3 days. Once an alert is generated and a ticket created the SOC will begin investigation and analysis. Additionally there will be devices that maybe only send a log once every few months such as backup firewalls or failover proxies, in this case, a permanent suppression will be created to prevent false positive tickets being created. Any device not designated as high, medium, or low will not be ticketed against.

*Note*: Depending on your SIEM, there can be several ways to configure this type of alert, some may be fancier where others may not have the capability at all. You cannot provide security monitoring for devices that do not send you logs.

## STAKEHOLDERS: SECURITY AND IT

*Detect condition*: If a system is configured to send logs, it will be rated high, medium, or low. These ratings are based on the expected number of logs over the time period configured and is not a priority or severity associated with the device itself, just an expected log frequency.

> Rule#1: Security device outage
> If device = "High" and log count = 0 in 5 min
> Then create ticket
> Rule#2: If device = "Medium" and log count = 0 in 24-h
> Then create ticket
> Rule#3: If device = "Low" and log count = 0 in 72-h
> Then create ticket

## USE CASE RULE SUMMARY

The use cases just described are basic in nature, they are a good example of the simple items that a SOC is going to have configured and be able to monitor for on a daily basis. It also demonstrates a nice and easy way to document your use cases that you can share with your customers and auditors but also use the documentation to review with stakeholders, engineers, and security researchers in your organization to ensure you are configured to capture the right types of events for the right reasons. The documentation is also a great reference for your SOC analysts and great training information for new SOC employees. Also if you encounter any issues or you discover that the tools are not triggering on the right thresholds or you are not seeing the right kinds of logs then it will give you an opportunity to review the logic in your use case and match it up against the configuration of all the systems involved in an effort to resolve any issues in configuration. Many times I will add flow charts and diagrams to use cases so that all the rules can be seen together and the logic and flow of the information is presented in an organized and relevant way.

There are plenty of resource on the internet that will not only give you great ideas on what rules and use cases to build but they will even tell you the types of devices you need to collect logs from and what specific events you need to be looking for in order to make the use cases and rules work properly. Just as a quick added benefit, here are a few other items the SOC can get tickets for that you may want to think about configuring and creating use cases for. Again, not a complete list but just a few extra items to start off the conversation on what is right for your SOC and what types of use cases you can build for your rules.

- Malicious SQL commands issued by external, internal users, or administrators
- Cross site scripting attempts
- Transmission of PCI, PII, ePHI data in plain text.
- Resource access outside business hours.
- Sensitive resource access failure by user.
- Privileged user access to sensitive resource
- User logged in locally and on VPN at the same time
- User logged into VPN from foreign country
- Brute force authentication attacks
  - SSH, LDAP, NetBIOS, and so on.
- Distributed denial of service attacks (DDoS)
- Common network attacks (e.g., IP spoofing, hijacking attempts, etc.)
- Acceptable Use Policy violations
  - Anonymous proxy use, BitTorrent, P2P, and so on.

Rules are not the only time you will want to build use cases. Reports can be another great item to document for auditors as well as customers and even for management. By documenting your reports into a use case, you can make sure that everyone understands the data that they can get from the SOC but once they get it they can have a reference as to what it actually means and how the information was derived. Having some context as to what information a report is showing or not showing is very important especially when you are trying to get key messages across to your customers. Although you may perfectly know how a report is generated, do not assume that everyone else does. We will discuss later in the chapter on metrics you can get pretty lost in reporting. Having well-documented use cases for your reports are not only professional but will also help clear up a lot of confusion. Take for example a simple report of the top vulnerabilities detected on your organizations network. You may think this is a simple report but how do you calculate the top? Is it the number of times an individual vulnerability is seen across the network of devices or is it the most critical and subsequently the highest priority vulnerabilities detected? Were there any filters to the report, such as only Windows devices or only desktops or was it the entire network. Often when I go into a new SOC environment I start to look at reports and metrics and have no idea what they are tracking. It takes a while to understand it all and to understand what the SOC is trying to report on and why. The reports need to be designed to be factual and supportive of the data and the information it presents. It is not meant to pinpoint failures or to call out individuals that may not be doing their jobs. Ensure you work with your customers to get the right data built into your use cases for reporting before you start sending graphs and charts around. People may get the wrong idea of what you are trying to do, make sure you are viewing the reporting process as a service you are providing. Here are a few use cases for reports as some food for thought, the use cases are written as service documents and detail how the SOC supports the data and the efforts.

## USE CASE: TOP VULNERABILITIES DETECTED IN THE NETWORK

*Description*: The top vulnerabilities detected report is a series of several data points consolidated into a single page of relevant graphs. The first graph is a list of the top 10 vulnerabilities recommended for priority remediation on the network. This is a filtered list of the highest priority vulnerabilities detected on the highest number of individual systems. For each vulnerability, the number of hosts affected is shown. The list is sorted so that the highest number of systems detected for that vulnerability is at the top of the list. Implementing the remediations necessary to eliminate these vulnerabilities will have the greatest impact in significantly decreasing the vulnerability and risk to the network and the overall organization.

The second graph is a listing of the 10 most vulnerable subnets in the organization. This graphed report demonstrates where in the organization the most risks from vulnerabilities are currently residing. Subnets on this report need to have patch processes reviewed or have focused efforts to upgrade and patch the systems in those areas. The report is unfiltered and includes all devices grouped only by the IP subnet they reside on.

Third graph is a list of the top 10 devices that have the most vulnerabilities detected. This is an interesting chart to highlight systems that may have been forgotten or that are having issues and need specific attention to be remediated.

Last we will include a report of the least number of devices with open ports in an effort to detect anomalous services. Ports that are only open on a small limited number of unrelated systems could indicate the presence of malware or unauthorized applications running malicious services. The combination of all of these reports detail systems that are currently the most vulnerable and should be patched updated or removed from the network as soon as possible.

## STAKEHOLDERS: SECURITY, IT, AUDIT, AND MANAGEMENT

*Report notes*: Vulnerability scanning activities run on a 30-day rotation. All systems are scanned and data are refreshed every 30 days. The details of the report will be published and be made available for all interested parties and stakeholders every

30 days. If any teams or departments are involved in remediation activities, the SOC will support those efforts with ad-hoc scans and individualized reports to aid in the cleanup efforts. Additionally the SOC is available to discuss any issues or technical concerns related to the patching or applying of remediation's detailed in these reports.

## USE CASE REPORTING SUMMARY

Without going through many different examples I think you get the idea. Ensure your reports make sense. Make sure you have the right detail and that your filters and criteria for your graphs are easy to understand and transparent. Here are a few others with short descriptions to help you get started in your reporting use cases.

- User reports from:
  - DLP, spam filtering, web proxy, and so on.
  - Who has the highest number of violations and may need additional security training
- AV
  - Daily report of all cleans, deletes and quarantines
- Embargo Country activity
  - Weekly report of any email or non-email activity to any country IP addresses that are associated with the current embargo country list
- Password change needed
  - This weekly report checks whether a user account has not changed its password in 60 days (or how many ever days are important to you)
- Windows account lockouts by system
  - This report shows all the account lockouts on systems running Windows, sorted by system.
- Windows account lockouts by user
  - This report shows all the account lockouts on systems running Windows, sorted by user account.
- Third-party—administrative logins and logouts
  - This report shows administrative logins and logouts from third-party devices.
- Third-party—unsuccessful administrative logins
  - This report shows unsuccessful administrative logins from third-party assets that target key systems.
- Third-party—unsuccessful user logins
  - This report shows unsuccessful logins from third-party assets that target specific systems.
- Day/week/month report of issues
  - This report shows issues created in the last day/week/month as the result of rule actions that involve critical related content.

## EXPECTATIONS

A SOC is the primary team responsible for the active monitoring of an organizations infrastructure as part of an overall security department, security strategy, outsourced provider or a trusted third-party partner. It should be the expectation of any organization that the SOC has to be aware of any security situations that affects the organization it is charged with protecting, it is responsible for the monitoring of logs and security alerts and to facilitate required communication and remediation of analyzed incidents. But it cannot do everything alone; it is the entire organization and everyone in it that has the responsibility to maintain security. The organization for which a SOC functions in should have very specific expectations of what the SOC does and how. The SOC must be fully integrated into the larger organization, not just the larger security organization or even IT but the entire organization with transparent and easy information flow and involvement in business activities. Information about the organization needs to freely flow through the SOC in order to ensure that relevant information for detecting incidents is acted upon. As organizations continually fund the SOC, the expectations for results climb. The SOC needs to provide trained analysts in all areas important to the organization from managing malware infections to forensic analysis and intelligence gathering. The SOC needs to be on its toes and be capable of agile and dynamic incident response and be seasoned at handling certain types of incidents that are ultimately important to the organization. The SOC has to have great communication skills in order to bring cross-functional teams from many different departments together to work cohesively in the effort to resolve incidents. It is an easy measure of how successful a SOC is by how it is able to dynamically change membership of its incident handling teams and easily integrate people from all areas of the organization from one incident to another and be able to manage many different incidents all at different phases all at once. Integration of the team is essential to be effective in quickly addressing, containing, and remediating incidents in an organization and it should be the expectation of the organization that the SOC would drive this. Another important characteristic of an expectation an organization should have on a highly functioning and effective SOC is transparency. In order to be a good communicator and team player, the SOC must share its information. It should share its tools, data, reports, and any information it has that could benefit the organization as a whole or in part. For example, vulnerability-scanning tools have a great amount of valuable information in them, providing reports may not be enough. In the spirit of transparency and being good corporate citizens the SOC should share the vulnerability tools with the teams responsible for remediation. Let them have access, let them run their own reports and let them self-serve the information they need to be successful. Controlling who can run actual scans may be required but limiting access to information creates more problems than it solves. During attacks it should be expected that the SOC would share information about what is going on as well as the overall security of the business with all the members and stakeholders of the incident team and management. Holding back information will only serve to alienate groups; the flow of information needs to be proper and candid so that sound business decisions can be made. Security does not have to be secret internally to an organization or even externally in the proper forum and sharing environment.

There are a great many expectations that should be placed on a SOC in how it executes, in how it communicates and in how it protects an organization. The SOC you build should be as open as possible, be integrated into the organization and most of all transparent in its efforts.

# Infrastructure

When building a SOC, you not only need to think about all the security tools, systems, and infrastructure needed to protect your organization but you also need to think about all that is needed to support the center as well as the infrastructure the team is going to use to do its job. There are three specific and distinct areas of infrastructure that you must look at when planning your SOC.

- Support infrastructure

This infrastructure is really your SOC's eyes, ears, nose, and throat. These are all the things a SOC needs in order to be able to maintain access to and interact with all the other infrastructure devices, assets, and tools. If required, this will also contain the needed systems to maintain visual representation of real-time statistics such as video walls and projectors so that the SOC can react and be sensitive to potentially negative statistic fluctuations. These are the items along with other physical equipment that you would mostly find inside the SOC being used by the staff.

- Organizational security infrastructure

This infrastructure consists of the technology that is needed to protect your organization. This includes all the items out in the wilds of your network that need tender loving care and need to be reviewed by experts to ensure nothing bad is going on. This is the nuts and bolts of your security footprint and can consist of many, many different types of technologies applied in many different ways all in the effort to protect your organizations confidentiality, availability, and integrity, the triad of security goals. Your SOC may own and manage all or some of these devices or may just be the recipient of the systems technical output or logs.

- Operation center infrastructure

This is where we are going to spend most of our time in this chapter. Infrastructure needed to support your SOC is vital to your organizations security success. There are a lot of things to consider, a lot of important tools to review, and there are many different philosophies on how to approach these different topics. Typically these are the things that the SOC needs to operate but may be installed at remote locations, inside a data center or somewhere outside the physical SOC location.

The first area that we need to address is obviously your organization's overall security infrastructure; this includes any IDS, firewalls, web proxy systems, antivirus, data loss prevention systems, and so on that the SOC might be using or are even responsible for maintaining, see Appendix B. Second you need to look at any special requirements for servers the SOC will need such as the ticketing systems, a security event management system or any other specialized tools needing separate servers. You also need to consider if the SOC will operate its own private protected network and what impact that will have. Lastly you need to think about all the equipment your analysts and engineers will need. This includes not only the Macs or PCs at their desktops but also any video projectors, special monitors, or even separate Internet connections. All three of these technical areas, organizational security infrastructure, SOC infrastructure, and SOC support infrastructure must be addressed when building your SOC.

## ORGANIZATIONAL INFRASTRUCTURE > OPERATIONS INFRASTRUCTURE > SUPPORT INFRASTRUCTURE

If you ever thought you could just sit back and wait for the screen to tell you something bad happened on your network or with a host system and have lights and sirens go off when someone accesses something they should not, then you are about to have a rude awakening. In most cases, there is no silver bullet to security that will show you an attack has taken place. Most times to catch the bad guy an analyst will need to be patient and also be very determined not to give up looking for that "needle in a hay stack" that will lead them to find security issues needing to be addressed. When it comes to building a SOC, it can be as simple as one person looking at an IDS all day long or it can be as complex as a disperse team of 2500 people all managing and maintaining hundreds of different types of devices around the world. In either case, large or small, you have to take into consideration the same three areas of infrastructure when you are building your SOC.

## ORGANIZATIONAL SECURITY INFRASTRUCTURE

As defined above, the organizational infrastructure deployed at the enterprise level is the actual infrastructure you are going to use to protect all the required areas of your organization. These are the devices and technology that will be deployed across the entire enterprise in key locations that will perform the actual job of protecting, detecting, or stopping malicious behavior or attacks. This can be the firewall used at the perimeter or in your network or even at third-party companies and cloud service providers all the way to the antivirus software on a user's endpoint computer. When you look at a defense-in-depth approach to security, you will find many different systems that all need to be managed and monitored by trained security professionals to ensure they all work and are configured properly, they are being looked at and important alerts are being addressed. This section is not here to help you design or build the security of your network. Instead it is here for you to get a feeling, appreciate, or to help others understand the daunting task your SOC may face in managing and monitoring your organizations security. Some people believe that it is not a big deal to run a SOC, you just sit in front of the computer and read whatever the screen tells you and then call someone. I wish it was that easy because then we would not see so many data breaches in the news. When we look at a typical organizational security infrastructure, some people like to talk in terms of a defense-in-depth strategy because it is easy to break down the things needed for security into areas that will be deployed on the network infrastructure.

Let us take a quick look at some of the organizational security infrastructure that would be needed at various levels of that defense-in-depth strategy. This is not a complete or exhaustive list but rather just a sampling to help your thought process around what is really going to be needed by your SOC if you have to manage, maintain, or monitor all this stuff. Keep in mind that I am not going to explain the function of these devices but rather how these technologies are viewed from a SOC perspective or how they would integrate, be managed by, or be utilized within your SOC.

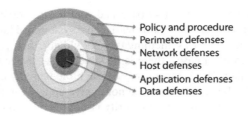

Policy and procedure
Perimeter defenses
Network defenses
Host defenses
Application defenses
Data defenses

# PERIMETER DEFENSES

At your perimeter, there are a few different types of technologies that you may want to use. But first understand that the perimeter is where your organizations control and management stop and some other service provider, business partner, or untrusted connection begins. The security model here is to prevent as much getting into your network as possible and detect all that you can if you cannot specifically stop it.

The first type of device in this area that you may think of is a firewall. Firewalls are vital to a SOC, they can tell you a lot about what is going on and what is coming into your network. The logs from a firewall need to be collected and analyzed, they are where you are going to find performance issues related to denial of service attacks, attempts by systems to violate access rules or devices being denied access due to many other reasons. But it is not always what is being denied on your firewall that is important. You almost always need firewall logs to help you determine the real IP address of an external system that is accessing your network if you are using Network Address Translation. When you translate real routable internet addresses to internal non-Internet routable addresses, you have to have a way to lookup the relationship to determine who is doing what. Without your firewall logs, the SOCs task of translating back and forth is going to be nearly impossible.

Next, we can think about a VPN or remote access system, this is where members of the organization will connect from outside the network to access internal resources. It is vital to maintain this system to ensure appropriate access is granted to users and that when people leave or no longer need the access it is revoked or taken away. So, monitoring users that access this resource is very important but also looking at where someone is accessing the system from may be even more important. If you see someone logging into the VPN from half-way around the world but they are currently in the office and you just saw them getting a cup of coffee then you may have a problem. Your SOC should be able to utilize these basic systems to gain valuable visibility into what security issues may be impacting your organizations network perimeter and who may be getting unauthorized access. Of course there are many more devices like proxy servers you may find in the perimeter of your network but let us move on.

## NETWORK DEFENSE

The next ring or layer deep in your defense strategy is the internal network. This is the internal portion of your organization that communicates together in potentially one or more different segments or areas. Security-relevant items you will typically find here are things like intrusion detection or prevention systems, network access control (NAC) systems, along with data loss prevention systems and behavioral or anomaly detection systems. IDSs should be set up wherever there is a network segment that can communicate with another network segment and data traffic passes between those two different networks or areas. This will act like a choke point and allow you to see all the network traffic that are successfully passed and evaluated by signatures internal to the IDS and determined if anything was bad or not. This could be traffic such as hackers trying to exploit vulnerabilities. The output of the IDS is vital for the SOC to review and evaluate but to also manage and to keep the system updated with the latest signatures to detect bad network traffic. NAC systems are also great at helping to prevent systems that are not owned by the organization to connect to an internal network. The SOC should keep a close eye on the changes to a network and what devices are connected or not connected. An attacker does not need to be outside the network in some far off place, they could be inside an organization's own four walls trying to get access to data and resources or they could be from an unattended conference room. Logs and alerts from these types of systems are important information that should be collected and analyzed by the SOC, this could also include systems that attempt to connect to any wireless networks or try to impersonate the real wireless network the organization is running.

## HOST DEFENSES

Quickly thinking about host defenses you would want your SOC to manage and monitor would include systems like antivirus, device controls for USBs or host-based data loss prevention systems. When antivirus software detects the presence of a virus there are a number of things that happen, one of which is hopefully cleaning the virus. But often times there are viruses that get detected that cannot be cleaned. There are many reasons for this but more importantly there has to be some notification of this type of condition that gets back to the SOC so that manual intervention can take place and the impacts of the virus will not cause any real issues. Often viruses are designed to steal data or open up doors to allow attackers easier access into protected networks. When data are going to leave your network, you should evaluate them to ensure they are supposed to leave and that they are being sent by the right person who has permission to send it and that its going to a known or reliable destination. Data loss prevention systems can operate at the network level and the host level, these systems are configured with rules to detect important data that an organization owns and ensure it is being moved across a network properly. The rules that these systems operate with have to be maintained and alerts for violations of those rules need to be reviewed and acted upon by the SOC.

## APPLICATION DEFENSES

Applications that perform critical functions or store important data for your organization need to be protected as well. These applications can live almost anywhere in your network at your organization from individual hosts to primary servers or mainframe computers. This is a fairly large and broad area for security as there are many different considerations in how to protect different applications but also for how a SOC would interface with those protection systems. It is important that applications are patched, a SOC that runs regular vulnerability scans should be able to detect when an application is out of date with its patches and escalate that information as a notification to the application owner in order to get it updated. Viruses, shellcode, and other malicious logic can take advantage of your applications and make them do things that they were not supposed to. Being able to detect when application files are inappropriately being modified or when a user keeps trying their password over and over again 1000 time per second are all things that the SOC needs to be on the look out for.

## DATA DEFENSE

You have all these layers of defense but it all comes down to the data and the resources storing that data. What kind of protections will you put in place to protect your data? Will you use file and volume encryption on your endpoint devices, secure vaulting on your servers, special group access, or even physical protections? Regardless of how you decide to protect your data, someone has to watch and react to alerts or modify the systems rules as needed.

## POLICIES AND PROCEDURES

Although not as technical as a ring like we have just been reviewing, policies and procedures will have large impacts to not only how your SOC operates but also what they are able to do and how they will do it. When you have a web proxy in place to protect your users from going to malicious sites, your SOC needs to review those events to ensure there are no infected systems with malicious software causing systems to access bad websites but your organization may also have policies on what can be download or what an employee is allowed to view on their computer. If you have a policy that says nobody is allowed to research guns and weapons while at work on a work computer then it may be the responsibility of your SOC to catch that and to properly report it to the HR department. There are many other policies and procedures that will impact the operation of your SOC, carefully review what your organization has and see what can be included into the SOC as part of their business objectives and help business controls. The policies and procedures will touch every aspect of not only how the SOC operates but how devices are configured, tuned, and deployed to protect against.

# SECURITY ARCHITECTURE

Now that we have talked about some of the enterprise level devices and organizational infrastructure out there that your SOC may be responsible for or get information from we need to talk about how this all comes together. If you were starting off from scratch or if you really need to take a good look at what you have and want to make sure you have the right equipment to protect your network, you would need the help of a security architect. This is someone who understands the needs and goals of the organization and who has a good understanding of where potential weaknesses could be. They will then work to recommend technology or configurations of existing systems to improve the overall security posture of a network. They will work with the larger IT organization to purchase, configure, and install security products that will monitor and protect the infrastructure. The architect should design countermeasures for different types of attacks such as unauthorized user access, data loss, hacking, malware, and many others. It is worth mentioning this role here because it is vital to the organization but will not always be a part of the typical SOC unless you are an MSSP. In many MSSPs, you will indeed find or should find security architects in the SOC. This does not mean that architects cannot be a part of the SOC but they are typically part of a larger security organization and will work along with the SOC to identify areas of weakness or areas that need improvement. These architects need to be responsible for understanding industry standards and best practices and be able to convert those to realistic technical controls. They have to keep up with not only networking trends but also emerging security technology as it relates to your core organizational security needs. They should be able to work effectively to help an organization design, size, and scale security solutions specific to organizational needs on a project by project basis or as part of an overall security strategy. Your architect will know what tools are out there to achieve security goals.

There is too much security technology that can be implemented at an organization to be covered in this one small chapter. Whether it is the access management system, network-based intrusion system, or core information technology infrastructure, you have to understand the size of the overall infrastructure you are protecting in order to make the right decisions on sizing your security solutions to be implemented. Basic example of this is if you plan to implement an access management system, you need to know how many users you have so that you can install the software on the right sized hardware meaning, memory, hard disk drive, as well as processing power, then you need to buy enough licenses to cover all of your users who will be accessing the system.

In keeping with the same example when we start to look at the structure required to run your SOC, we also need to know what the expectations are for the SOC in utilizing the implemented organizational security infrastructure. The requirements for your SOC will be very different if your access management system is fully automated opposed to a system where the SOC will be managing access grants and revocations from the system. You also have to consider if the access management system will talk to other systems such as sending logs to an SIEM infrastructure. So, for each

IT system implemented in your organization, you need to have an honest and open discussion about what needs to be protected how it is to be protected and what the expectations are for the SOC in protecting those systems. For some companies, this is a standard risk assessment. In many cases, there may be systems where the SOC may not be directly responsible for managing such as a web server, but there may be very real and specific requirements for the SOC to protect that web server from intrusions. Different organizations will employ different technologies for this purpose, all depending on the risk assessment of that device and the organizations desire to protect it. This could mean the implementation of application layer firewalls all the way to just collecting logs in a centralized log management system. But you do not need to boil the ocean when looking at your organizational infrastructure and how it is secured before you set up your SOC. You do, however, need to create a positive forum in your environment in which information technology, security, and business representatives can openly discuss what needs to be protected and what the risks are to an organization compared with the level of security currently being provided for a specific asset. Once you get a good idea about the entire organizational security infrastructure that needs to be either managed, control or utilized by your SOC can you then start to think about what is needed for your SOC in order to perform the job. Even if you think you have everything covered and you were correctly sized in your environment you still need to make sure that you allow enough capacity to grow. You want to make sure that as you develop your security infrastructure you are flexible enough to scale up or even down depending on your company or organizational needs and financial condition.

## SIEM/LOG MANAGEMENT

There are a ton of papers and books[1] written on the topic of SIEM or just security event management, whichever you choose to call it. There are also a ton of papers and books written about log management. Since both are very heavily covered topics there is no real reason to cover them in-depth in this book except for the fact that they are critical and extremely functional components to a SOC and deserve a review.

Years ago when the function of security was really just starting out people who were trying to protect a network from hackers would build a basic IDS or a file integrity checker. They would build this system, get it up and running, connect it to the right part of the network, and watch it like a hawk. Their eyes would be glued to the screen waiting for something to happen and then pounce on every alert like a cat chasing a mouse. After a while, it tends to get boring or you have to install several systems on different parts of your network and the review of the information gets very tedious. I am talking about a time when we did not have fancy graphical interfaces and webpages to look at. Everything was command line and stored in

[1]NIST SP 800-92, Guide to Computer Security Log Management, which is available at http://csrc.nist.gov/publications/PubsSPs.html.

files. When you have several different systems, going back and forth to each system looking for events and chasing down potential issues becomes difficult and very time consuming. To help resolve these issues programs were created to generate emails when changes were detected. Similar to the way email groups worked these messages could be sent for every alert or digest versions could be sent once a day. This helped make things a bit more manageable but there was just too much information to consume. Now, fast forward time to today where we have more advanced systems each with their own graphical interface, dashboards, and charts along with raw data visualizers, all viewed as a web page or inside a custom application, it does not make things any easier. Although these systems have come a long way to provide better value in managing their data and events, a typical security infrastructure can employ hundreds of different types of security systems, and thousands of rules that all generate an amazing number of events 24 h a day. To really manage these events properly you need to be able to prioritize and address as many of the most critical ones as close to near real time as possible. SIEM tools have really helped in this area. By creating a system that can consume events from hundreds of different types of devices and systems and then build rules around those events, the SIEM has become what is known as a force multiplier, meaning it can make a few people do the job of many. By collecting all these events and building rules around them, you can really ensure that your SOC works what you want as a priority and stays on top of events. The SIEM can handle reporting to your ticket system and even perform any additional communication or notifications you need. Today, a SOC that operates without some kind of a SIEM tool is seriously handicapped. A SIEM tool is one of the best ways to utilize security intelligence data to proactively monitor for suspicious indications of threats. Additionally a SIEM tool is going to be able to provide you a significant ability in metrics reporting and security analytics that may be required to not only spot problem areas but to also provide reports to management. I am not saying that every organization needs to go out and buy their SOC the best tool money can afford, and there are even some low cost if not free ones out there, you can definitely find champagne on a beer budget, but to not aggregate and collect events from your security tools into a central repository that has been built with your organizations workflow, priorities, and objectives in mind will significantly reduce the efficiency of your SOC and reduce the effectiveness of your overall security strategy.

Log management is a bit of a different story and I want to separate it out from SIEM because they are really two entirely different things. Some people believe or understand log management and SIEM to be relatively the same but they are really not and should not be considered the same in any way. I would like to place a clear definition on each for the purpose of how a SOC and your organization should view these systems.

SIEM should be considered as a system that is capable of the short-term collection and storage of security-relevant data and information that has functions and controls to aggregate like events, correlate multiple events in a series or chain in order to build new security-relevant events to be investigated by trained security personnel. High speed and performance are going to be your two primary concerns for the hardware running your SIEM solution.

Log management should be considered as a system that is capable of the long-term protected collection and storage of complete raw event data that has advanced search and reporting capabilities for auditors to ensure compliance with organizational controls and for security personnel to perform forensic and historical research. Large storage and backup capabilities are going to be your areas of focus for your log management solution.

All too often I see organizations trying to use a log management system to perform the tasks that a SIEM was created to do and vice versa. This does not mean that the two types of systems do not have similar capabilities but they will usually approach the problems from different perspectives. A system that is designed to evaluate events against hundreds of rules at high speeds will be a very expensive system to use as a log aggregation repository. A log management solution should be able to store logs at a much cheaper cost.

Let us look at a typical scenario where this difference can be expressed. When a hacker attacks a server, there can be hundreds of unique requests to that server being made and can typically be very noisy as far as the volume of events. In a log management system, this noise can be very difficult to see with thousands of other logs all being collected at the same time. With a SIEM tool, rules can be created to see this type of activity automatically and create a single new alert that notifies your SOC that a potential attack is in progress. A more difficult example of this may be an attacker who tries to disguise a server attack by initiating requests very slowly and waiting long amounts of time between attack requests. In this case, reviewing a single day or week's worth of logs may not show you any recognizable trends, like a needle in the haystack. But with the right rules and properly trained SOC staff, they will be able to recognize these trends when they are analyzed over a week, or month inside a SIEM. The attackers source IP address may even be automatically captured by the SIEM tool immediately upon the first detected event and then as the attacker gets more aggressive or performs other threat-based events the system will automatically raise the criticality of what that IP address is doing on the network to raise the awareness, whereas the log management system will just simply collect all the events.

I do not want to diminish the needs of collecting logs at all, it is a vital part of any complete and robust security operation. You must be able to collect the right data in your logs, monitor for anomalies and store them for a reasonable amount of time. Not only do logs need to be collected they also need to be protected especially if an attacker is able to compromise a server. A log management system serves a great purpose as it gives you the ability to move log files off of a system so that an attacker who wishes to cover their tracks cannot alter those logs. This goes well beyond setting permissions on a system log or encrypting the logs, it takes them well out of reach by ensuring they are safe on a completely separate system. Most all servers and systems today provide some kind of log or Syslog[2] capability and these logs are

---

[2]Syslog is defined in IETF RFC 3164, The BSD Syslog Protocol, which is available at http://www.ietf.org/rfc/rfc3164.txt

what tell you something has gone wrong. The logs, regardless of how or if you collect them will tell you very important information, if configured correctly. They can tell you when suspicious activities have occurred and that something requires further investigation, they can also tell you what an attacker is doing by recording their commands or actions. Last but not least, your logs can become the subject of legal proceedings and therefore should be captured and stored in a safe and sound place. Most larger organizations will have audit departments that will work with a SOC and will help provide guidance on what reporting they need, how long to store the logs and what kind of storage system is acceptable from a legal perspective.

SIEM and log management can become a very expensive, systems can generate a ton of logs and these logs take up huge amounts of storage. For larger systems, this could be billions of events per day and when designing a system, it is very easy to under estimate the space that would be required to keep these systems running. Typically auditors and regulators like to see storage of specific logs for a year or more, when looking at the storage needs for billions of daily events over the course of a year the storage will get expensive. A log management system will understand the long-term storage needs and will be able to address that with data compression and other interesting and inexpensive ways to achieve your goals. The storage needs can fluctuate depending on what you are doing and what investigations you are performing, for example, you may decide to pump up the log detail on a specific device to get more information temporarily, this can easily become a concern for storage. Administrators of these systems have to closely monitor the size of the storage systems in the log management and SIEM environments to ensure they continue to operate properly. It is also worthwhile to note that as an organization grows systems, servers and networking equipment being used in an organization can grow in numbers or drastically increase in event rates, you need to take that into account and plan for storage growth in these tools and consistently revisit those plans. To help combat increasing log sizes and running out of storage, your SOC should work with your organization and auditors if you have them, to level set what is actually needed, and what can be removed from being captured in the logs. What is relevant and what can be eliminated are important items to review as some types of network devices and servers will allow you to select what types of events get logged and have the capability to turn off what you do not want. By eliminating what you do not need will help you store those important events at a lower cost. Do not just collect everything, make sure that your SOC, engineering, and management work together to ensure you get what you need.

# OPERATION CENTER INFRASTRUCTURE
## TICKETING SYSTEMS

An issue tracking system or ticket system is a vital part of your operation center. You need to be able to create, update, and resolve reported issues as well as track work progress. Just using a single security tool in your infrastructure may not be sufficient to properly analyze an event, though using all of the tools you have available combined to effectively monitor the network will empower the analyst to be successful. Each analyst over time will develop his or her own style of monitoring. Using a ticketing system will allow for a central repository of all notes and data used to perform each events analysis. This will not specifically instruct an analyst on how to do a particular job but help contribute to a better understanding of work flow and best practices and will allow others to follow behind them, read their notes, and validate their findings.

A ticket system can often also contain a knowledge base containing information on resolutions to common problems or may even have indicators about what true positive event looks like opposed to a false positive and can include ticket numbers that were previously solved as actual references. Consistent use of a ticket tracking system is considered one of the fundamentals of a good operation team. As such, we are going to spend some good time talking about different systems and what are some needed and optional components to your ticketing system for your SOC. This is such a vital resource to the SOC that you need to spend some good time thinking about what the requirements are before you implement anything. You need to know what the SOC team members will need and what kind of metrics you would like to get out of the system.

One of the primary features of a ticket system that you should look at is its ability to capture analyst's notes. This is critical as you analyze events, you need to make sure that notes are properly captured, time stamped, and easy to follow. The flow of notes can be cumbersome, you need to make sure you know what works for you. One time I worked in a SOC that had a ticket system that took me forever to find notes, they were buried somewhere and you could only see one note at a time. So I had to open the note, see if it was the one I wanted, then close it and open another. Each opened a new screen, it was a huge hassle even after I figured out how it worked. Some systems make you click on every note to see what is written, whereas other system list out all the notes in a very long linier way then there are other systems that have separate notes but as you click on each a text box activates with the information that you can easily see.

If you have a lot of devices in your security infrastructure or are protecting a large device list then it may be important for you to have your ticket system include an asset database to collect information on devices under management or being protected by the SOC. This is optional as this can also be accomplished if your organization already has an asset database so your needs may vary. Having an asset database included in your ticket system may afford you additional automation, workflows or easier access to information customized inside every ticket.

An array of communication methods such as text, email, or SMS text is also a major requirement you should think about with your ticket system so that you can automatically notify people of required actions. Additionally you will want to see what other systems or integrations are possible with your ticket system. For example, maybe your ticket system can automatically communicate with a change database or asset database. This will help you deconflict issues that arise looking like a security problem but is really an authorized change. There may be many different types of communication integrations possible with your ticket system so spend some time evaluating the possibilities as this will only extend your capabilities and improve the performance of your SOC.

A good basic ticket system will allow team members to create new entries that are individually numbered for easy tracing, and then allow the members of the SOC to make free form text entries regarding a specific case, events, or issue. The ticket system should track who made the entry, what time and date the entry was made and allow for different ticket statuses. Ticket statuses can be as simple and as basic as open or closed but can be also be very complex and detailed such as "waiting for system administrator call back" or "escalated to management".

Event analysis/investigation is a time-sensitive process and crucial information can be flushed or overwritten from security devices or sensors lacking large storage devices. if the processes take too long to retrieve the information you need. No matter what, you are going to work against the clock if you are under attack and you want to reduce the impact of that attack. Quickly reacting to threats and attacks may allow you to get an intrusion prevention block in place or shut down a system to prevent the spread or escalation of an attack. The SOC needs to always perform work quickly, but not hastily. They should not have to think about the current process and what the next steps should be, the ticket systems and workflows should be there to support them. In order to make your ticketing system work best for you, think about your events and what problems or malicious activities might cause a certain set of system alerts to be ticketed, then build your ticketing system to match those events and the workflow you will need to be the best at effective analysis, communication and ultimate conclusion of those events your SOC will address.

When an analyst has used all of the security tools available to them and determined that an incident has occurred or further validation is needed, entering information into a ticket should always be the next feasible step an analyst will need to do. It is crucial that all of the information available is put in the event ticket that was generated or created and the information should be in great detail. Capture all of the logs, screen shots, and network flows as possible during the investigation and include it in the ticket. There should be no issue with information overload inside your ticketing system. The robust information you include in each and every ticket will only help when more than one person in the SOC gets assigned to work a ticket so that everyone can better understand what the original analyst was seeing or what they are basing decisions on. You should also consider that tickets may need to be reviewed hours, days, or even months after an incident and it can be difficult to remember all the gory details, good data in your ticket will help. Multiple people working a ticket is common as this can happen for example, if an event gets created during first shift and another analyst picks up and works the event on second shift. Or if an analyst needs to escalate a ticket to a more senior person such as an engineer, that second person who gets the escalation should not have to redo all the original research as all the required information needs to be in the ticket.

You should also consider using the concept of queues. This will allow you to split up your tickets into different areas for either team focus or organization. For example, you may want a general queue where all tickets get automatically created or created by your tier-1 analysts. Next you may want a separate engineering queue, this is where your analysts can place existing tickets that need the attention of the engineering team. This type of queuing will allow different teams to focus and see only the tickets they are concerned about and remove extra information and noise that they do not.

## BUILDING THE TICKET SYSTEM

There are many different ticket systems out there to choose from. There are free and open source ticket systems and also very expensive ones that you can choose. From a technical or implementation perspective, there are many different decisions about features, functionality, licensing, support, and platform that you will need to consider.

But, before we dive deep into what your ticket system should look like or do for you, your first step should be to see if there is anything that is already being used in your organization that you could leverage and utilize for your own needs. It may be a very simple process and much cheaper to work with an already established system in your organization. By working inside an established system you can gain significant advantages as there may be existing support structures and knowledgeable people that you can work with on training, design and development in getting new queues and workflows built just for your SOCs use. By utilizing an existing ticket system you will be able to easily move tickets around your organization for when issues need to be addressed by teams outside your SOC or if issues arise that external teams want the SOC to address.

One drawback of using an existing system that you will need to ponder is the security and permissions of how the system is managed. What I mean by this is you need to carefully review who will have access to your tickets and your queues. For the most part having people who are not in the SOC look at tickets will not be a big deal but if your SOC is performing investigations on employees of the company then very tight controls will need to be placed on this data. Investigations in a SOC can and regularly will contain information about users but may not be because of something that a user directly did. For example, assume a user visited a normal and typical news website that happed to display a link or advertisement that was detected by your security infrastructure as malicious. An alert may be generated and a subsequent ticket created. Then inside this ticket, an investigation would be performed that would include the users browser activity, their system logs or antivirus scans plus a bunch of other things depending on your tool sets. All of this investigative activity would be performed to ensure that the computing assets and network components are safe and free of malware but will have little or nothing to do with the actual user. To the casual or mistaken uninformed onlooker, it could be interpreted that the user did something bad, rumors, and water cooler talk could start and even though the user may never have not known their activity was being investigated people around them could build an unfair negative opinion about them. Without going into another long example, imagine if the SOC was investigating someone for insider threat, stealing data, or unethical behavior. Bottom line is that if you are going to use a ticket system that is already widely used in your organization, make sure that access is well understood, appropriate, logged, and controlled.

When you decide that you want to have your own brand new ticket system either because I scared you off from using the one your organization already has or there is nothing so you need to start from scratch anyway, the first thing you want to think about with a ticket system is its ease of use. An overly complex system or one that does not visually flow properly or make sense will be difficult to use and train people to be successful. The last thing you want is for investigations to get lost, and for your SOC to spend more time using and working the ticket system then analyzing security issues.

Next you will want to think about how you view information and may create different views to support various activities or different uses. For example, your main screen may show you a list of all open tickets but will give your SOC analysts the ability to sort those tickets by date created, criticality or any other criteria you want.

Here is a simple ticket view:

| Ticket # | Status | Date | Time | Subject |
| --- | --- | --- | --- | --- |
| 1875 | NEW | 6/9/14 | 12:47 | MS-SQL Buffer overflow |
| 1877 | OPEN | 6/9/14 | 12:59 | Website block |
| 1881 | NEW | 6/9/14 | 13:46 | Unauthorized FTP transfer |
| 1882 | NEW | 6/9/14 | 14:02 | Virus found |
| 1888 | NEW | 6/9/14 | 14:02 | Denied IP by policy |

The ability to include tickets or give the SOC users the ability to change the filter of what is being displayed to different statuses may also be something you will want to consider. You might also want to allow for the inclusion of other fields to be viewed. This could be items like the last modified date, the name of the analyst that owns the ticket if it was previously opened and so on. When filtering you may want to only see tickets that are new and nobody has addressed yet, or maybe you want to only see tickets that you own or have been working on. Another option you may also want to think about are using different colors of text to help highlight critical tickets, new tickets, or a tickets that need some kind of special attention.

Here, is the simple example again but with color, the color can be automatic workflow built into your ticket system to help point what the priority events are based on criticality or some automated workflow logic. You will need to make sure you document your workflow so that everyone clearly understands what things mean and how it all happens. In the example below, the different colored text of ticket 1875 may indicate that the ticket has been in a "NEW" status for too long and someone needs to open it and address it. While ticket 1882, that is all shaded in, may indicate a critical event that needs to be address before all others. Do not be afraid to use different colors to mean different things as long as you do not make it too complex. The idea is to be able to quickly highlight the important tickets when viewing a large list. At one SOC, the fact that tickets were red was not enough, they used the system's ability to blink/flash the ticket text on and off to add an extra sense of urgency on that item. Hopefully your ticket system will be versatile enough for you to be creative on how to color coordinate your ticket views. Remember, make sure that the colors of all the views make sense and are easy to use or are customizable by the user to their preference.

| Ticket # | Status | Date | Time | Subject |
|----------|--------|--------|-------|--------------------------|
| 1875 | NEW | 6/9/14 | 12:47 | MS-SQL Buffer overflow |
| 1877 | OPEN | 6/9/14 | 12:59 | Website block |
| 1881 | NEW | 6/9/14 | 13:46 | Unauthorized FTP transfer |
| 1882 | NEW | 6/9/14 | 14:02 | Virus found |
| 1888 | NEW | 6/9/14 | 14:02 | Denied IP by policy |

The basic fields that you should have in your ticket system are fairly straightforward. Even though the various fields should be standardized, typically ticket systems are not designed for a SOC but rather a more general purpose like a help desk or call center, so there will be a fair amount of customization you will want to make and will need to think about. In addition to the various important fields of information, you may want to customize workflow to streamline a process or ensure compliance with required steps you want your analysts to take.

Let us take a look at some of the primary fields your SOC will rely on and may or may not be part of a standard ticket system installation.

## SUBJECT

This may seem like a no brainer but the actual subject of a ticket is very important. When you are looking at the queue of your ticket systems, you may see rows and rows of tickets and if they all have the same subject then how would you know what ticket you need or would like to work on. The subject of the ticket can be passed to the ticket system by the device that generated the original event. In the case of a SIEM tool, you may even have the ability to customize this field's value. If for example you were sending IDS alerts directly to your ticketing system then the subject field may just be the name of the signature that fired such as "MSSQL Overflow", "New server on network" or "Virus found". If you are able to customize the output of the system that generates an event or if you are going to manually create an event, try and keep the subjects standardized. This way, as you look through tickets or search historical tickets you will find it much easier to get what you want. Some

SOC environments may want to have the source IP address of the device that caused the alarm as part of the subject. That way if you have multiple tickets with the same alert name you can quickly see if it is all coming being caused by the same device or multiple devices.

Example:

| Ticket # | Status | Date | Time | Subject |
|---|---|---|---|---|
| 1875 | NEW | 6/9/14 | 12:47 | MS-SQL Buffer overflow – 192.168.10.51 |
| 1876 | NEW | 6/9/14 | 12:47 | MS-SQL Buffer overflow – 192.168.10.51 |
| 1877 | NEW | 6/9/14 | 12:47 | MS-SQL Buffer overflow – 192.168.10.51 |
| 1878 | NEW | 6/9/14 | 12:47 | MS-SQL Buffer overflow – 192.168.10.51 |
| 1879 | NEW | 6/9/14 | 12:47 | MS-SQL Buffer overflow – 192.168.10.51 |
| 1894 | NEW | 6/9/14 | 12:48 | CMD.EXE execution – 192.168.10.51 |

Once you are able to find a ticket you need to work on you should be able to select that ticket to begin work and perform your analysis. Once you select a ticket it should open up to the "ticket view". This is a view where you can see all the important elements of your event. It should be arranged in a way that is easy for an analyst to quickly assess the event and make quick decisions on what to do next. It could include asset information, and knowledgebase information all on the same screen as the basic event information.

In most cases, your event information and details should be on the top and the rest of the majority of the screen should be dedicated to allowing the analyst to make notes, upload documents, and perform actions on the ticket such as escalating it, changing its status, or even closing it.

## PARSED VALUES FROM EVENTS

Your ticket system may have the ability to parse, chop, or read raw events that gets sent to it. When it reads these events, it can place key information into separate fields of the ticket. This is extremely valuable as it allows you to perform key reporting or search for specific elements of events and build metrics or to even spot trends. Values such as Source IP, Destination IP, Source Port, Destination Port, and of course the time the actual event occurred are all values that you should be able to read from a raw event and place into its proper place. Parsing can be valuable when you want to custom design your ticket view as we discussed above. Parsing events will allow you to put important data elements into the correct locations for easy viewing and searching.

## TIME TICKET CREATED

For automatically generated tickets, the time a ticket is created is typically later than the actual time an event was generated. It takes some time for a security device on a remote network to generate a log, have that log get sent either directly to the ticketing system, or be processed in a central log management or correlation engine. Knowing the time difference between when an event was generated and when a ticket was created can be very important especially if the time difference is hours not seconds or minutes. This may indicate problems on your network or some difficulty in processing. This lag is a metric that you should watch very carefully, it may help you to spot busy devices, or configuration errors with your security devices or even network congestion at a customer site. You need to learn what the normal deviation is and monitor or watch for any significant changes.

In the case of tickets that get manually generated, the ticket created time is also important because that will be the start of any event. This is where the timeline begins and without this it will be very difficult to figure out the chain of events when you start putting all your notes into the logs of the tickets. Sometimes analysts will do some research or complete an investigation prior to creating a ticket. Do not let this happen, anyone performing an investigation needs to have an open ticket first. This not only helps you track time people are spending on tickets doing analysis but it also allows your SOC supervisors the ability to watch the ticket queue to see who is working on what. Not only does it help them see what everyone is working on but if there is a ticket that stays open for a while it will allow the supervisor to check in with the analyst working on it to see what is going on and make sure they have all the resources they need and to make sure they are not dealing with a issues that will require additional attention from other SOC resources or engineers. Additionally if an analyst works an issue outside of the ticket system, you will lose track of what they are doing and will not know how to properly apply your resources. When an analyst is done with his research they may open a ticket and then just dump all their notes into that ticket and then close it. The results of that will make it look like they only had the ticket open for a minute but in reality they worked the issue reported inside that ticket for 2 h. It is very hard to capture the actual time worked on an individual ticket but as your build your system it is something you may want to keep in mind, or the system you select may have enhanced capabilities that allow you better visibility and reporting into how much time is actually spent on any given ticket. Time tracking systems built into your ticketing software can pay big dividends for you when creating metrics and evaluating your SOC. This is critical for resource planning and evaluating where bottlenecks may be in your processes. For more information on these types of metrics, refer to the chapter metrics. In the end, you really want to ensure your analysts are working inside the ticket system because things happen, documents get closed and information gets lost, or people get pulled in multiple directions and then it is difficult to go back to what you were doing if you did not keep accurate records.

# USER\GROUP\QUEUE

Tickets can be broken down and organized in many different ways. You need to make sure your organization of open tickets make sense and that they are easy to find, track, and address. All tickets except new tickets should be assigned to either a user or a queue. So when a new ticket is created, if it was created by a user, than that ticket should be assigned to that user automatically or if it was automatically generated then the ticket owner should be blank and it should be in a primary queue waiting for an analyst to open it and address it. If a ticket gets transferred to another group or queue then the ownership should be that queue until another user opens it. The history of actions, notes and ownership should all be logged and tracked inside the ticket for easy viewing. You may have different groups in your SOC such as your tier-1 or tier-2 analysts, engineering, or management and each of these groups should be a different ticket group in your ticket system.

*Key point*: The more granular the queue you can create the better metrics you can generate to see what is going on. But the more granular the queues, the harder it is for people to notice tickets that may be waiting for their attention. Make sure the division of groups and queues make sense for your workflow and reporting purposes.

Under each group there may be different queues for that group to organize tickets. Depending on your workflow you may only have one global queue for everyone to work out of but if you do have different requirements here is a quick example of what a group and queue structure may look like.

- Tier-1
  - General queue (all new tickets)
  - Health queue (security device or internal system issues)
  - Waiting for callback (tickets that have been addressed but waiting on an external resource to call/email back)
- Tier-2
  - Main escalation queue (location of general tickets that are being escalated to the tier-2 team)
  - Health queue (security device or system issues)
  - Waiting for callback (tickets that have been addressed but waiting on an external resource to call/email back)
- Engineering
  - Main escalation queue (location of general tickets that are being escalated to the engineering team)
  - Device based queues (individual queues based off of device type)
  - Provision/decommission (location of tickets for the installation of new devices or the removal of old ones)
  - Global issues (Tickets that effect overall service or delivery of service)
- Management/team leads
  - Main escalation queue (location of general tickets that are being escalated to management)

- Customer complaints (tickets that need loving care)
- Unresolvable issues (tickets that cannot be resolved due to technical issues, limited information or outages)

## SOURCE (SIEM, EMAIL, PHONE)

Ticket generation should come from many different sources. The ability to generate tickets from email messages is almost a no brainier. Emails can be automated from your security devices or they can come from users or customers. Tracking emails by converting them into tickets is a great way to ensure that all communications coming into your SOC are addressed and resolved professionally. Security systems like SIEM system or log management systems will have their own ability to create rules that trigger some action. That action could be a direct connection to your ticket system and have a new ticket opened that needs to be evaluated. The tight integration of your SIEM system and your ticket system is invaluable. Some SIEM systems include their own light weight incident management tracking system but you really need a way to handle tickets and incidents competently, so make sure you are able to effectively get important data from your SIEM to your ticket system. There are also automated ways to integrate your phone system with your ticket system. These integration systems are really nice for organizations that have a heavy call volume or in a MSSP operation, especially when an analyst is able to answer the phone and have a new ticket automatically open with the customer details already populated. This is a great way to make the SOC more efficient and provide great customer service. It also helps the SOC management ensure that all phone calls are tracked and logged appropriately in the ticket system for later review and to ensure that all work being performed in the SOC is being tracked. The sources of your tickets are an important value to keep track of and should have a field in your ticket system. You need to know where your tickets are being generated from for several reasons. First, if you are getting a ton of junk or false positive tickets being generated you should know where they are coming from. If you have many different systems all automatically reporting and sending in information to generate tickets and you do not have the source information then it will be extremely difficult to know what system needs to be adjusted to resolve or tune the problem. You also need to know how your SOC is being informed of issues that need to be addressed. If you are properly engaged with your organization and have effectively communicated what you do, what your specialties and responsibilities are then your tickets should not all come from your automated tools. You should expect a percentage of your tickets to be coming in from phone calls, emails, your portal system, and possibly ticket escalations from outside the SOC. It is very important to track these sources so that you can run effective metrics to determine and evaluate where your most critical or even reliable source of events are coming from. Additionally you should be able to run reports on the kinds of issues you are getting from each source so that you can better understand the value you are getting from that device or team.

# CATEGORY

An incident should be categorized as one of the categories as listed in the below table based on the type of incident. These categories are fairly standard in the industry and are regularly used by computer emergency response teams everywhere. the table provides a listing of the different categories and a definition/description of each category.

| Category | Name | Description |
|----------|------|-------------|
| CAT 1 | Root-level compromise | This category is used when an individual gains unauthorized root-level access (logical or physical) to the organization's network, any of the systems, applications, data, or other resources. |
| CAT 2 | User-level access | This category is used when an individual gains unauthorized user-level access (logical or physical) to the organizations network, any of the systems, applications, data, or other resources. |
| CAT 3 | Attempted access | This category is used when an unauthorized user attempts to gain unauthorized access to the organization's assets (local or remote) |
| CAT 4 | Denial of service (DoS) | An attack that *successfully* prevents or impairs the normal authorized functionality of networks, systems or applications by exhausting resources. This activity includes being the victim or participating in the DoS. |
| CAT 5 | Poor security practice | This category is used when misuse or unauthorized use of an organization's information technology assets is discovered. Also, covers violation of the organizations computer security policies such as weak password, or misconfigured system. |
| CAT 6 | Scanning/ probing | This category includes any activity that seeks to access or identify a company or organizations computer, open ports, protocols, services, or any combination for exploit. This activity does not directly result in a compromise or DOS. |
| CAT 7 | Malicious code | *Successful* installation of malicious software (e.g., virus, worm, Trojan horse, or other malware) that infects an operating system or application. |
| CAT 8 | Unknown | This category can be used for a ticket that does not currently have a determination of what is happening. A ticket with this category selection cannot be closed until a specific category has been determined |
| CAT 9 | Exercise | Since categories will be used for metrics, any tickets generated while exercising or testing should be closed with this category in order to keep these types of events separate from all the real events. |
| CAT 0 | Discard | This category should be used for falsely generated tickets, bad tickets, or any tickets that should just be discarded and not counted. |

## STATUS

The individual status of ticket is important, it tells you very quickly what is going on with that issue and when combined with other key values it can really help you to manage your flow and rate of ticket closures. You will have to think about what values will make sense to you as your SOC gets going but there are a few basic ones you can start with.

- New—The value of any ticket that was just created and has had no work done or nobody has touched it yet.
- Assigned—Someone is currently assigned to the ticket work may or may not have begun on it.
- In progress—Tickets that are being worked on but that may be scheduled for resolution during a change window or at some agreed upon time.
- On hold—Tickets that cannot be completed right now, something is needed or other actions need to happen before these tickets can move forward.
- Reopened—This is a ticket that was previously resolved and closed but had to be reopened for some reason.
- Resolved—Tickets that are presumed to be closed and have a clear resolution.

It may be a good idea to set time limits on tickets or even force workflow for tickets in different states so that nothing gets lost or forgotten. For tickets put into an "On hold" status maybe you can force a user selectable timeout. So when a user puts a ticket on hold they have to select a specific date and time the status will automatically change from "on hold" to "In progress" or "New". Then you can put specific time limits on tickets that are "in progress" and change their color to signify that they have not been addressed or looked at in too long of a time period. Your imagination can run wild with possibilities, make sure your ticket system is capable of meeting your imaginative needs in this area.

## REASON CODES

Not every system uses reason codes but it is a great way to help build metrics or gain better visibility into why a ticket is in a particular state. For example, if you have a ticket that was resolved, why or how was it actually resolved is a bit of a mystery unless you open the ticket and look for a "reason" as to how it was deemed to be resolved. By using reason codes it will help you understand specific states of your tickets and also give you nice clues for tickets that may be in the wrong state or need additional work. A good example of a ticket that is properly resolved would have a reason code of "Infection Cleaned". An example of a ticket in the wrong state would be a ticket that is marked resolved but has a reason code of "waiting for call back". Running reports that show different statuses and their associated reason codes will help you see what is going on very quickly. We talk more about metrics in a different chapter but it should be easy to see how valuable combining fields help build a very clear picture of what is going on. The reason codes should make sense to your workflow and mean something if you want to pull reports and build metrics. As a quick example, searching for every ticket in a given month that has a reason code of "Infection Cleaned" could be used very effectively. Those may not only be tickets you want to report on but also review to find out what is causing all the infections or what is missing to allow viruses to get in.

Here are a few reason codes that will help you get started

- Waiting for external ticket update
  - This is good if you are using a different ticket system than the rest of your organization and you want to keep checking the other system or you are waiting for an email to be generated to let you know when your ticket in the other system has been updated. It would be a good idea to also document what the external ticket number is so that you have an easy cross-reference.
- Waiting for a child ticket to close
  - This can indicate that another subordinate ticket is linked to the parent ticket and a child ticket issue will need to be resolved before the parent ticket can be closed. This is good if you have an incident that spans multiple devices, a primary ticket can be created for the main event while individual tickets are created for the review of each potentially effected system.
- Waiting for call back
  - A call from the user or another support group is expected to update or confirm that the issue has been resolved.
- System not vulnerable
  - After your investigation into an event, you determine that the system has been fully checked and is not vulnerable to whatever attack or events alert triggered.
- No infection found
  - For virus alerts, the system has been checked and no infection has been found.
- Infection cleaned
  - For virus alerts, the system has been checked and the infection was cleaned.
- System remediated
  - The system has been checked and a patch, software upgrade, or configuration change has been applied to correct the vulnerability or issue.
- False positive
  - A triggered alert without the presence of proper evidence to support the alert.
- Confirmed security incident
  - Evidence has been collected to support that a security incident has occurred. Tickets with this reason code should have a complete root cause analysis.
- In progress
  - Evidence to support the alert is actively being gathered.

- Review ticket/needs follow-up
  - More evidence is needed within the ticket to support the alert or an assigned group needs to review the information.
- Signature tuned
  - The generating source system signature or rule has been tuned and will not generate another alert like this one.

## ACKNOWLEDGMENT/TICKET FEEDBACK

There are two external communication mechanisms that I grouped together but are actually completely separate functions you may want for your ticket system. For acknowledgement, you may want a customer, device owner, or even an internal SOC analyst to acknowledge the creation of a new ticket that was generated in your system. This can be a great customer notification mechanism that alerts them to a potential issue that your SOC is working on and gives them an opportunity to weigh in on the issue right from the beginning. When a customer gets a notification they may look at it and immediately know why the ticket was generated and can help you close it quickly. In the acknowledgement function, you can track to see how long it takes someone to respond and you will have good metrics on response times to your issues. Also, if you require him or her to click on something to record the acknowledgement, it is a good way to make sure you confirm they know about the issue. The acknowledgement could just be a simple reply to an email, click to a website or logging into a portal to view the issue that generated the ticket. Since your SOC will be either working with external customers to your organization or internal customers inside you may want the ability to customize acknowledgements based off of customer or department preferences. May be it is critical that for every ticket generated in the SOC for your organization's web servers, the web team needs to actually acknowledge the ticket whereas another external customer may just want to be notified with no acknowledgement. Customization of how your ticket system interacts with people is vital to the level of customer service you want to provide.

Acknowledgement is typically at the beginning of the process of working an issue but ticket feedback is at the end. It is always a good idea to try and find out how you are doing and by giving people a quick short survey whenever you close a ticket can be extremely helpful. You will want to make sure that you can customize this feature as well or it can become a burden quicker than it can be helpful. Make sure that you are asking the right questions for the survey and change the questions often so that you are getting a good review of different parts of the service you are offering. Also, be mindful of peoples email inbox, do not flood them with a ton of surveys, try to get some built in capabilities to limit how many surveys you send someone out of your ticket system in a span of time. Otherwise people will just ignore these requests as an annoyance.

## WORKFLOW AND AUTOMATION

In order to make your ticket system more capable and really aid your analysts, you will need to add some workflow and automation. Workflow can consist of predefined tasks that need to be completed for the type of ticket an analyst is working on. The tasks will need to be performed in order, will dictate the specific details of what needs to be done, and will require input for the task to be completed. This can help if you need to collect specific information for tickets and want to ensure that each analyst collects all the required information and in the correct order prior to closing a ticket. It will also make sure that information is collected and posted to a ticket in an organized and expected way.

Automation is a great way to aid in the regular analysis of information. For example if you could automate the login process to a specific system or external device from the ticket system, it would save you a ton of time having to look up login details. I am not condoning hardcoded password here, I am assuming there is some secure functions happening in the background. For example, if your ticket system had an asset database and when a ticket was generated for a specific device in that database, you automatically had a remote desktop button that you could press. Another good automation idea maybe that when a ticket is generated for an IDS event, the ticket system will automatically pull health information from the device that was the suspected target of the attack and post those details into the ticket notes. It could tell your health information of the device like if the device is still up and online, CPU statistics, network statistics, and so on. This may give your analyst a quick bit of information to tell them if there was any impact associated with the event. The ticket system you evaluate may have many different automation and external system integration capabilities, spend time evaluating these features, and see what you may be able to take advantage of. Having this type of automation will reduce the analyst's manual involvement in gathering data and information by having the system execute rules that automatically perform an action on a ticket when certain conditions are met. There is nothing quite like opening up a ticket to see all the research you need right in front of you, there ready to be evaluated without lifting a finger.

*Key point*: Count your mouse clicks, if it takes to many clicks to get information or you cannot quickly find information to analyze a ticket then you are wasting time. Figure out how to automate tasks, reduce the number of mouse clicks it takes to perform tasks, and make your SOC faster through automation.

## PORTAL INTERFACE

You may think that discussing a portal interface is kind of odd in this section but it is very worthy topic right here. Most ticket systems these days will have some kind of web interface. Even if the ticket system you select does not operate completely through the web, there will typically be some kind of interface that you can leverage.

This is a great feature to offer your internal or external customers. If you are able to give customers an account so that they can see all their tickets, interact with your SOC by placing notes in tickets or be able to even pull custom reports you will be giving them a great self-service capability and making your SOC more efficient at the same time. The portal does not have to be just for tickets, you can use it for posting special information, posting client specific reports or generic reports for all customers to review. You can use the portal to sell additional services or make sure all customers have key contact information to work with in the SOC. Your portal can be anything you want, but having your ticket system be integrated with that portal can really add to the professionalism of your SOC and provide customers with great value.

## MOBILE DEVICES

Being able to respond to tickets or just having the ability to quickly look at new tickets once it is generated can mean the difference between saving your organization from a significant breach or being able to finish your lunch. There are many technologies out today that allow you to securely connect to your ticket system and see basic information that allow you to make split second decisions on whether or not something needs to be addressed right away or if it can sit for the time being. As was mentioned previously, your ticket system should have the ability to set a criticality levels to the ticket. The ticket system can email specific types of events to you based on rules you create or for more serious events or special events you should be able to create text alerts as well. These types of remote alerts should be configurable not just to one person but an entire group of people or specifically assigned people based on rules. You should also be able to acknowledge or respond to tickets just by replying to emails and of course all of this interaction should be automatically recorded in the logs of the ticket.

Additionally you may want a mobile application for customers so they can monitor their security posture. This could be done with a small dashboard that details how many open tickets they have, the criticality of those tickets and even the event generation rates over the course of a day, week, or month.

## SUPPORT INFRASTRUCTURE

It all starts off with the SOC computer, many times I have been asked, "What's better for a security analyst to use, Mac or a PC?" What makes this question so difficult is that many organizations have a standard, and because the standard exists, all departments inside of an organization should comply with organizational standards. For many years, now most enterprises have been using Microsoft Windows devices as the common go to platform for most employees. These organizations have spent a lot of time and money building corporate infrastructure to support and manage a PC environment. So because these corporate infrastructures already exist to support the PC environment, the security analyst wishing to utilize a different platform such as a Mac or even a Linux platform could prove to be challenging. I really do not care to be in the middle of this debate other than to say that some of the best analysts I have worked with will of course have their favorites, but will confidently be able to operate inside any platform or all platforms. In many cases, they will utilize a Mac or PC and Linux operating system in one way or another each and every day in order perform their core job functions. I am sure nobody reading this book will thank me for this section because I know that I am not providing any real definitive answer, nor am I loading up any arguments for one operating system opposed to another. The reality is that I do not see any SOC truly being successful without having access to multiple if not many versions and distributions of different operating systems if not for testing purposes than for special analysis functions. For example, there are many tools written for the Linux platform that make forensic analysis easier when dealing with certain types of cases. The Windows operating systems maybe better when trying to perform malware analysis. Finally the Mac OS X operating system may be easier to work with as it combines many features of the other operating systems but is also extremely capable of running several virtual machines with different operating systems all at the same time.

## PHYSICAL

There is a lot to think about when you are designing the physical layout of your SOC. As with any build out of any space there are a ton of considerations that have to be made, many more than this book could detail. Instead of diving too deep into physical space considerations I am only going to touch lightly on some options and important considerations that you should think about, but again this is no way a comprehensive list by any means. Keep in mind that if you are providing a SOC as a service to external customers or you may want to showcase your SOC to internal or external customers then the aesthetics become very important. Your SOC should reflect the work you do and the quality of the services you provide. Be proud of what you do!

Typically organizations will give all employees a desk, computer, desk phone, and any other desk accessories someone may need to perform the basics of the job they were hired to do. In a SOC that may not be the case and you need to think carefully about the environment that you create to ensure it is comfortable and healthy. Some of you that have never worked in an operation center before many think I am a bit weird about now to bring up comfort and health but it is a real concern that you have to consider. For other more experienced people who have worked a few years in an operations center you know exactly what I am talking about. Working in an operation center is not for everyone and the decisions you make here could be some of the biggest differences in being able to retain good talented people or even keep your SOC up and running.

Take for example a SOC that is chartered to run 24×7 on three shifts 365 days a year or two shifts for 16 h 7 days a week. You would not necessarily give everyone that works in your SOC their own desk, phone, and stapler. Instead you would create shared workspace so that you could reduce costs and reduce the size requirements of your space. Regardless of the physical layout of the SOC it makes perfect sense to utilize shared space if you are running multiple shifts. One of the very first lessons I learned managing a shared space work environment is to always be mindful of health concerns. One person coming into the SOC with a common cold could wipe out all your staff for a few weeks. You may think this is normal for any work environment but in a shared space, operational environment it is intensified. Multiple people are using the same handset on phones, a quick call is one thing but if your SOC analysts are spending a good amount of time on escalation calls or support calls then for the next shift to come in and pick up the same phone is kind of unpleasant. People are sitting at a computer for an 8 h shift using a mouse that someone else was just using for 8 h. Does it make you feel a bit sick thinking about using a mouse that someone else's sweaty hands were just using for the last 8 h? There are other considerations but these two alone are a huge way to pass on germs, virus, and sicknesses to each other. To combat these issues, there are a few easy things that you may want to do. First, consider allowing SOC staff to either bring in their own compatible headsets and mice at their cost to use for work or provide them a standard model of each. During each shift change, each analyst would change over to his or her personal headsets and mice. This could also be a design consideration for the desks and consoles that you would purchase for the SOC. You needed to make sure that the USB ports and phone ports are accessible enough to allow for easy changes or purchase quick connect cables to perform the same function. Moving slightly away from the phones and mice, the desk surfaces were also a major concern. People regularly will eat at their desk during work, whether it be a quick snack or a major meal. Typically not a big deal but now your SOC desks are cafeteria tables and need to be taken care of as well so that people do not get sick. Think about it, do you really want to come to work and sit at a nasty desk that someone was just using who may not have the best personal grooming habits and use their phone and mouse and eat your lunch right where they ate there is a few hours ago? I know that I do not what to go anywhere near that place. Anyway, I think I have grossed everyone out by now just by thinking about this but this is a serious issue and if one person gets sick in an environment like this then you are going to quickly find yourself with an extremely light staffing level as everyone is going to be calling in sick. Depending on the size of your SOC, sometimes it may seem that as soon everyone gets over one round of colds it starts back up again. Allowing people to use personal headsets and mice is one way to combat a part of this issue but you also need to make sure you keep your SOC clean. You may think that regular cleaning would resolve this issue but in a 24×7 SOC there is almost no down time.

Do not let people leave food around. I have a few good stories about this one, as I am sure many other people do as well, people that have worked with me in the past may be chuckling, as I know there are a few pictures out there that bring this point home very graphically. So make sure that you have adequate garbage facilities or plenty of caution tape. You may also want to think about not allowing food or drinks into the SOC but this could prove to be challenging as well.

Ensure that your organization's facility services has access to your SOC and is able to get in to clean and vacuum on a regular basis just like they normally would any other part of the organization. This all sounds logical but in some of the secure and cleared facilities I have been in I have found it to not be so easy. Plus, you have to remember that depending on your SOC schedule there could be people working around the clock so what is the best time to make noise vacuuming and cleaning. If you are in a secure space the cleaning crew may be required to be escorted at all times but any classified or sensitive processing has to stop and be covered up while they are in the room. Finally, and this is no joke, at one SOC I managed I actually had a budget line item for disinfectant wipes and sprays. I had a regular shipment of wipes brought into the SOC and spread around the various workstations so that during each shift change over people could wipe down and disinfect their areas.

Ventilation is also a key aspect to your SOC space. Most SOC's are behind closed doors or in secure areas and as such needs extra ventilation. There will always be tons of computers in your SOC unless you are using remote technology so you need good airflow for the systems but your people need air as well. By having good airflow and ventilation, you will keep your systems cool and your SOC healthy.

Comfort is another area of concern that you need to spend some time and focus on. The job of working in a SOC primarily consists of sitting in a seat and staring at a monitor for 8 h. There are some very serious ergonomic considerations that need to be addressed. I have found that comfort is an individual taste and that tastes can rapidly change. I am in no way an ergonomist but I do know that issues such as Carpal tunnel syndrome, Tendonitis, and Tension in the neck and shoulders are very real and serious issues that need to be taken into consideration. The quality and efficiency of the work being done may improve in a carefully planned ergonomic and comfortable work environment. Additionally, health care costs may be reduced, and worker morale may be greatly improved by taking your time in this area when designing your SOC. When looking at chairs, I have spent tons of money on high quality top of the line ergonomic chairs for the SOC just to have people swap them out with crappy old chairs from other parts of the organization. Some people like cloth, others like leather and some like mesh, some like adjustable arm rests while others like adjustable reclining. I have personally tried several so-called "8-h" chairs and I could not sit in them for 8 min. Honestly I am convinced that you will never get this right and it is better to have a sampling of chairs so that people can have the option to switch off from time to time which is probably your safest bet. There is no denying, you have to watch the chair issue, sometimes people can get very possessive about chairs and there always seems to be a time in the SOC where there is a single coveted chair. I have actually seen people arrive to work early for their shift just to claim a favorite chair before anyone else does. I have also seen people get upset because someone changed the settings on "their" chair because they had it perfect last time they were on shift. As if you did not already have enough to worry about in a SOC but I would be surprised if at some point down the road, you do not have a "chair issue". In the next chapter, we discuss some fun ways to combat this issue.

Monitors are also another concern that you have to address in the SOC. It has been widely argued that staring at a computer screen for eight hours or more a day, every day will not harm your eyes from a medical standpoint; but, ultimately it could contribute to eyestrain or "tired" eyes. We have all had those days where it feels like our eyes are going pop out of our head if we stare at the screen for one more second, but we push through it and move on, because there is so much to do. To help combat these issues, make sure your SOC staff is taking breaks every hour if for nothing else then rest their eyes by briefly focusing on other things, this should go a long way in to reducing eye fatigue but also keep them relaxed and focused while working. This could even be considered exercise for the eyes. By adjust the lighting in the SOC to keep it at a comfortable level, too much light causes strain to your eyes when you look at the screen. Too little light will make it difficult to read papers and books on your desk. Most SOC's I have built or been in keep it pretty dark where most of the lighting comes from everyone's computer screens or the large video walls and/or projected wall images. In some cases, SOC employees will bring in small desk lamps to augment their light if they feel they need it. It is also important to keep your monitor clean and free of dust as these tiny particles can contribute to eyestrain when trying to focus on the screen. Finally, consider the mounting of the screens. Fixed mounting can be very hard to deal with as people shift positions all day long, monitors would be best mounted on free swinging arms if possible to give people the greatest range of motion and ability to adjust to their position, height and distance they want to be from the actual screen. Also, considering that your staff are highly trained security wizards you should safely assume that the bigger the monitor the better and nobody should have less than 2 per machine. Video real-estate (size of actual viewing space) is something that most everyone in security takes full advantage of.

Some people may find it hard to work in this type of environment due to the lack of personal space. When people float from desk to desk or share a desk area with other people an individual does not really have a place to hang his or her hat. This problem can be hard to deal with especially if SOC employees are regularly meeting with or visiting other employees in other parts of the company who may have personalized cubes or offices with windows. It can be fairly undignified for an individual to not have an identity or a place to call his or her own at work. Unfortunately in a shared workspace environment this is something hard to combat. You may have some creative ideas of your own but I equate this to grade school or high school where you switch from class to class and do not really have a desk of your own to keep your favorite pen and notebook. One idea you can try is to have desk draws at each workstation or console and make sure you assign a draw to each individual so they can keep their stuff in a central location. Another idea is to have personal lockers for people to store stuff. Having personal storage is important, you want people to have books, reference materials, notebooks or other items that may help them with their job. But sometimes it is not necessary to carry these things home every day, instead people need a place to store stuff that they can feel confident will not be disturbed by others. SOC people are a special breed, give them some space and let them have some ability to customize their environment, it will be best for everyone involved.

Do not lock down SOC computers to much, these are trusted security professionals and you should therefore trust that they can have some flexibility in their computer environment without damaging anything. I am not saying that everyone should be a domain admin, but some custom applications shared across the SOC and some ability to customize the environment should be allowed. Roaming profiles in a SOC is a great thing if you can support it. By allowing your SOC employees to customize their profiles you are in effect allowing them to personalize their living space and that space will follow them around no matter what workstation or console they need to log into, this also works great in remote desktop or terminal service environments. Because as security professionals we all live on the computer, and we like the programs that we like and the SOC should be allowed to use just about any software they need to get the job done, within reason.

You can have fun and laugh about some of this but I will honestly tell you that a clean and healthy work environment with some ability to make personal customizations will create a significant and positive impact to your organization.

As for the layout of your SOC, you may decide to keep your SOC open and free flowing. This is ideal to help keep the SOC from becoming stale and looking like a regular office with cubes. In an open environment the idea is to eliminate many of the barriers that create that office style environment in the first place. Getting rid of cubicles and replacing them with desks or modern work area furniture creates open spaces which is an environment that allows employees to interact with one another, share ideas and interact. Console desks are a great idea and accommodate flat panel monitors and hide all the cables required to run multiple computers. You want to take a look at all the possible furniture options from traditional to specialty console furniture. You want to ensure people have enough storage to eliminate daily build-up of clutter

Space is not usually an abundant commodity, plan carefully when building your SOC and purchasing furniture. There are a lot of space saving options that can maximize the number of people you can accommodate with the least amount of floor space, offering a clean and uncluttered workspace. Another option is to create clusters, at the same time as keeping the physical layout as open as possible, you can also give emphasis to teamwork and cooperation for select groups of people such as tier 1 or 2 analysts and engineers by keeping them localized to specific areas. Clustering desks throughout the office, you can create teams to spur competition as well as cooperation. This also gives teams the ability to discuss issues and work together without interfering or bothering other teams or nearby people who may not be involved in the issues the team is currently working on. Open spaces tend to cause people to swarm and issue, where several people overhear a conversation or issue and the swarm together to contribute or help resolve the issue. This is great teamwork and can sometimes help expedite the resolution of issues as well as provide a training mechanism for less experienced people. But there are diminishing returns when too many people are involved and other issues get dropped. Clustering helps eliminate that problem by keeping swarms localized to specific teams or groups. I am not partial to one or the other, the decision depends on what you have to work with, the size of your teams and your furniture choices.

If you are looking to build a bigger SOC then a more traditional operation center built on a stadium model may be more of what you need. In this layout you would have a large video wall and rows of desks or consoles positioned in the room to give everyone a good view of the wall. In some cases the floor will be sloped so as the front desks are lower than the back to give it a stacked or stadium feel. In the back of the room, you would have management desks or offices for supervisors or watch officers. You may even have small conference rooms in the back as well. In working in a busy SOC with lots of people walking around you need to take great care in not only how you position the furniture but that you have the proper ventilation for all the computer systems and that cables are neatly tucked away.

## PRIVATE SOC NETWORK

There is no doubt that your SOC will have special computing needs. The software that will be used to access security devices and resources are going to be very different than what is installed in the rest of an organization. The information and data the SOC will be looking at is sensitive if not extremely critical to an organization. Knowing all that plus the fact that in some cases your SOC analysts may have administrative credentials to lots of IT systems it is extremely important to ensure that all the security systems, your SOC users and their equipment are very secure and protected. In larger SOC environments and at MSSP organizations it is not uncommon to have resources fully dedicated to the security of the SOC. These resources would work as a regular analyst or engineer but would be solely dedicated to supporting the security of the SOC, this could include the networking of system resources, the management of computers, laptops, and servers, and the safeguarding of data. You could almost picture this as a SOC inside a SOC. When deciding on if a SOC should operate on a completely separate network or just a private virtual network take data flow into consideration. I have seen situations where and IDS event was generated and when that single event was sent to the SOC it passed by another IDS sensor and generated another alert as the second IDS system detected the bad data being transferred as well and had the same rule configured. Having a private network is not a must have item especially for smaller organizations. But just because your SOC is focused on security and you have extremely smart security people working there does not mean they are not susceptible to attacks. Attackers will target users in the SOC just like any other user in your organization but there will be increased focused attacks on your SOC by attackers looking to gain internal network knowledge or credentials to key systems. To better protect your organization and to give your SOC a bit more freedom a separate network infrastructure with proper firewalls and security controls should be used. This also helps separate your SOC and their equipment from directly being exposed to key business resources and systems.

## VIDEO WALLS

These are often very impressive in a SOC and can also be very expensive. Although a video wall is another optional component for running a SOC you may have very good reasons to use one. There is a wide range of sizes and resolutions as well as different technologies to build a video wall. Having visualizations of big data sets that engage with your analysts and engineers daily activities can be invaluable especially if it enables them to make real-time decisions. From cubes to long stretches of seamless border LEDs there are almost an endless array of options these days. The video walls can be used to display metrics to indicate performance health of customers systems, changes in network activity or special alarms generated out of the SOC's ticketing system. The screens of the wall could also be configured to display important news channels or the entire screen could be utilized to present training videos to the entire group. The screens should be standardized and organized as we will discuss during the chapter on metrics but keep in mind that there are no set rules as to what you can do and the screens can be changed to suit your needs of the day.

## VIDEO PROJECTORS

Projectors are an absolutely viable option as opposed to a complete video wall or in addition to a video wall. There are projectors that are designed for 24/7 continuous use if that is how you are running your SOC. This could be a great cost effective alternative to more expensive video walls. Additionally video projectors can be more versatile in that the size of the screen can be adjusted as your needs change.

## LABS

The building of lab can be a vital part of any SOC and a critical tool used every single day if done correctly. A lab environment is typically a self-contained network that includes many different types of devices, virtual machines and may even include a separate Internet connections all built for multiple purposes. The lab can be used to train new analysts on how to manage and maintain equipment that you use on your network. It can contain the equipment necessary for analysts to train towards certifications and you can even use the lab for people to learn new skills that will help advance their careers. It can also be used by engineers to try new mitigation technics or test newly developed IDS signatures before sending them to production equipment. The lab is a great place to try new things that is consequence free if things going bad. These SOC labs can also be used to develop security intelligence by trying new exploits and performing security research and testing.

The value of real hands on experience cannot be matched and with a lab you can give people that experience at any time.

Labs can quickly become very expensive so you will have to build it wisely. To give your SOC the ability to manage and maintain equipment in a lab environment is a huge gift that will pay big dividends. Those dividends will be paid in the form of better-trained staff, better execution of changes and management of your security infrastructure.

The lab environment can also be used to test changes to your critical infrastructure before you do it in your production environment. This will give you a higher degree of confidence that changes are implemented with a lower risk of causing negative impact to your organization.

In your lab you can have virtual systems that contain specialized software and different operating systems for people to try or use. Depending on the size and ability of your lab infrastructure, you can give everyone in your SOC their own server to use and play with. Allow them to develop new tools, test out new skills or install different hacker tools to see what the capabilities are. You can help train your SOC staff to perform different tasks that may be needed from time to time like performing vulnerability scans or even give them the ability to do penetration tests of other systems in the lab. For your analysts you may want to consider training them on passive tools that would aid them in their jobs like being able to port scan systems to see what is responding or banner grabbing of known open ports to help figure out what application a server is running. These are all things that can be done in a safe environment in the lab. When your SOC is dealing with more real and live incidents such as malware analysis or performing forensics, a lab is a great tool to be able to contain these types of activities so that it would not affect normal SOC operations if something bad got loose. When looking to purchase new equipment to add to your security infrastructure you can install demo versions of the systems in your lab and perform tests to see how it works and test its reactions to your simulated environment. Additionally you can use the resources of your lab to test your staff with exercises and training materials that will be elaborated on in a later chapter. There is no right recipe for the building of labs, just make sure that if you are going to build one that its proportional to your SOC organization and that you build clear roles and responsibilities and ensure its properly maintained.

There is a lot that goes into what you need to build your SOC. There are 3 distinctly separate areas you need to consider, organizational security infrastructure, operation center infrastructure and support infrastructure. When you evaluate the needs of your organization first it will help dictate what you need in your SOC to support those organizational needs. Then the support infrastructure needed for your SOC will almost design itself but putting good upfront time and creative efforts into that support structure will enable your SOC to perform at the peak of its ability.

The SOC will never run out of things to do as attackers get more sophisticated and running a good SOC will increase your organizations ability to detect and respond to those attacks. With the right tools and right reporting you will quickly gain a positive opinion of the SOC outside your organization regarding what you are doing for them that will result in additional tasks and responsibilities. The infrastructure you design that runs and supports your SOC is just like building a house, you want to ensure you have a good foundation. Do not be afraid to use what you have, no reason to run out a make tons of purchases. Building your SOC can be an iterative and incremental process that grows and builds. It is ok to start small and add people, processes and technology as you mature your organization and develop your goals. It is also ok to look for tools and products that are a champagne taste on a beer budget to get you going, just make sure you are not sacrificing on key features that you will need to be successful. Your organization may just be building its security infrastructure so build your SOC along with it, make sure you are efficient and have all the tools to be successful. I did not even come close to discussing all that is need to support a SOC or an organizations security infrastructure but I hope that I have at least got you going in a good direction, have provided you with some deep thoughts on direction and have given you some insight into some key considerations.

# Organizational structure

## CHAPTER CONTENTS

When it comes to organizational structure, one of the questions I hear the most is who should a SOC report to? The issue and topic of where a SOC belongs in an organization can be very political and a hot topic. Typically before I answer a question like this, I would need to know more information about the organization, but it seems to always typically lead to the same answer. If you are questioning whether your SOC is reporting up through the correct management chain, then you are probably not happy with your management or leadership. When you start to focus on management outside the confines of the immediate SOC, then there are problems that need to be dealt with and addressed overall. There are many reasons why a SOC would report up through a different management chain in different organizations and each may have its benefits as well as drawbacks.

Organizations are challenged in today's technology environment in that new products are popping up every day with a cool new toy or feature that users want or even demand that their organizations support. Technology for organizations has evolved into a highly distributed, mobile centric and global footprint that not only has to work for every user but also has to be scalable and accessible from almost everywhere in the world. Adding to the fact that technology is changing at a break neck speed, security and security-related organizations, especially SOCs, are still a relatively new entity. The SOC as we know it today has not been around that long as a standard department in an organization comparative to IT, marketing or public relations. These nuances make the placement of security and its operation center in a bit of limbo and up for interpretation by the organization that runs one. Ultimately there are no right or wrong answers, as different organizations have different needs, but at the same time healthy organizations with supportive management that work well with its staff will ultimately be successful no matter what the overall organizational reporting structure is.

Really, whom a SOC reports to is not as important as the security mission and goals the SOC needs to perform and provide for the business or organization. Focusing internally to the SOC, there are many different ways you can structure your SOC to provide the best value. Over the next chapter, we are going to explore the role of the SOC in the organization in greater details and then we will take a look at different options for how to structure the SOC internally. How you structure the SOC is vitally important to ensure you are keeping in alignment with your customers, objectives, and organizational goals. When building a SOC, you need to ensure that you are able to bridge any gaps between the business and technology while focusing on addressing the risks of your organization.

Security operations have ever growing tasks and responsibilities from network security and application security to intrusion detection and risk management. Add into the mix that some SOCs will be asked to perform encryption, user management, eDiscovery, and web content filtering, it's easy to see that security will touch every aspect of a business. Even though the SOC's role is very technical, educational training and policy development are also being required of the operations teams and are a cornerstone to a good security program. Depending on the focus of the SOC and the current needs of an organization, the logical reporting structure may change and should change when it makes sense.

One of the greatest challenges security managers and their operations teams face is getting recognition from senior or executive management. Organizational security is not just an IT issue as it has great impacts on the business and the overall organization and as such must receive attention from the highest levels in any organization. The SOC and the larger security department must work closely with business leaders, legal, HR, internal and external audit groups, compliance, physical security, and of course IT managers to develop a comprehensive approach to managing risks associated and becoming interconnected inside the organizations. Using metrics, as we will discuss later in the book, is a great way to get some of the efforts of the SOC out into the general organization. But organizationally, the SOC needs to be in the right place to ensure that it's supported and that its higher-level management supports it fully and gives it the right visibility in the larger overall organization. If the SOC is doing what it is supposed to be doing and generating the right reports, then the business will notice.

There are a number of different reporting structures that are possible, and each organization will have to figure out what is best. Whether the SOC reports through IT, legal, compliance, finance, audit, or another arrangement is made, there will always be impassioned arguments as to why it is best that security be situated in one of these departments. Regardless of where security is in the organization, there must be a level of independence to avoid any actual or perceived conflicts of interest, and the team must be able to work with the larger organization in order to strike a balance between the risks of the organization and business need. There should be regular updates on security with metrics to an organization Board of Directors or senior executive leaders who are ultimately responsible for the acceptance of risk, especially in regulated industries such as financial services, energy, and healthcare.

Organizations these days must ensure that sufficient security is in place to minimize risk to an acceptable level, and only the leaders of an organization can know what that level really is, if they are properly advised. In order to ensure that senior leaders are indeed properly advised, they have to make sure that regardless of how the reporting structure is designed, the security organization including the SOC reports high enough in an organization to have the respect, political influence, and visibility it needs in order to be effective. We will discuss positions along with roles and responsibilities of individuals later in the chapter on staffing, but it is also important to acknowledge here that security operations must have a strong leader, be it a SOC manager, a director or the chief information security officer (CISO). A security leader needs to be not only a strong advocate for the security mission but has to also be highly technical and an effective communicator. The leader needs to be able to translate important security issues received from the SOC's highly technical resources and communicate those issues as effective business risks, objectives, and responsibilities that are suitable for executive leadership to understand and appreciate. Additionally, technical skills of the security leader must be sharp enough to communicate executive leadership concerns into objectives that are effectively transferred to and developed with SOC staff that must implement and execute.

Over the last few years, security professionals have seen their tool sets grow at an amazing pace. The modern cyber threat and increasing skills of the advisory have demanded that defensive systems designed to protect our networks be quickly deployed and professionally configured to prevent what seems like an almost inevitable breach. In some cases, budgets for security to make capital purchases are increasing and in other cases, organizations are fighting to hold on to existing budget to maintain what they already have, yet it never seems like enough. But as tools are added to defend organizational networks, we also need to maintain those tools, manage the tools, and monitor their outputs. You could have a security team armed with arguably the right tools but nobody to truly harness their full potential, and that would be a waste.

In order to run and maintain a successful security organization and an effective operations center, you need to annex your resources from the entire organization you work for. It is everyone's responsibility to protect the organization where they work, so help them be a part of the solution. This goes beyond security awareness training; make people an extension of your team. When developing policies or new security programs, engage your business and bring people together from many different areas of your organization. This extended team can help to provide insight into how they use technology every day, how they can help the organization be more secure, and how to best implement technology in a secure way. Train them on how to best help your SOC and how to be a part of the solution, but listen to them and learn about them as well. It is not always about bits and bytes and the latest zero-day exploit; it is about how we interact with people and technology. Allow IT teams to get involved in your security processes and tools, let them help guide you, let them use the tools you have, show them how powerful the tools are, and allow them to be partners. For example, do not just provide security metrics but give people access to your metrics tools. You have to weave the security fabric into all of IT and an organizations business. It is no longer about intrusion detection or prevention; it is about network architecture, patching, DNS, proxies, among many other things, but most importantly it is about people. Get out into your businesses community and see how security can positively affect them and learn what you can do to help enable the business no matter where security organizationally reports to, and they will help enable you and your security programs.

An organization can never hire enough people to get the job of security done. Instead, SOCs need to ensure they elicit the support of the entire organization. Putting processes into place for users to report security issues to the SOC and training users not only on security awareness but also on what to look out for and what to report are a great boost to an organization's security program. Enabling and arming users with essential information on security will not only help keep your organization safer, but it will effectively expand your security team and become a force multiplier. Not everyone needs to be a skilled analyst, but if users get strange emails, unrecognized attachments, or have unexplained things happening on their computer and know (whatever your processes is) to contact the SOC, contact IT, or open a help desk ticket, then the result will be an investigation closer to the time of the incident and an increased chance to prevent a bigger issue by either blocking or remediating risks or by communicating to the user population about a current threat to watch out for.

SOCs that get buried in an organization typically do not have the real support to be effective and will not likely be able to gain the respect of other IT groups and as a result, will be shielded from senior executives and other organizational leaders. This leads to important security issues going un-noticed and significant breaches can occur. The senior management needs to support an appropriately sized security organization and program with the right skilled resources in order to be successful. It also needs to fund the security program appropriately and if security spending has been inadequate or non-existent, then it may take a few years of higher-than-normal spending to catch up to where you need to be. This does not mean that you need to hire an army of people; instead, it may be that you just need to give the responsibility of security as an additional duty to someone in IT, or maybe that is all you can do. But having at least just that one person spend some time on the issue will help the organization start to understand the magnitude of the task or the seriousness of the issues. Additionally, focus on educating the senior executives and organizational leaders, as well as the security team, on the linking of good security with good quality business and then link individual success to good security practices. An organization needs to also enforce policies when bad behavior occurs in the area of security. if not, then nobody will take it seriously and security will just be brushed aside.

## DIFFERENT REPORTING LINES

Typical, SOCs have no reporting lines inside an organization. By that I mean internally, a SOC has some typical organizational structures, but where a SOC lives in an overall organization varies greatly. Different organizations will have a SOC reporting up through a wide range of structures, and it seems that no two organizations are alike. Sometimes this is due to who senior leadership feels is a strong enough executive to oversee the operation and ensure the objectives of the group are met. In other organizations, the SOC or security would come under the IT department just because it makes sense. Whereas organizations that have suffered large breaches may have the SOC report up through the legal department or an audit and compliance group. In larger organizations, a SOC would report up through a CISO management organization. A CISO could have any number of different managers they report to in an organization, even in some cases you may see them reporting directly to the CEO. There are some impacts and implications into how a SOC reports up through an organization. Ultimately, as mentioned before, security must support business initiatives and be an enabler for the business. A clear mismatch in reporting lines and overall department responsibility is a recipe for a SOC and an entire security program that is destined to fail. Do not have security for the sake of security; instead, develop data classification and information risk or operational risk management processes to direct resources toward the protection of agreed-upon risks, and protect the critical assets deployed in an organization. Lastly, ensure that your SOC has the authority to make or impact change in the organization as it relates to containment and recovery activity to protect an organization.

## LEGAL

In some cases where the security of an organization or the lack of appropriate security controls may have caused significant issues, the management and oversight of security may need to come under the direct control and administration of the legal department. This does not mean that anyone in legal knows about security or has special skills to improve security, but security will hopefully get the focus and support it needs to resolve any current significant issues trending in the organization. The legal department may also need to work closely with security or directly control the security organization during a significant breach that is in the public eye. This could be because the legal ramifications, regulatory violations, or the potential significant loss of business security actions are not handled properly or taken seriously. Additionally, if an IT organization's lack of focus or mismanagement of security is seen as the cause to significant compromises and breaches, then legal may need to take over the direct administration and control of security to ensure that the right risks are being addressed in the priority directed by senior leaders and not of the general business or IT, a very quick way to make security a priority for everyone. The tolerance of security issues and risks may be very low and the timeline to implement changes in an unhealthy and politically charged organization may be difficult. Bringing security under the direct purview of legal will help cut through any cultural challenges. If there is no security organization to begin with and a significant issue occurs, then an organization's board of directors or senior leaders may demand the immediate establishment and building of a security organization that would include a SOC. This is typically an extreme condition, and a security group with an operations function is not correctly aligned in this configuration. Direct legal oversight is a heavy-handed way to enforce immediate and significant change in an organization. This is an approach that is not meant to make friends; it is a way to implement immediate and decisive change.

Once significant changes have been made and organizational objectives have been accomplished, then alternative long-term and sustainable reporting-structure changes should be made in order to have security become a regular part of the organization and culture. Eventually, an organization would need to heal the wounds of its significant security issues and work collectively to integrate or reintegrate security into the normal fabric of a successfully operating organization. Organizations that move from an improvised, fire-fighting launch of its implement of security and work to develop sustainable security programs that are cost-efficient and quality driven will accomplish greater benefits and reduce costs to the entire organization. Where security moves to will depend on the needs of security, the structure of the organization, and the overall maturity level of the different departments.

## CISO

The CISO should ultimately be in charge of and responsible for security and as such, a SOC. If in smaller to medium-sized businesses there is no real security group or department, then the SOC is the entire security organization or vice versa. This means that the SOC manager would also be the CISO. The CISO position is still a relatively new role in many organizations. How serious security is to an organization and how closely that organization wants to manage its risks will determine how high up in an organization a CISO will report to. In some cases where the primary business of the organization is security or managing security for customers or if security is a true success factor for an organization, the CISO could be seen reporting directly to the CEO. Even without a direct reporting line, the CISO should have regular meetings with the CEO, board of directors, and other senior executives to ensure that security risks and successes are being discussed, acknowledged, and addressed at the highest level of any organization. As a company progresses forward, typically new technology can help with innovation by bringing new products to the market, improving on existing products, opening up new revenue streams, or modernizing existing ones. Security teams and operation groups should enable this forward technical progress by figuring out ways to implement it securely instead of slowing progress or impeding progress. A CISO and his or her organizational leaders need to be able to direct technical staff to ensure that business objectives and risk tolerances are met. Attacks and attack groups are ever increasing in sophistication, and technical staff that is part of a CISO's organization need to be focused on cyber security operations and keeping up with new and changing threat trends.

Further, a CISO needs to be able to speak to senior members of an organization and in some situations a board of directors. This is no easy task, as the person filling the CISO role needs to be able to articulate complex technical issues and risks effectively and in a way that is clear, quick to the point, can be well understood, and does not cause any unnecessary panic. Not only do the CISOs need to be good communicators at this level, but they also need to ensure they understand their audience and make the right decisions on what to bring to their attention. More often than not, a CISO may only get a small amount of time every few months to be in front of a board, and he or she needs to know how to make it time well spent. The CISO needs to ensure that he or she has an organization that makes sense and that works effectively to address the goals of the organization and that it is being heard.

## CIO

The Chief Information Officer (CIO) as an executive level member of an organizational leadership group and the senior leader for IT is the typical place where you would find CISO, the security organization, and the SOC. This makes the most sense for the majority of organizations, as the security teams must work effectively alongside the IT teams. IT being responsible for the implementation and management of technology and the SOC being responsible for monitoring and managing security on their technology is a natural partnership. An organization that is security operations focused would report through IT, and may be a part of an overall infrastructure and operations department. It would be primarily focused on deploying, managing, and monitoring of security tools and technologies within the IT environment. Because of this it would lead the organization to focus on best-of-breed products, cost efficiency, and integration with existing tools and technologies.

Unfortunately security and IT being under the same organizational umbrella also brings great challenges that should be addressed. Unfortunately a CIO who has the clear direction to deliver IT solutions may not properly balance security risks that add additional requirements or impediments in implementations to projects and as such could introduce great risk to an organization. This can be seen happening when a CIO's main focus is the implementation of projects on a timeline target while reducing costs, instead of implementing effective technology timely and under budget while reducing risk. If an organization wants a great CIO, not a good one but a great one, then his or her task should not be to just reduce costs but also to reduce unnecessary risk to the organization as well. Having security operations report in a management chain under the CIO can be a conflict of interest and may cause significant separation-of-duties issues. Oftentimes security metrics can be taken as a report card on how well IT is doing, and a CIO who wants to hide those shortcomings or security issues can do so especially if security does not have the right visibility in an organization. Not all CIO's are bad, but the days where a CIO can ignore security or not be security focused are essentially over regardless if security reports are up to them or not.

## COMPLIANCE

In one of the most mature types of organizations, a well-funded and focused audit and compliance department could be a beneficial group to house a security team and security operations. Typically, this organization would have an operational mission but would be more strategy focused on security and is much more concerned with meeting business objectives while assigning all security priorities based on risk and compliance. In this type of organization, there would be a large focus on aligning the organization on governance, risk, and compliance (GRC) metrics along with reporting. This type of department is more progressive and forward looking and has more of a capability to be proactive in managing security as its focus is really to try to anticipate threats and organizational needs. For security professionals, this sounds like the best place to be and it can be, but there are, just as there is with all things, some drawbacks. Namely, if your organization is still building, implementing technology or bolting on security to IT infrastructure, then the reporting lines of this type of structure are going to inhibit a close relationship with IT. This is not the environment you want while you are building a security program, as it is a maturity level that good organizations need to grow into. For example, whereas compliance may not have the capital to spend on infrastructure, existing IT budgets could cover many security tools and infrastructure that may need to be purchased. But if the organization is mature and the entire security infrastructure is implemented, then you may be making a great move. Moving a security operations group or an entire security team will not happen overnight because most people view security as an IT function, but as people take on risk functions and those roles are more formalized, responsibilities will change and evolve.

To help with this evolution, senior security managers and / or CISOs need to make sure they are running effective continuous improvement programs and have metrics that ensure security focus areas are inline with the overall organizational objectives. Additionally, do not operate in a bubble; network and share with other security professionals in other organizations to help develop ideas, solutions, and measurements so that everyone can grow and learn from one another.

## SOC ORGANIZATION

Now that we have discussed where a SOC reports to and even discussed a larger security organization, it is time to focus deeper into the SOC. This should be not just where a SOC reports to inside an organization, but it is time to cover the overall organizational structure of the SOC. Depending on your organization and your needs, you may have big differences in not only the structure but also some of the roles and responsibilities that are placed in the SOC as opposed to the roles that are placed elsewhere. We cover individual roles and responsibilities in the chapter on staffing, so here we are going to primarily focus on the groups, teams, and structure. In a typical SOC, you would see three different and distinct groups that are all responsible for working together and have tasks and goals that are interwoven. As shown in the chart below, a SOC should consist of an analyst layer and an engineering layer at a minimum. In a traditional SOC, you would have your level 1/level 2 analysts, engineers, and then a management layer.

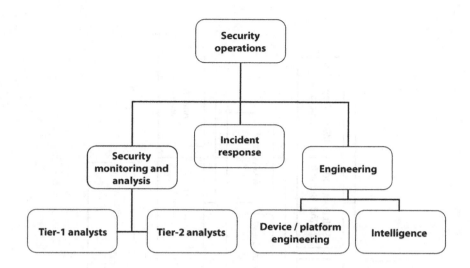

You can also split out your engineering group into functional areas such as device-based or platform-based. This means that you may have engineers that specialize in a specific device function like IDS or are more focused on windows security at the software or host level. Also as part of engineering, you may want to break out intelligence into its own group to give them the ability to explore, learn, and investigate to get all the new information they can in order to feed back the relevant information and intelligence back into the SOC ecosystem. The chapter on intelligence details a lot about the efforts of intelligence building in a SOC. This group can either be under the engineering organization or on its own, and depending on how your build your SOC it could even be operated under an analysis group. Either way, the goals and objectives of any team need to be communicated in an easy way and managed appropriately to be successful.

In a larger SOC environment, you may find many other roles and groups being formed in order to expand and build on key activities. This could include everything from an architecture group all the way to a metrics and reporting group. As the SOC expands and requirements build, the functions that were once performed by a single person will have to be expanded out to multiple people. This is a natural growth pattern and is important for the maturity of the SOC. It is important for leadership to not only recognize when growth into other areas is required but to also pre-plan for that growth. The pre-planning should help ensure that the proper funding, space, and equipment are available and that departments like HR are involved so they can help to establish the proper job descriptions and compensation structures and to coordinate interviews. Do not be afraid to explore and change roles, job descriptions, and organizational structure. Re-defining your SOC and changing things around can be a good way to mature the organization because it gives people an opportunity to rise up to new challenges and shine or emerge as a leader under new direction and focus. Shifting management and people in different roles or areas helps to see who can perform and under what conditions people thrive the best.

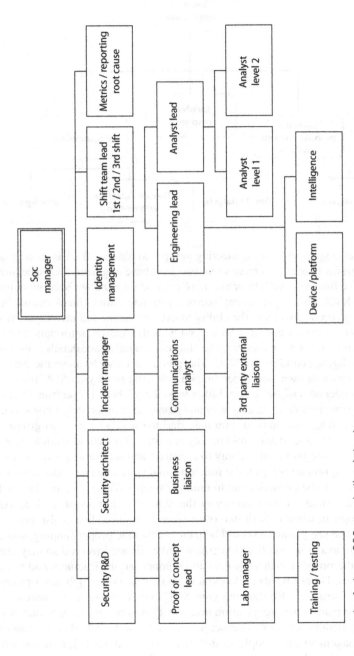

An example of a larger SOC organizational structure

The organizational structure of one SOC to the next is going to be very different. It should mimic the requirements and focus that an organization has on the SOC and the SOC's ability to execute with the resources it has available. If you are a SOC in the government, there may be significantly different requirements than if your SOC was inside an educational organization. You will find similarities as well as differences in the way you build the SOC and those differences should be in meeting the needs of the organization and not necessarily the needs of security. What that means is that your SOC has to take care of security whether facing known or emerging threats and should be agile enough to perform those functions every day, but more long-term organizational expansion happens slowly. Do not make gaps in security a resource issue. Prioritize properly, execute, and plan appropriately.

## ENGINEERING

The main support for the overall SOC and analysts comes from the security engineering team. The engineers can be engaged in multiple different areas and broken out into several teams depending on the organizational requirements and current focus areas. Primarily, the engineering group should be responsible for the security infrastructure that has been deployed across the enterprise to protect the organization. This would include the care and feeding of those devices to include any signature and rule creation as well, and it typically includes the new deployment of security infrastructure. Engineering can be broken up into several areas such as maintenance and intelligence. The engineering team could also be where you find your forensic and malware analysis experts. Depending on the size of your organization, security implementation may be the function of an architecture team that works directly for a chief technology officer, but it would be the SOC or the larger security team that would direct the use and ultimately operate the systems being installed. It would be the SOC engineering team who would work directly with the architecture group on the installation of a new system or new security device. Engineering is also a likely place to have a liaison for IT change management. This individual would not only participate in the organizational change management processes but would also maintain an internal change process for the SOC team. This would include ensuring that all changes to security infrastructure are documented and that any changes that would affect the larger organization are properly communicated and approved prior to implementation.

Engineering being a highly technical organization can also play the role of developing security standards and evaluation systems against those standards. They would build and generate documentation on how new technology should be secured and what settings would be required for safe and secure operations. For example, if IT decides to implement a new mobile device management system, there should be collaboration with security architecture and engineering, where security engineering would evaluate the solution against any existing organizational security documentation and then provide a whitepaper on how the new solution should be configured.

Then IT and a system architecture group can implement the new solution and meet business objectives and security engineering can come back around at the end of the implementation to see whether the security objectives were met or additional changes need to be made. Additionally, engineering would keep tabs on all of an organization's technology, and as new vulnerabilities and security issues are discovered, the team could make key recommendations to a security architecture group who could evaluate the implementation impact and timelines.

One of the key and primary goals of the engineering team is to support the analyst team. The engineering group would be the third tier or in most cases the final escalation tier of an issue prior to going outside the organization. The engineer's role in this case is to help investigate why something is not working, how an event was generated, or even why an event was generated in the first place. Engineering would support security architecture as part of the SOC or a system architecture group as part of an IT team. The engineers would be able to help architecture understand the proper intent of a security standard and provide clarification to standards from a technical perspective when needed. Additionally, when there is a significant environment change or a new infrastructure being designed, architecture may call upon the engineering team to help provide technical guidance on the capabilities and capacity of the existing security infrastructure. This is also a valuable partnership as engineering may be able to help spot operational trouble areas with an implementation plan prior to executing, saving an organization time.

Security engineering teams in a SOC should also work closely with IT and be very knowledgeable about an organization's overall IT infrastructure. This way when things are being analyzed in the SOC, engineering can make quick determinations on the behavior of systems and know whether something is just not right and warrants a further and deeper review.

## SECURITY ARCHITECTURE

This team inside the SOC (not all architecture teams are in a SOC) is developed to ensure that the required level of security assurance as defined by organizational policy and standards is fulfilled. It would also be this team's role and responsibility to develop and administer an exception process. This is a process where when technology is implemented that will not or cannot meet the standards, a risk-based process kicks in and the deficiency gets documented. Then it would be the architecture teams along with the engineering teams working together to see whether there is an acceptable mitigating control or compensating countermeasure that could be implemented to reduce the risks. If an exception is needed, the architecture team would lead an exception review board that consists of multiple groups, including groups in IT and in the business, to review and approve. This is done in an effort to minimize security risks to the ongoing operation of the organization and in new implementation of technology for the organization. By working closely with the SOC analysts and engineering teams, the architecture team would bring forward security initiatives that are developed to provide better visibility to analysts or close gaps in security found by engineering or anyone else for that matter. This team should work with a larger architecture team or IT implementation team to review system and technical designs to ensure that they meet or exceed security guidance in their deployment and configuration plans. The team would also be a liaison to the organization and different business units within an organization and would consult on how new technology implementations would be secured. The team would also be able to take new changes going on in the business back to the SOC so that the overall team could prepare or at least be aware of changes that may affect the monitoring and the management of security infrastructure. The security architecture team would also be a helping hand to the legal department in ensuring that contracts and agreements have proper security considerations built in. When working with third party technology providers, this relationship becomes especially useful if any specific security controls or changes need to be implemented to support the relationship. Another aspect of this beneficial relationship is that during acquisitions and mergers, security architecture can help design a process that on boards or slowly severs a relationship that keeps both organizations secure while meeting the needs of any legal contracts. The team can also make sure that any legal contracts contain appropriate language for third parties to maintain security standards that are equal to or that exceed the standards of the organization. This way, the external relationships do not become a risky program and it also ensures that any required monitoring of third party network or user activity is known and agreed to. From a security perspective, the security architecture team should be the knowledge source for the implementation of any technical controls for regulatory compliance. The team would provide the needed guidance to the engineering teams or IT for any new concerns or the resolving of open compliance items. Security architecture would also work closely with the audit and compliance departments to ensure that the required reports are being generated and that metrics are developed to support the audit and compliance initiatives. These tasks can be performed from a single team or separate teams that roll up into a larger architecture group. If different business units seem to be heavily engaged in technical projects, it may make sense to have permanent architects be assigned to those groups and just let them be the single point of contact for those groups into security operations.

## SECURITY MONITORING AND ANALYSIS

This is the main area that makes up the operational capability of a SOC. A large portion of this entire book is dedicated to what this team is focused on inside the SOC. The overall structure of this team is dependent on the size and number of tasks that the analysts need to perform. It is also largely dependent on how many shifts there will be and how many people will be on each shift. Primarily, the tasks that are going to be performed in this group are the monitoring of the networks and ensuring that the assets of the organization are safe from malicious attacks internally as well as externally. The makeup of the team needs to lend itself to be the first responders to event escalations and to address all critical security incidents. The team may also have a group or crew that is solely responsible for scanning and monitoring for vulnerabilities and analyzing what those weaknesses expose from a risk perspective in relation to the rest of the organization. A larger extent of what the monitoring team or any organization for that matter should be focused on is detailed in Appendix A. The tools and devices that can be used to defend and detect an organization from a security perspective are detailed in Appendix B.

Analysts can be broken down into triage or tier one and escalation analysts in tier two or senior analysts. Again, depending on the focus of your SOC activities you may want to split your analysts up into business areas. For example, you may have one set of analysts who watch international traffic and another set who watch only domestic traffic. The breakout could also be by different business groups. This can be effective if the types of traffic and systems being monitored are so different that the singular focus of an analyst needs to be on that area only to ensure that nothing is missed or that a specific analyst team is well versed in the technology being used in that specific group or area. Another effective split in monitoring may be by classification, if one group monitors public or general systems and another monitors classified or sensitive systems. Organizations that make a technical product or provide a technical service to customers may find that two distinct monitoring and escalation groups are needed but that still work closely together. For example, a vendor that provides technical products and services may want an architecture and product security expert team that is focused on the items necessary to guide the development of a secure product and deliver secure services but also be able to respond to customers' issues if security issues occur or vulnerabilities are discovered. This is a split focus on the vendor's products in one team and its own network in another team.

A good example of how different security operations teams can split focus yet still work side by side is how the U.S. Government and military operate. For example, the U.S. Army, Air Force, and Navy each has its own operation centers responsible for monitoring the networks of its own service groups. They do this while the U.S. Department of Defense has its own team that coordinates across all the U.S. military teams as well as monitoring of their own networks.

## RESPONSIBILITY

In any organization and in any structure, the SOC has to have a clearly defined, delegated, and even documented list of responsibilities. The key place to document the SOC's responsibilities would be in the organization's policies. Depending on how your organization operates and the various teams and departments you have, the policy could say many different things. Ideally, you would want to start off with the fact that your SOC has the clearly stated mission to monitor and respond to all digital-based network and system security issues. This prevents any other department in your organization from deciding to just start its own SOC. Next, you will want to have a list of other departments and what their responsibility is to support the SOC efforts.

For example, if your SOC does not own or have the ability to modify firewall policy, then critical block requests made to the IT networking team should be addressed in a timely manner. But if the IT networking team does not have a clear responsibility to respond to the SOC, then the efforts of the SOC to block or mitigate and attack could go un-addressed. Not all of these responsibilities need to be documented in policy. The leaders of the SOC or a larger security organization need to spend the time to sit with each group it would require services and response from and clearly document what each group's roles and responsibilities would be. Then, internal SLAs and SLOs could be established to ensure that there are measureable success criteria. Everyone needs to work together to achieve the same goals for the organization. Clearly documenting responsibilities is a great way of not only defining what you need but also working with other groups to help you determine what they can offer to you as well.

## AUTHORITY

What does your SOC have the authority to do for your organization? Just because you have the responsibility to monitor a few systems and devices does not give you the authority to do anything with that information. The SOC needs to have the support from senior executives, directors, and the rest of management to act on behalf of the organization in the interest of protecting them from risks associated with cyber threats and attacks. That authority should be known and defined so that when the SOC needs something, it can get it. For example, when someone in the SOC notices that a critical asset on the network is not configured to send its logs to the central log management system or the SEIM, then the SOC should have the authority to make the proper requests to have that system properly configured. System administrators should not push back thinking that they do not have to send their logs because the SOC does not have the authority to request those types of actions. This just makes everything less efficient and creates problems. The SOC needs to have visibility into as much activity as possible in order to protect its organization from harm. This does not mean the SOC should collect every type of log from every system, but needed logs that are necessary to get critical information should be easily obtainable if the SOC is given the proper authority.

There are many other types of authority your SOC should have depending on its responsibility and its capability to defend your organization and reduce risk. Detail the authority your SOC needs and work with the management to gain approval before issues occur and systems are needlessly compromised.

## FULFILLING NEEDS

Along with responsibility and authority, a clear definition of the organizational needs should be documented, but many times people do not go in-depth with this. You can consider this a charter or mission statement for your SOC. Once you have a clearly defined mission statement, the SOC can list all of its services and its service catalog for departments or groups to see. The organizational needs are typically derived from and driven by security risk either known or perceived by the organization. The SOC should only perform activities that respond to the underlying organizational risks and needs of the organization as clearly defined. If the SOC is able to build new use cases, communicate needs in areas it is currently not focused on, and gain buy-in from organizational leaders, then it can expand its role and capabilities in those areas. In addition to focusing on needs, a continuous assessment of security posture, the current industry risks, and any audit findings should be used as a foundation for adding to SOC activities. This evaluation process and SOC capabilities need to be revisited periodically to ensure that the SOC functions are still needed and that the resources are appropriate to accomplish tasks. The senior leaders in security operations must be certain the SOC is meeting the strategic needs of the organization on a regular basis.

Making your SOC a part of the organization and its critical mission will be far more effective if it is properly supported than if you just bury the group under several layers of misaligned management. Some functions can be outsourced, but ultimately, someone in your organization needs to take responsibility and have the authority to coordinate, communicate, and take action on incidents that arise out of monitoring and managing risk.

# Your most valuable resource is your people

5

## CHAPTER CONTENTS

Building a SOC is not an easy task, certainly not easy when all you hear is that there is a massive shortage of security experts and if you can find one, he or she will come at an exceptionally high cost. At the time of writing this chapter, it is true that well-trained security professionals are far and few between and they are expensive, but that does not mean it is impossible to find great people for your SOC or to secure your organization.

The first thing you need to do is evaluate the skill sets you would like to have in order to make sure you are really looking for exactly what you need. All too often when I look at a security organization and an operation center, their open requisitions for new employees go unfilled for long periods of time. Typically, the answer to these unfilled positions is that they cannot find the right qualified candidate. But when looking a bit deeper, I usually can find that they looking for someone who just does not exist. For example, their job descriptions may detail a role for a junior analyst but requires a master's degree and 10 plus years of experience along with a ton of industry certifications. It is great that they have high ambitions, but this is a bit unbalanced and would not necessarily attract the right candidates to the job. Sometimes this can happen in an organization where HR requires specific education or industry experience in order to command the types of salaries that are needed to attract security professionals. Since cyber security professionals are still somewhat new roles in organizations, there are not very many precedents set for salary or compensation levels across different types of industries. This means that HR is forced to try and find other similar roles to model benefit packages after and although they may find similar technical descriptions of these roles, they are actually quite different. These disconnects can happen for a number of reasons, but as universities have started building programs and are granting degrees in these specialty areas, these issues are beginning to get resolved. Let us take a closer look at some of the representative positions in a SOC and some of what the real requirements are for various positions you may find in a typical SOC. We will review some of the technical and soft skills required to be successful in these positions and let us also look at some of the basic job descriptions and associated job postings that you can use to attract top talent.

Where you get your people from is also very important to understand before you start writing job descriptions. There are four main ways to get a new person to work in your SOC.

- Off the street
- From another internal department
- Contractors
- Managed security services provider

First you can hire them right off the street as most organizations traditionally do. This is always a gamble because you only have basic references, phone calls, or interview meetings you have had with the individual to determine his or her personality, technical strengths and willingness to be part of the team. It is hard to determine what is real or what is showmanship when you are putting someone through the interview process. Make sure that you expose potential candidates to as many people as reasonably possible during your interviews to gain a well-rounded perspective. Make sure you meet together as a team, if possible, to discuss the candidate and see if there is a good fit culturally as well as technically. Do not discount people that have desire or passion for learning and cyber security. One of the best ways to build a loyal, highly trained staff is to grow them organically inside your SOC. If you are able to keep people engaged and interested and you have the ability to invest in their knowledge, then you will reap the rewards of growing your own cyber security professionals in your SOC. Not only should you focus on external resources but you should focus on growing all your staff to make them the best operations team you can. When you focus on expanding their skills, you will be able to retain them as valued employees. People want to grow and if they become stagnant in your organization, then you will see a high rate of turnover. Do not be scared to invest in your people. It is true that some will take their skills and leave, but the better you treat them and the more you invest in them. the more you will be able to retain them.

Next you can bring someone into your SOC who is from another department of your organization. This could be someone from IT or another technical area who is interested in cyber security and wants to explore other technical spaces than the one he or she is in now. Bringing existing employees into your SOC, especially people from IT, can be an incredibly positive boost to an operation's organization. They may already know a lot about the IT infrastructure and the key people that your SOC will have to work with. They may be well liked and respected in the organization with established relationships and can help pave the way for a new organization such as a SOC that is being formed. I cannot stress enough the value of having an existing employee coming to work in your SOC. For a new SOC or new security program just starting up, getting existing people in the organization who know the ropes to help get you get going is a must have. Security is not always looked upon favorably as your organization may require the SOC to watch what people are doing. I do not mean spy on people and certainly there are some different privacy laws from country to country that prevent the actual watching of people, but as rules are broken, events are triggered that will cause an investigation. That is not such a big deal, but catch someone doing something wrong and it becomes a very big deal. Not only that, but when the SOC finds vulnerabilities or sees attacks on the network, people in IT may not view the SOC's investigations and the answering of questions as their favorite things to do during the day. Having people on staff with already established relationships in the organization can help smooth over these types of issues before they become bigger problems. Not only that, but existing employees may know what different servers are used for and what oddly named servers are for and who is responsible for managing them. These are all things that the SOC will have to figure out, but having someone on the team who already knows and has some of this knowledge will help the SOC progress and mature faster in gaining the required familiarity it needs to protect the network.

A SOC can also hire a professional services organization to place contractors in key roles. These contractors will typically be more senior security analysts or engineers who have been in the same role at other companies and have general knowledge of the tasks that need to be performed in a SOC environment. Not only have these contractors likely done a role at another company previously, but they also will typically be trained by the contracting company to ensure that their clients are getting a seasoned resource for the time they are onsite providing value for that customer. Contractors are not always the best solution because you have to pay them to learn your processes and procedures and help them learn where everything is, but that is typically offset by the skills they can quickly bring to the table. The right contracting agency that specializes in cyber security staff augmentation will have a deep well of resources that can be tapped for almost any need. Have a new intrusion detection system being installed or need help implementing a new intelligence program? Provide the contracting agency with your specialized needs, and they will work to find someone who can get the job done. Staff augmentation agreements with contracting companies can be for general analysis roles to help build up your staff temporarily or can be for the implementation of specific projects. Most of the time you will also get the option to hire a person full time from the contracting agency if you really get along with them and believe a more long-term relationship is beneficial. There will be costs associated with hiring a contractor full time so make sure that if you are going to use this option, you understand those charges up front.

Managed Security Services (MSS) is something that we will discuss in more length during another chapter, but it is worth it to mention that organizations can be very successful using a provider. Although an MSS can also provide professional services engagements and staff augmentation, in this case we are talking about not hiring someone to work internal but instead removing the function internally and outsourcing. In this situation, you will outsource specific functions to an external organization and only have response requirements for the activity when the MSS finds something that requires your attention. The MSS will provide the resource coverage you need remotely and will take over the key functions you need to have managed. They will do this with highly qualified and specialized employees that may be unavailable or unaffordable for some organizations. The key to a successful MSS relationship is being a good partner and making sure your expectations are reasonable by only outsourcing functions that lend themselves to easy execution without intimate knowledge of your organization or business.

## OPERATIONAL SECURITY

When you are out there in the market for new staff to fill your SOC, make sure you think about the operational security of your organization. I know that there is a working balance, but you should put some thought into what you want to tell people and what should be kept a secret as to how you run your operations as this is a way to further protect your organization. For example, if you need a front line tier 1 analyst in your SOC and you create a job description stating all the vendor names of all the security products you use and would require a junior analyst to have experience with, you may be giving away a bit too much. By listing all these products, you are giving away potential social engineering, marketing, and intelligence information that an attacker can use, and you may also create a bias to potential candidates. Maybe a potential candidate has great experience, but because you are using one type of antivirus product in your organization versus another, it may make them skip over applying for your job posting. I know this seems silly as they should just be glad you are using antivirus, but do not lose out because of brand recognition or vendor preferences. On the other hand, it is ok to discuss what compliance or regulatory requirements you have as knowledge of those programs is helpful when framing out work that needs to be done in security. Being familiar with programs such as the Payment Card Industry (PCI) Data Security Standard and the Sarbanes–Oxley Act of 2002 (SOX) helps to give you a good gauge as to a person's experience and his or her capabilities in helping your organization stay compliant. Again, when you are looking for a more junior person, having knowledge of products and programs is what you want; for example, familiarity with antivirus is what you want, and the specifics of the product they will get when they are on the job with you. Additionally, how you use the product, what your processes are, and the tasks you are going to require them to perform will almost always be new to them because they are your processes and nobody else's. Of course there will always be similarities from organization to organization that are using the same tool sets, but you will almost always have some distinctions that are specific to your operations or your organization. Also, when an attacker may be looking to infiltrate your organization's network, knowing that you use one brand of IDS versus another may give them an advantage in crafting their attacks to help them be more successful in being able to get past the kind of IDS they know you use. You need to think about what information is important for all job descriptions, not just junior analysts. A person's exposure to SEIM, firewalls, data loss prevention systems or whatever is vitally important, their knowledge of specific brands may not, but that will be up to you. If you really do need someone who has mastery level skills in a particular brand of SEIM, then think about getting an outside hiring agency to market the role for you. That way people will not be able to directly associate your internal operational security controls to the security of your specific organization.

## CULTURE

The culture that develops in a SOC is fairly unique. It is true that when you have any group of people that all work closely together at length, they will develop their own culture, will enjoy a specific sense of humor, and have shared personal feelings and developed trust. But in the case of a SOC, it may be different; it may be more of a group culture of acceptance, knowledge, and general weirdness. There are people that will thrive in these types of environments and those that will not. In larger SOC's that run 24×7 operations, people may not have real personal space. They may share a desk and a computer with people who work on other shifts. They use the same keyboard and mouse as the others and will work on some of the same projects, tasks, and tickets and at times may even operate as if they shared the same brain. Anyone who is lazy or messy will be spotted right away. Someone who is a clean freak sitting at a desk right after someone who is a slob is a type of the cultural and interpersonal clashes that you will need to deal with in a SOC. As a SOC grows and matures, everyone in the SOC grows and matures. When one person in a SOC learns something new and shares it, everyone in the SOC learns something new. Everyone who lives in a SOC will benefit from the knowledge brought in from the outside and from creative people who figure out how to do things better and then share those skills. This happens much in the same way as when one person comes to work sick and a few days later everyone in the SOC is sick. It did not take us long at one high security SOC to figure out that we needed hand sanitizer right next to the biometric hand scanner that everyone used to gain access to the operations floor.

Not unlike other areas of IT, people who are focused on cyber security are very passionate. There is a sense of pride in making sure that the network and all its resources are protected. Bringing someone new into this culture is not always easy. In great SOC cultures that I have worked in, you know it just clicks, you have fun, you respect the people you work with and you learn something new everyday that you go to work. And when you have stayed in touch with the people you have worked with for over 10 years after you left that SOC, then you know you had and still have something special.

A single bad apple can absolutely poison the well in a SOC, so you have to be careful. When a person is not pulling his or her weight, not properly documenting tickets, showing up late, or passing work off to others, the moral in the SOC can go down fast and people can start to gang up on the offender. Unlike other work environments where some of this may go unnoticed, in a SOC it will become very obvious to team members who are picking up the slack. Make sure you stop this early because as things become toxic, work will suffer.

The cultural fit is extremely important in a SOC environment. People have to work very close to each other and will work under some extreme conditions that can also be very high stress. Making sure you have the right personality mix is vitally important.

## PERSONALITY

Personality is a key ingredient for an individual in a SOC environment. You need to find people that are naturally curious and want to uncover the real or root cause of events. These are your modern day Sherlock Holmes who will leave no stone or packet of data unturned in order to get not just an answer but the right answer that satisfies their curiosity. People that thrive in a SOC environment do not need their own office and like working together as a team. They are able to ask for help appropriately and when needed, and will always look for opportunities to share their knowledge in order to better the group. In some very positively charged SOC environments I have been in, positive competition was also a large part of the personality of the people. They would compete to see who could find the most zero day exploits, or who could write the best intrusion detection signatures, or who could develop the best rules to capture new hacking attempts or abnormally behaving devices. They would also attack each other in a lab for bragging rights. This was all in great fun and not only did it inspire people to learn, but it also helped in developing leaders and trainers, not to mention how it benefited and advanced the security of the organization. Without positive personalities like this in the SOC to drive development, innovation, and inspiration your SOC will get stagnant, stale, and filled with people coming in every day to punch a clock.

## CORE SKILL SETS

There are some basic skill sets you should look for in someone you are considering to work in your SOC. These skills are the basic core skill sets that anyone in any position in your SOC should have, and this includes management. One of the basic skill sets that are important for people in a SOC to know at a minimum is rudimentary networking. They should know IP addressing, basic routing, and basic protocol information. They should understand what protocols are and how they operate as well as what ports they use. They do not necessarily need to know an extensive list of ports and protocols, but the more common ones are fine. Do not interview someone just to blow him or her away technically, which is not fair. Instead, gauge where they are and determine if they are trainable to the position you need. Next, they should understand some simple attack methodologies like brute force, overflows, and denial of service as well as how some types of malware work. These simple attacks combined with basic networking skills will give anyone in the SOC a running start when the first real event comes in that they need to address. Obviously the more advanced a person is in these areas the better he or she will be, but do not discount a potential candidate who does not have advanced skills in these topics but has a strong willingness to learn. When we get to the chapter on training, you will see how easy it is to bring people in and give them the skills they need to be successful. You need to be able to get junior analysts in the door and invest time and knowledge on them. I have many, many examples where I have brought someone into a SOC as a junior analyst. They have only had a basic understanding of IT in general but because of their positive personality, drive, determination, and willingness to learn, not only did they come in to the organization and do a great job, they excelled, exceeded expectations, and rose through the ranks to become some of the best platform, intelligence, or general cyber security engineers in the business. So an individual coming into a SOC needs to have a good attitude in order to be successful but also having had some exposure to some programing languages, hex code, and the use of command line instruction from different platforms are a big help as well. Even though you may need a more seasoned and senior person today, look to promote from within and develop your staff to take on greater roles and responsibilities, and then hiring may be easier as you will be freed up to find people who you can train.

To break it all down, here are some of the core skill sets needed for an individual to be successful starting out in a SOC:

- Basic networking
- Simple attack methodologies
- General understanding of malware
- Must have a passion for technology
- Must be genuinely curious
- Should be good at deductive reasoning and critical thinking
- Be creative
- Have a general quest to learn and gain knowledge

### Roles and responsibilities

In a typical SOC, there are various job functions and roles inside those functions that you need to have in order to build out your operation center. We talk more about organizational structure later, but this is as good a time as any to look at a basic organizational chart to frame out the positions we are going to discuss. Each position, although related to each other, is very different and will have a different focus and different skill sets. As such, each position should have a different job description, and individuals in those positions should be held accountable for very different goals and objectives.

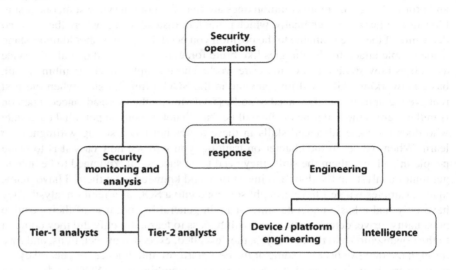

You start off with you basic analyst; this role is your front line initial triage staff. Their jobs are very regimented and prescriptive. They are to do what is documented and nothing else. Anything outside what is documented needs to be escalated. Your second layer or tier 2 is your senior analyst. These folks are there to take more complex escalations from your front line and quickly resolve any issues they can. They also need to make critical decisions to escalate problems to an engineering group or to an incident response lead if the problem deems it. Their position is also prescriptive but has room for flexibility and they have decision capability for escalation purposes. An incident response lead can function in many different capacities depending on the situation. They are there to control the flow of information between analysts, engineers, management, and the customer. They should follow very prescriptive processes to ensure that everyone follows the right process and that all key decision makers are properly informed during crisis times. Engineers can be broken down in many ways and depending on your organization, you may have many groups or just one group. Either way, your engineers should be your most technically skilled SOC staff in a specific area. They operate at a descriptive as opposed to prescriptive level. They will typically be writing rules, building infrastructure, solving problems, and working with vendors to address functional or implementation issues. They can also be research engineers that focus on security intelligence or special projects needed at your organization. Depending on the size of your SOC, you may also have a layer of management in the basic design. If you run several shifts for 24×7 coverage, then you may need a shift supervisor, someone who makes sure that tickets are addressed properly during shift hours. This is also someone who can take customer escalations and deal with management problems as they arise, such as employees calling in sick. The shift supervisor should be one of your best technical analysts who can operate at an engineering level but wants to take their career on a management track. This way they can jump into any issue and make sure that each team is moving along smoothly during that shift. They will also be the liaison for management to report issues, communicate objectives, and resolve any potential problem areas. In addition to shift supervisors, you can have team leads that are directly responsible for individual team performance. These are individuals who work inside a team such as engineering but manage the people, projects, and workflow in that group on a daily basis.

Lastly, there is the SOC manager. This person is responsible for the entire operations of the SOC and will typically have all shift supervisors and team leads reporting into him or her, again depending on the size of your operations team.

You may have many other types of positions in your SOC. This is just a basic framework to begin the conversation of the roles and what the staff should look like from a skills perspective and how you should view them. The perfect SOC employee will be one that you grow and you keep engaged and keep happy, and they will in turn help keep your organization secure.

## ANALYSTS

Your first line staff—the people that answer the phone, triage most of your issues, and review most all your events—are your security analysts. There are many different types of analysts you may have, but your most junior analysts are tier 1/level 1 or the first tier of people who evaluate events. They are the first to open a ticket and peek inside to see what is going on. Your tier 1 analysts are typically not given very much flexibility in how they handle issues. They are given a rigid and prescriptive approach in dealing with events. They are to follow predefined and documented procedures and escalate anything that does not fit the norm to a second tier or a tier 2 senior analyst. It is critical to train your analysts on how to spot problem areas in order for them to be the first and best line of defense for your organization. The more time you spend training your front line analysts, the easier it will be to protect your organization and run an efficient SOC. You also need to listen to your front line analysts. They will tell you where they are wasting their time, how to improve processes, and what they could be doing to make things better and more secure. Give them the opportunity to help shape the SOC, as it should be your hope that one day your front line SOC analysts will become your trusted engineers or managers. I will also argue that you should never hire tier 2 senior analysts. The skills that make a senior analyst are specific to your operation and the operation of your processes, programs, and procedures. While it is true that you can hire people that have more technical skills and require less training, technically there may be no end to the training you can give someone on soft skills that will help them. Being an effective analyst requires a good balance between being technically competent and being able to work with people. A senior analyst will have these skills, will understand the finer points of your processes, and will be able to execute key tasks with finesse, a style that nobody off the street will be able to do until they really learn the ropes of your organization.

When thinking about this position and what you need the role to perform for you, think about the technology that they will need to interact with. Will they access devices directly, will they just work out of a ticket system and nothing more, or in smaller SOCs will your tier 1 and tier 2 really be the same people? Although it is nice to have clearly defined roles with junior people working alongside more senior people, it is sometimes a luxury as not all organizations can afford an army of cyber warriors. This does not mean the job descriptions change or that the functions are different; you just need to combine the functions and merge the responsibilities into one person's core competencies.

Sample job description and posting for a tier 1 or 2 analyst includes key technology that the particular SOC is focused on from an organizational perspective but as mentioned above, the names of the specific vendors or products are omitted. The omission of product and vendor names does not diminish the description; in fact, it makes it more focused and more to the point as you are not instantly drawn into thinking about the products but focused more on the skills.

## SECURITY ANALYST—JOB DESCRIPTION

DESCRIPTION:

This position manages and monitors events from internal security devices, and authentication services associated with the organization's security controls. Incumbents will possess strong technical analytical skills while providing accurate analysis of security-related problems. They have a well-rounded networking background and are responsible for performing extensive troubleshooting of customer issues in the fast-paced SOC. This individual is user focused and works to resolve user needs in a timely manner. These needs may involve resolving hardware/software failures, investigating and responding to security threats, and making change requests to the security policy of company devices.

ESSENTIAL DUTIES AND RESPONSIBILITIES:

Provide technical support for an on call $24\times7\times365$ basis. This involves handling events such as identifying user security issues, extensive troubleshooting, and coordinating resolution or restore using a variety of applications and testing tools. The events can include hardware/software failures as well as security breaches, threats, or network connectivity issues. Regularly provide high-level proactive technical support, including security configurations, security policy modification recommendation, and diagnostics of remote network security issues.

Professionally and courteously answer inbound security-related calls and provide customers with the best possible customer service and experience, create tickets, fill out necessary checklist paperwork, generate trouble tickets for all work and informational requests, handle security-related user complaints, and escalate according to established procedures.

Ensure that the company is implementing best practice security policies that address business needs while protecting vital corporate assets.

Individual must be able to perform with minimal supervision of routine duties;

must demonstrate ability to solve practical problems and deal with a variety of concrete variables in situations where only limited standardization exists; interpret instructions furnished in written, oral, diagram, or schedule formats; and be able to handle multiple tasks simultaneously.

EDUCATION:

Associate Degree or equivalent experience Special consideration given to relevant industry certifications

Typically, 2–4 years related experience required.

FUNCTIONAL/TECHNICAL KNOWLEDGE/SKILLS:

- Background in networking or security to include intrusion detection/prevention.
- Excellent written, verbal communication and organizational skills.
- Knowledge and experience with PCs, LAN topologies, routers, hubs, and terminal servers.
- Knowledge of security applications such as IDS, Security Event Management and anomaly detection tools.
- Knowledge of VPN technology.
- Knowledge of trouble ticketing systems/CRM.
- Understanding of the operation of test and analysis equipment such as protocol analyzers, LAN/WAN sniffers, and so on.
- Ability to read and interpret network diagrams.
- Ability to read and understand packet captures
- Basic understanding of the OSI model.
- Strong interpersonal and user service skills.
- Knowledge of Unix and Windows operating Systems.
- Experience with processes in functional areas (i.e., trouble management, fault management, and incident management).
- Understanding of network management concepts and software, including SNMP.

# SECURITY ENGINEERING

When you look to fill the role of security engineering, your descriptions are going to vary greatly. Engineers can be highly specialized and focused on the very specific needs of your organization. They can be platform focused such as IDS, proxy, or Data Loss Prevention or they can be threat based for the purpose of building intelligence. You may even have network or system engineers that are more IT focused and support the SOC and all its equipment. You have to keep in mind that with your engineering staff, their main purpose is to support the SOC who in turn supports the customer weather internal or external. So it is important that your engineers understand that with every device they deploy, ever rule they create, every piece of intelligence they collect, the analysts will be on the front end of their efforts, and will be responsible for acting on whatever they put in place. Although your security engineers are highly technical and will work on long projects they should not operate in a bubble and need to keep focus on the rest of the organization. This will become obvious when an engineer creates a new rule in a SEIM environment that generates thousands of false positive events that flood your ticket system all for your analysts to fix. As uncle Ben said to Spider-man, "With great power comes great responsibility". Your engineers will have great power over your security infrastructure, make sure they are responsible and accountable.

Engineers should be responsible for looking over tickets that have been closed by the SOC analysts. They should review a specific percentage of tickets each week to ensure that not only are the analysts properly working the tickets but that they agree with the analysis conclusion that was used to close the ticket. This exercise will help not only build better quality control into the overall SOC system but it will help highlight areas that the engineers need to train the analysts on or even areas where the engineers need to fix a system to make things easier or to work better for the analysts.

Sample job description and posting for an engineer, again this will include technology but will not specifically call out brands or products. Below is an example of a job description and posting for a security engineer who has overall critical responsibility for the management and configuration of host-level security on an organizations server network. This could easily be transitioned to be a job for an engineer focused on intrusion detection, intelligence, or Security Event Management.

## SECURITY OPERATIONS ENGINEER—JOB DESCRIPTION

DESCRIPTION:

This position manages and monitors events and performance from host-based security products associated with the company's security controls. Incumbents will possess strong technical analytical skills while providing accurate analysis of security-related problems. They have a well-rounded networking background and are responsible for performing extensive troubleshooting of customer issues in the fast-paced SOC. This individual is user focused and works to resolve user needs in a timely manner. These needs may involve resolving hardware/software failures, investigating and responding to security threats escalated from the analysis group, and making change requests to the security configuration and policy of company devices. Candidates will be the subject matter expert on the team for patching, application whitelisting, hardening, scanning and monitoring as well as security metrics for all severs on the organizations network.

ESSENTIAL DUTIES AND RESPONSIBILITIES:

Provide technical support for an on call 24×7×365 basis. This involves handling events arising from the SOC to perform extensive troubleshooting, and coordinating resolution or restoration of primary responsible systems. Engineer will have overall responsibility for configuration control architecture and software management tools, including but not limited to the knowledge, configuration, and deployment of application whitelisting software tools, and server configuration control software. Duties will include the research, design, test and recommendation of security controls for the organizations server and storage infrastructure. Responsibilities will include the monitoring and metrics associated with security controls to ensure controls are tuned for peak effectiveness.

Additionally, duties will require the evaluation, recommendation, and adjustment of work processes as necessary to correct adverse trends. Candidates must have extensive knowledge of industry accepted standards for system hardening and be able to tune systems to the extent practicable to prevent non-authorized personnel from accessing server infrastructure while ensuring full business functionality.

Candidate will be required to work closely with operations teams to develop processes and security standards for the organizations virtual and physical server environments. Measure, identify, and remediate servers that do not meet security standards. Will be required to work closely with analysts in the SOC to identify and address threats in a timely manner and to troubleshoot and resolve operational issues involving security controls.

Engineers in this role are required to participate in troubleshooting efforts and must be able to perform technical writing, participate in briefings, as well as be a mentor for peer engineers and analysts. It should be expected that management from time to time would assign special projects.

EDUCATION:

Education Level Preferred: Bachelor degree in Computer Engineering, Computer Science, or Information Systems Special consideration given to relevant industry certifications

Minimum of 5 years server security experience in mid-sized to large it organizations.

FUNCTIONAL/TECHNICAL KNOWLEDGE/SKILLS:

- Must have experience with security-related technologies including Active Directory, host-based firewalls, host-based intrusion detection systems, application white listing, server configuration controls, logging and monitoring tools, antivirus, and antivirus systems.
- Must have in depth, hands-on experience with security features and system administration of Linux, UNIX, and Windows operating systems.
- Must have an understanding of security vulnerabilities in common operating systems, web and applications servers, including knowledge of remediation procedures.
- Experience or understanding of NERC, PCI, and SOX compliance standards.
- Experience analyzing new requirements and making security recommendations based on business objectives.
- Must have experience implementing and maintaining security controls and best practices.
- Must possess excellent communication skills and ability to cooperate with other business functions.

## SECURITY ARCHITECT

Although the security architect is not always in the basic SOC organizational chart, it is worth putting a bit in about this role. The architect can be a critical function in a SOC environment and needs to work closely with a SOC. This role can either be managed inside the SOC under an engineering function or can be outside but still under an information security department or CISO function. An architect must be laser focused on the operational functions of any infrastructure or control that they are recommending for implementation. An infrastructure that is not properly managed or the output not properly addressed is a waste of time and the results from those efforts will be lost. The architect must understand how the SOC works and be in lock step with the operations team. They need to ensure that any new technology can be properly managed in the operations center, which is fully integrated with the SOC tool sets and that the proper training and support functions exist for the ongoing care and feeding of that new technology.

## SECURITY ARCHITECT—JOB DESCRIPTION

DESCRIPTION:

The security architect will achieve organizational security goals by determining technical security requirements, planning, and guiding the implementation of security systems. The incumbent will enhance security team accomplishments and competence by planning the delivery of solutions, answering technical and procedural questions for less-experienced team members, teaching improved processes, and mentoring others. Architecture will determine security requirements by evaluating business strategies and requirements, researching information security standards, and conducting system security and vulnerability analyses. Risk assessments and the studying of proposed architecture/platform of business systems will support any identified integration issues. Lastly, the architect must verify installed security systems by developing and implementing test scripts to ensure the success of requirements being met.

ESSENTIAL DUTIES AND RESPONSIBILITIES:

Analyze and design security solutions for business and organizational applications and infrastructure, and provide expertise and consulting to internal or external clients. Will identify and document information security risks and propose mitigating or compensating controls based of best practices, industry standards, or regulatory requirements. Will have the responsibility for understanding complex business needs, requirements, and project scopes, with a focus on information security requirements. Will research, design, and develop new information security controls and will have the ability to assess current IT environments and make recommendations to increase security. Will work closely with compliance, IT, and security organizations to achieve goals.

EDUCATION:

Bachelor's Degree in information systems Special consideration given to relevant industry certifications

5+ years of experience as an information security engineer/architect

FUNCTIONAL/TECHNICAL KNOWLEDGE/SKILLS:

- Background in networking or security to include intrusion detection/prevention.
- Excellent written, verbal communication, and organizational skills.
- Knowledge and experience with PCs, LAN topologies, routers, hubs, and terminal servers.
- Broad knowledge of many aspects of information security with in-depth understanding and hands on experience in many of the following areas: firewalls, proxies, IDS/IPS, VPN, virtualization, authentication technologies, content filtering, DLP, PKI and encryption technologies
- Deep knowledge of industry regulations and requirements such as PCI-DSS, HIPAA as well as ISO27001, NIST, and so on.
- Experience developing information security policy, planning, and rollout of products to achieve organizational regulation and policy goals.
- Experience designing and deploying security solutions
  - To include:
    - Building requests for information (RFI) for vendors
    - Performing proof of concept tests (PoC)
    - Vendor selection
- Ability to produce high quality technical documentation and Detailed solution design documentation
- Should have ability to multitask and adapt to the changing demands of the organization
- Will need to work with multiple teams and cross functional groups of individuals with no direct management responsibility.

## SOC TEAM LEAD

I cannot say enough how important the SOC team leads are in your SOC and in your overall organization. These are the key people that you will need to ensure that everything is running smooth and that issues are being addressed appropriately, they are the ones driving the ship. Your team leads may be a single-shift supervisor or could be stove piped into different functional areas such as an analyst lead, and incident lead and an engineering lead. The larger the SOC the more leads you may want to have to manage individual functional teams, so depending on what makes sense to you and the roles you need you will split these job functions out. Ultimately you need to have a single person who is responsible for what happens on a shift and this is going to either be a lead or a senior lead. A senior lead may be whom all the other leads report to if you need more than one team lead. When looking at the SOC team lead, this should be the single person who is operationally responsible for what is going on during a shift across all teams. This person will ultimately reports to the SOC manager and who will be responsible for executing on the SOC managements requirements.

The lead must be able to do almost every job proficiently and in most cases better than anyone else in the SOC. Not only is this one of the most technically competent an experienced people in the SOC but they must also be very aware of any and all situations happening in the SOC. They need to have sharp instincts to know when an analyst or engineer is having trouble and be able to step in to provide guidance. The team leads are not only your top technical people but they are also management. Because they are management they need to have people and management skills to ensure that everything runs smooth. Your team leads are going to be the leads for just about everything such as scheduling, training, work load and the handing out of any special projects. They will also be the people that should recommend individuals for promotions and raises during review times. These are the lieutenants of the technical front line and need to be able to keep cool at times of extreme stress like when a major incident is happening. They will direct operations and ensure that all requirements are taken care of and that processes are followed, all the while providing support and cover as needed.

Quality control is another area that should be the responsibility of the team leads. They should be responsible for reviewing tickets in the system and spot-checking the work of the analysts. They should review a set percentage of tickets every week to ensure that quality work is being accomplished and they should be looking to see if there are common errors or issues that may require additional training for either individuals or the group as a whole. These spot checks could revel that people are not following process but it is also a great way to see if there are any tickets being improperly addressed or filed or even lost in the system.

## SOC TEAM LEAD—JOB DESCRIPTION

DESCRIPTION:

This is a team leader position with high visibility and significant responsibility supporting the SOC. This individual is responsible for providing direction, leadership, and mentorship to technical and non-technical personnel within the operations environment. The individual should have excellent customer service, analytical and troubleshooting skills along with the ability to work under pressure. It is a key requirement of this position to be able to quickly and efficiently resolve security issues while maintaining high levels of operational metrics. It is imperative that support for internal colleagues is provided as well to include, but not be limited to, supporting escalated ticket-based work, providing training on various security devices and concepts, and creating documentation to better achieve operational goals.

ESSENTIAL DUTIES AND RESPONSIBILITIES:

- Responsible for leading a team of personnel in a SOC environment
- Be able to prioritize and direct workflow
- Addressing technical and non-technical escalations
- Coordinate and schedule shift coverage, and assign resources for special projects
- Meet service level agreements
- Help establish and enforce policy and procedure
- Coach and mentor all levels of skills sets within the team

EDUCATION:

Education Level Preferred: Bachelor degree in Computer Engineering, Computer Science, or Information Systems Special consideration given to relevant industry certifications

Possess current certifications for enterprise level security platforms

Minimum of 5 years server security experience in mid-sized to large IT organizations.

FUNCTIONAL/TECHNICAL KNOWLEDGE/SKILLS:

- Must have experience with security-related technologies including active directory, host-based firewalls, host-based intrusion detection systems, application white listing, server configuration controls, logging and monitoring tools, antivirus, and antivirus systems, network monitoring and network-based security facilities.
- Extensive experience with firewall technology
- Extensive experience managing operational teams
- Past experience managing crisis teams and performing incident response
- Generally familiar with basic scripting/programming: Examples such as: PERL, BASH, SQL
- Ability to coach and mentor all levels of skillsets within the team
- Intermediate to advanced level device configuration changes, network troubleshooting, and security-related issues
- Advanced knowledge of Linux administration with command line and system knowledge
- Excellent problem solving skills and keen ability to diagnose and troubleshoot technical issues
- Dedication to client service and passion for learning
- Well spoken, articulate, attention to detail, with excellent writing abilities
- Must be able to communicate technical details in a clear manner
- Ability to manage multiple projects

## SOC MANAGEMENT

Not unlike the SOC team leads people in SOC management rolls need to also be technical, they need to be able to translate organizational objectives into technical controls that everyone in the SOC can understand. They need to also understand technical issues being dealt with during an incident or when supporting critical infrastructure issues. The SOC manager needs to know their people really well and be able to think on their toes. During incident repose or times of crisis they need to be able to put the right people in the right places at the right time to efficiently and effectively deal with any issues that may arise in order to prevent or limit any exposure an organization may have during an attack or breach. In working with the team leads, they need to address organizational concerns, grow the team's collective knowledge and ensure that the entire operations group is meeting or exceeding standards. Additionally, management needs to be responsible for deploying, maintaining, tuning, monitoring and managing all aspects of the organizations SOC. Additionally, the SOC manager has to be a liaison between the operations team and the rest of the organization. In some cases, the SOC manager may also need to be the primary point person for any external agencies or governing authorities. This is very important when incidents have a criminal implication or when auditors come in to check on regulatory controls. All of that has to be properly managed and controlled so that the organization can maintain its compliance and ensure that there is cooperation with any authorities that may need to be involved in incidents.

The SOC manager is also the key person responsible for all the metrics in the SOC. This would be to ensure that the SOC is operating effectively, efficiently, and that the metrics demonstrate an acceptable level of performance. The manager needs to also perform predictive analysis to ensure they are brining in the right staff to fill critical roles, promoting the right people and ultimately achieving organizational security objectives. Management should also always be on the lookout for new ways to build metrics that demonstrate effectiveness or weaknesses and use these tools at all levels of the SOC to help engage everyone to better bring them into alignment with expectations.

The SOC manager needs to also work with the rest of the organization and if available a larger security organization to identify areas where the SOC is causing problem or for areas of opportunity for the SOC to further help meet security objectives. A SOC can create problems for other groups such as IT, in that escalations may need to be handled better or information flow needs to be done differently. In these cases, it is important that the SOC manager work with these external teams to understand what they need or how the SOC can work with them better so as to not cause issues and make life easier for everyone involved. Additionally the person in this role needs to be an evangelist for the operations group and ensure that the right amount of publicity is being heard internally to the rest of the organization. All too often the SOC goes unnoticed behind closed doors unless there is an issue or someone is helping to promote the great work everyone is doing in security operations. A SOC manager must create value out of the SOC for the organization, effectively communicate that value, and provide people with the tools and products that demonstrate that exceptional value. The manager who is able to place the interests of their customers internal or external, clients, and other groups in the organizations first will succeed the best.

In a later chapter, we talk more about structure and reporting but it is important to think about how a SOC manager plays a role in the overall organization. This person could be the CISO for a smaller organization or report into a larger security or IT department.

## SOC MANAGER—JOB DESCRIPTION

DESCRIPTION:

Lead and manages the efforts to integrate, implement, and maintain the organizations security infrastructure and operationalize the security requirements and goals of the organization. Provide technical and operational oversight for security tool deployment and implementation. Continuously monitor levels of service of the SOC as well as interpret and prioritize overall threat levels through use of metrics from the analysis of intrusion detection systems, firewalls, and other boundary protection and security devices as well as any other security incident management products deployed to protect the confidentiality, integrity, and availability of resources. Recognize potential, successful, and unsuccessful intrusion attempts and compromises thorough review and analyses of relevant SOC reporting, event detail and summary information. Must provide oversight for incident management and response, security investigations and forensics, vulnerability management, remediation assistance, intelligence gathering and dissemination, threat scenario modeling, impact assessments, and security exercise preparedness. Ensure the integrity and protection of networks, systems, and applications by technical enforcement of organizational security policies. Monitor and proactively mitigate information security risks and adjust posture as needed to continually strengthen the fidelity of attack detection. Provide briefings at various levels of management regarding ongoing security incidents and operational metrics. Establish reporting and information sharing relationships with governing and partner organizations, and other appropriate external agencies and organizations for the purpose of tracking threats or sharing common security incidents. Develop and maintain processes and procedures used to manage operations and incident response process and a root cause continuous improvement program. Develop and maintain reporting metrics and mechanisms used to execute and measure SOC activities. Maintain and enhance the security roadmap used to provide technical, personnel and procedural growth and the implementation of new tools and techniques. Develop papers, briefings and technical marketing materials designed to show the value of the security operations and the individual tools deployed in the organization. Provide executive level briefings regarding status of the SOC implementation, effectiveness of security tools and infrastructure, areas of concerns, ongoing project status and cost benefit analysis for the use of the SOC and the cost avoidance of detected and mitigated security incidents. Work within a 24/7 shift-scheduled security operations environment.

ESSENTIAL DUTIES AND RESPONSIBLITIES:

This role is responsible for the visibility of organizational security controls to protect the environment and all security technology data outputs that terminate in the operations center. They must effectively ensure operational control or "watch" of the environment, developing and integrating all security processes, and threat intelligence services. This includes formalization and ownership of a SOC capabilities and responding to all security incidents. This role is responsible for the successful operations and expertise of all security technologies and establishing escalation processes for those selected security incidents that have been deemed critical.

This role will also manage penetration and vulnerability testing activities and will ensure the Security Architecture and Engineering teams work together to provide feedback on the "health" of the enterprise security baseline based on those tests. This role develops and communicates requirements for security technology automation and works with IT, business representatives, HR, architecture, and audit teams on the overall solution set for design specification, technology selection, and security objective development. This is a heavily metrics-driven operations role that provides a critical data and reporting foundation as direct inputs to the overall risk management function. This role will influence and drive the overall enterprise information security strategy.

The ideal candidate has a proven history in enterprise security operations managing technical staff. The SOC manager will have strong level of technical depth in information security and is focused on driving metrics-driven results. The ideal candidate is output driven and able to leverage multiple forms of communication to articulate complex concepts with proficiency to both technical contributors and executive management.

EDUCATION:

Bachelor's degree in a technical engineering or IT-related field or equivalent and 8+ years related experience. Related experience includes senior level SOC analyst, SOC shift manager, or team lead. Incident response and handling experience required. Requires background in in the following domains; security products and technologies; security engineering, networking protocols and data center management; security analysis and investigations.

FUNCTIONAL/TECHNICAL KNOWLEDGE/SKILLS:

- Leadership and management in an enterprise security operations role.
- Familiarity with operating enterprise security technologies and establishing enterprise security processes.
- Experience with advanced threat management.
- Experience with cloud, mobile, SIEM, and open source security technologies.
- Experience integrating heterogeneous operational security technologies.
- Familiarity and experience standards frameworks ISO, NIST, ITIL, and so on.
- Development of detailed metrics and reporting for executive management.
- Candidate must possess excellent written visualization and verbal communication skills.
- Experience in security operations within a 24×7 environment.
- Strong knowledge of information security principles and industry best practices.
- Experience with computer forensics

Shall we play a game? (War Games, 1983)

## SOC GAMES

Now that we have reviewed all the personnel and their functions in the SOC, we now have to get them to start protecting our organization and we need to keep them engaged. We know who the players are, what their functions are and what they are supposed to be focused on accomplishing in the SOC. But let us be real honest for a moment, depending on the size of your SOC and the size of the organization you are protecting or if you are a managed security services provider, the daily grind of working in an operations center can be very boring at times with limited sprits of excitement, it is like fishing without the sun and beer. Analysts review tickets and decode packets of data and try to find out if the bad things their systems are telling them that happened really did happen or if it is just a false positive. Typically the work should be a dull roar unless you are dealing with active threats on the front line and engaged in crazy attacks and breaches every day as some MSSP organizations are. For an analyst that is required to work tickets and may even have a quota of tickets they need to work are going to suffer eye strain and after a time will want to start to skipping steps just to get the work done. Another thing that might happen is that they analysts will only pick the tickets they want to work on instead of the tickets that are a priority to work on. This does not do anyone any good and drastic mistakes can occur, things can get missed or signs of larger issues can go ignored. To combat the eye strain, and sometimes repetitive work people have to do in the SOC the management team needs to come up with creative ways to give them frequent breaks, help keep people engaged, excited, and also progressing in their career.

One of the ways to help keep people sharp and engaged is to play fun games that help keep the focus on the prize of securing the organizations environment. To start you could run a contest that keeps score of analysts and engineers ability to stop specific types of threats. The more creative you are the better it will be and the more fun you can have with it. This could be games that run a full month with a total scoring system or a one hit wonder with a single prize at the end. You can allow people to wear funny hats or dress causal for a month and you could even award the winners with an assigned parking space until someone beats their score or maybe until another winner is announced.

The cricket dartboard game is a good example of how you could accomplish this. You assign different types of true positive events to a value that aligns with your organizations security policies, for example: The numbers 20 thru 15 and the bull's eye are used and are assigned a specific true and validated event that an analyst or engineer needs to find. Anyone can "hit" any number in any order but once an individual has scored three hits on the same number that number is closed for them and they cannot score any longer on that value. A player who has closed all of the numbers by finding these types of events first wins the game.

> Bulls eye = Unauthorized data transfer out of the network
> 20 = Detection of advanced persistent threat (APT)
> 19 = Successful use of default passwords on the network
> 18 = Successful cross site scripting attack
> 17 = Phishing email found with malware
> 16 = Unauthorized device found on the network
> 15 = Active virus found on system

You can also provide a double and triple score for each of these based on who the user is or how serious the event is. For example, if someone finds a virus talking to a command and control server on the CEO's laptop (or if you are in the military you can do it by rank) that may be an instant triple 15. Or for example, if it is determined that an Advanced Persistent Threat actor has compromised a system and you have evidence that they tried to move laterally to another system then that may be a double 20. You will have to come up with your own system and score values but you should be able to see how this could be an easy and fun game to play. You should also add a prize value to winning, for example you could take the first three people to complete the board out for a nice dinner or give the first winner $500, second winner $250 and the third place winner $100. Either way, it is something that can help keep people engaged, get them thinking about different types of threats and will make them seek out different types of events that are important to the organization and not just work the issues they are comfortable working, or focus on one specific issue that may be in their comfort zone.

First one to root wins!

Defending your network or servers from being breached by a hacker or by advanced persistent threat actors should be amongst one of your biggest concerns. Or if you are trying to strengthen your controls because this has already happened once before and now you realize that you are more of a target now than you were before then you can set a bounty on a specific event that would find evidence that this is type of activity is taking place. The contest would simply be the first person that finds an unauthorized external actor accessing an internal system or server with administrative level credentials wins. Of course you never want to see this happen but we all know that having a system compromised is not a matter of if but when. So when this does happen, are you able to detect it and is the unauthorized access at an administrative level. In different SOCs, I have tried this game with a $1,000 prize to the first person that was able to find this activity on the network. It was a great motivator and the direct result was that analysts and engineers were evaluating and analyzing events and tickets to a depth that were never seen before. They were really taking the time to ensure that they knew what was going on and why something was happening in the hopes it would lead them to the prize. The direct benefit to the organization was a better quality of analysis on tickets and a nice motivator for the staff. The positive effects lasted long after the contest was over because the analysts were more educated in evaluating these types of events and the quality of work in the related type of tickets improved tremendously.

Other simple games can be played as a group that will help motivate your SOC to support them in avoid the day-to-day grind. You could offer them simple rewards like bringing in food for lunch if they meet or exceed specific Service Level Agreement goals like answering the phone by the third ring 100% of the time in a week. Another goal may be to ensure every new ticket is addressed in 15 min or less for a month. The prizes and contests should be customized to your SOC and what will motivate your people. Take a look at your metrics or your security goals and you will easily find areas that will need improvement, then try to see how you can rap those improvement areas into very specific targets. Then ask your team what they want for a prize and see what kind of answers you get, you may find that they would love to have a more comfortable chair, or a bigger desk. If your SOC manager or even your CEO has a really comfortable chair, maybe you can offer up your CEO's chair for a week to the winner. Not every game has to have a cash value, make it fun and be consistent, you could do a game every month or just on special occasions or when you see issues and need a shot of motivation. Be creative, just because the SOC has a serious role does not mean you cannot have fun while you are keeping watch of the network.

## SPECIAL PROJECTS

Sometimes games are just not enough and will certainly not resolve all problems. Sometimes people in a SOC just need a break and need to get away from the ticket queue for a while. This could become a big moral issue and when people really start to get eyestrain and board as an analyst they will want to move on and leave the organization. If you are properly investing time and money into training your staff then you will not want them to move on so you need to keep them interested and engaged. One great way to do this is to assign special projects. There is almost never a shortage of things to do in a SOC or in the overall security organization so special projects should always be available, if not then there may be something else wrong. Anyway, figuring out a list of special projects that needs to get done is a great way to not only help mature your SOC and move forward but giving out those special projects can greatly help and motivate people in your SOC. By giving someone a special project even a short-term special project you are telling them that you are confident in their abilities and that they have skills that you would like for them to utilize. Not only should they be excited to take on a special project but this should also be a nice break from working a ticket queue for a while. Special projects can really be almost anything and will greatly depend on what your needs are for your SOC and your organization. But they could be something as simple as updating training documentation or building a new training program or as complex as helping an engineer with a new product implementation. Another great project is the developing or exploring of new metrics or reports or even giving someone the opportunity to build new visual displays for the SOC video wall or projectors. These are just really simple ideas but I am sure you could find better ones in your SOC. The special projects can be simple or complex, they can be a way for you to see if an individual is ready for advancement or just a way to help break up the work load and definitely a great way for you to help give people a break from a relentless queue of tickets.

## DO NOT FORGET YOUR PEOPLE

You SOC will only work as hard as you work for them. People like to be recognized for the work they do, sometimes they want this a bit too often or even when they do not deserve it but that is just human nature. Sometimes people working for an organization think they should get an award for just showing up to work on time. Whereas other people pull their own weight as well as the weight of several other people and never get recognized for all that they do. The people who work in a SOC environment need to constantly dig deeper, they need to be on the lookout for attacks coming from every direction and they need to be able to detect and defend against it all whereas the attacker just need to be right once. The members of a SOC have to monitor several to several hundreds if not thousands of servers when an attacker just needs to focus on one. The people in a SOC work hard to keep their skills up and constantly learn new things so that they can be better prepared for whatever comes their way. A SOC can see hundreds or even thousands of events populated into tickets a day out of billions of possible logs but an attacker just needs to hide one malicious payload inside one needle in that haystack. Analysts and engineers need to remain focused and ensure they get the best fidelity they can with the tools they are given or have designed. Make sure you take care of your SOC so that they can take care of the entire organization.

Some organizations have formal recognition programs such as employee of the month. If they do, then it is important that SOC management make sure that every single month someone from the SOC team is nominated. Continue to nominate people even if the nominations are not accepted. It may seem like a small thing but to some people simple recognition goes a long way and management should never miss an opportunity to positively recognize the efforts of individuals. Other organizations have informal recognition programs that allow anyone to nominate any other person for a nominal cash reward for going above and beyond. These programs should be popular and encouraged by management. If none of these formal organizational programs exist, management can still take the initiative to support the SOC and do special things as a group. The SOC is a team, they work hard together so getting them involved in team or group activities should not be very difficult. Plan a team BBQ or cookout during working hours and rotate people from the SOC to take a break outside for a while. Since most SOCs are dark and closed off rooms this should be a welcomed change on a nice day. If you run a 24×7 SOC, plan on doing the cookout later in the day so that your first and second shift can overlap. For the third shift you can do an early morning cookout before the other shifts. I know cooking steaks at 7:00AM may not be the most appetizing things for you but I am sure the people who have to work the overnight shift will appreciate it. If doing a big BBQ or cookout is just not possible then there is always the ability to bring in Pizza, or have you ever thought about how many burgers you can get from the drive through window for only one dollar each, it is a lot and you can feed quite a large SOC for very little money. Food is typically always a welcome treat in a SOC, so do not think you need to go overboard to recognize the efforts of the SOC, sometimes it is the small things that go the furthest.

As it has been mentioned before there will come a time in which the organization your SOC is working to protect will be successfully attacked and compromised. Keep in mind that this is not the time to beat up the SOC, instead you need to look at how it happened, perform root cause analysis and ensure that the SOC has the right tools, processes, and procedures to prevent it from happening again. Additionally you should think about what would have happened if the SOC were not there and what kind of chaos would have ensued if professionals were not available to find the issue, even if it was after the fact. The SOC will not always protect the organization from every attack but will be able to defend against most. They should be able to detect and limit the exposure from a successful attack while being able to direct incident response and help guide any recovery efforts.

# Daily operations

## CHAPTER CONTENTS

A SOC is not your normal business office atmosphere where people show up to their offices or cubicles everyday on mostly their own schedule or within an acceptable time range. In most office environments, people can customize or personalize their offices or cubes to give them a sense of comfort or a feeling of home. In a typical SOC that operates 24×7 that is not possible, shifts will share desks and computers where personalization is difficult or impossible. The life of someone who works in a SOC is different, make no mistake about it, no matter how it looks or what the space is that you use, if you have a SOC, it is going to be different. Your SOC is on the front line protecting your company by paying close attention to details while rushing to address all priority events stacking up in the ticket queue. It needs to be different, the environment needs to be open, people need to work together, work with each other and count on each other for knowledge, direction, and information. Your SOC needs to be a supportive environment where people are challenged so they can grow and so they come in every day ready to find that needle in a haystack.

It is an interesting ecosystem that needs to be protected and understood to ensure that your staff continue to perform at their best. Your daily operations are critical to the flow of this ecosystem. You have to be mindful of the work tempo, the workload, and individual relationships between people on-shift, between shifts, and with management. Set up your operational schedule up front but do not be afraid to experiment and try new things, as no two SOCs are ever alike.

The SOC is charged with the responsibility of being the first responders to information security incidents and events, they are also protectors of the organizations infrastructure, data and, in some cases, the personal electronic protection of the organizations employees and members. Analysts and engineers need to be held to high standards of conduct, integrity, and job knowledge. As such there are specific expectations and routine daily tasks that need to be performed to ensure that operations happen smooth and efficiently. To ensure continuity and job process integrity are maintained by everyone in the SOC and across all SOC shifts or all geographically separated SOCs. Specific policy and procedures need to be developed in the SOC and documented for everyone to follow. One of the most important of these policies and processes is the SOC daily standard operations procedure (SOP) that provides guidelines for everyone to follow. This chapter represents some of the items you will want to consider implementing in your SOC as part of the daily SOP. It is not meant to be all inclusive as your organization will have other considerations or items that are specific that will need to be included here.

# PROBLEM AND CHANGE EVENT COMMUNICATIONS
## MASTER STATION LOGS

Sometimes referred to as an analyst log, a Master Station Log (MSL) is a great way to capture events that happen outside of a ticketing system or does not have a place to be ticketed such as something that occurs around the SOC but has no place for a true record to be stored. Additionally, the MSL is a great place to highlight items of importance that need to be communicated across multiple teams, shifts, or SOCs. The MSL can be a simple text document that is shared, a workgroup based website like SharePoint or a formal software application that is installed on a server. Either way, the MSL is the official narrative record maintained to document and communicate significant events. As a minimum, like a mini ticketing system, all the entries should contain, the time of the entry, the name of individual making the entry, and the specific details relative to the entry. These entries are necessary for internal communication between shifts and the security groups to affectively monitor ongoing organizational issues that could affect security visibility or the operations in general. It is also a good tool in helping to bridge the gap between shifts or SOCs when issues span multiple time zones or have a lasting impact from one shift to the next.

The events below are an example of what should be reported at a minimum within the MSL.

- Network outage—Any disruption in services that affects the organizations users the ability to perform their job function such as the loss of LAN, WAN, or VPN connection.
- Security outage—Any disruption in security equipment or networks that reduce the visibility of the SOC and limits the ability to perform security services.
- Patching/update notifications from IT or security engineering—Any patching/ update notifications to include but not limited to IDS updates, SIEM rule updates, security system reboots, or major maintenance and upgrades. This should include expected service and server down times and what loss of functionality should be expected.
- Hardware failure—server, router, or switch that is has been determined as down or offline and could be degrading performance or causing latency in event detection.
- Special visitors to the SOC such as management, contractors, or auditors.
- Environmental issues such as construction, heating and cooling issues.
- Special announcements made by management

A team leader at the end of every shift should email the MSL or a copy out to the entire SOC organization. This will help ensure that everyone is on the same page and that items that need to be closely watched are documented and communicated effectively. It should be everyone in the SOCs responsibility to review the MSL upon start of their shift to ensure they are familiar with anything that may affect their ability to perform their job function or for anything that they may need to be addressed while on shift. It should also be very easy for SOC leadership to read three reports from the previous three shifts and be completely up to date on what is going on and any issues the SOC is currently facing.

## SHIFT TURN OVERS

Shift turnover is an extremely important part of the shift in a SOC. This is the chaotic time where one shift of people is ending their day and the next shift of people has arrived to start their day. Procedures for performing a shift change should be agreed upon by all the team leads and then posted, trained, and adopted by all members of the SOC. Everyone should know the process to start a new shift and exit the old shift to ensure that there is a clean handoff and that all the required important information is passed along.

To help facilitate the handoff process, each shift should be scheduled with an approximately 15–30 min overlap. This allows for a bit of flexibility in case there are ongoing issues that people need to finish up or if there are unforeseen issues with people showing up on time. The process should start off with all SOC employees spending the first 10 min of his or her shift communicating with the analyst or engineer they are replacing regarding special concerns or critical information. While this conversation is happening, the outgoing analyst or engineer should be finishing up any tickets or calls they may be engaged in and then focus on cleaning their work area for the next person.

The senior shift lead would be responsible for putting together a turn over report that would be emailed to everyone along with the MSL. The shift lead should gather everyone from the shift prior to them leaving for the day and interview each person in a quick stand-up round robin fashion. If any analyst or engineer has a specific issue or items of importance then they communicate it in this rapid-fire forum. The team lead should make notes, ask questions and ensure that they have all the information they need to pass along and ensure that items are addressed properly. Depending on your SOC you may want to formalize roles for this end of shift stand-up report. You could include specific metrics like the number of open events that are being left for the next shift to address, or any specific outages or viruses that are causing problems. Set a specific starting time for the shift change meeting for each shift and enforce it consistently. Make sure you emphasize how important it is for everyone to attend and to not hold up the group, everyone wants to leave work at the end of their shift so being held up by one person is not fair. Because one shift is ending and another shift is starting, the meeting must be completed in a timely manner as to not interrupt the work of the incoming shift and you do not want this to go very long, just long enough to transfer the important details.

The senior lead gathers all the information deemed important to the oncoming shift from the analysts, engineers, and intelligence teams and generates an end of shift email report. The turn over email report will need to be emailed to all SOC analysts, SOC management, or anyone else that would benefit from the information daily at the end of each shift. It should at the minimum captured any critical events that happened on shift that the oncoming shift needs to make a priority, a brief rundown of shift happenings such as system changes, signature updates, rule modifications to SIEM tools, a list of tickets that was worked and that need continued investigation, any other information that the current shift might think will be helpful to the oncoming shift and last but not least it should include relevant cyber intelligence or attack trends that may impact ticket-able events that the shift will likely see.

Between the SOC shift report and the MSL, it all seems like a lot of information and can even be information overload. If you have never been a part of the process before or you are new to the SOC it will be overload but you will quickly get the hang of it and will be able to quickly pick out the important bits that relate to you fairly easy. These reports will change over time and I encourage everyone to try and make these processes better and find better ways to pass on information. More is better when you are doing your shift change, just try and work on how to present the information as best and clear as possible to ensure that everyone has a good grasp on what is going on and what is required for them on their shift.

Each shift coming into the SOC needs to perform some procedures to ensure that everything is setup and working properly. As we discussed, there will already be a hand off process so the incoming shift should be fully updated in the previous shifts activities. The next set of tasks they need to perform is to ensure that all required tools and systems are properly functioning. They should reset the video wall and any projectors to make sure that nothing is hung or stuck, the shift team should check the phones, network connections or any other important technology. If you not running a 24×7 SOC then you need to make sure that phone lines ring into the SOC instead of going to voicemail or an on-call pager. A written process should be created that each shift follows and any issues or discrepancies should be noted or escalated to the proper people to be resolved. Another important consideration is if your handoffs are problematic and items are being dropped or lost, consider staggering your team leads. Have the team leads shifts start and end a few hours overlapped into each shift. That way you have a single team lead spanning two partial shifts as continuity. Also as we will discuss later, having different people in different roles work different length shifts may also help with continuity between shifts. For example if you have the majority of your shift working 8 h but two people work 12's then they can help with the change overs.

## DAILY OPERATIONS CALLS

Depending on the activity level in your SOC or current threat level of your organization you may want to institute a daily operations call. This call would be for your SOC management, team leads or engineering leads that need to perform a verbal review of the day's activities or expectations for incoming shifts. It could be a stopgap measure for management to get better control and visibility into daily operations or it could be a permanent tool that is used to keep everyone in the loop as to what is going on for hot items in the SOC. This is very different from a shift change process, as it will include people who are either not in the SOC or not even be in operations, it could include leads from sales, customer service or IT, depending on your organization. The daily operations call is a management review where SOC leadership gets to report on highlights of the day to management. This could include internal or external customer issues, missed SLAs, ongoing incidents or upcoming events that are significant to the operations team such as network maintenance or outages that may impact operations. The SOC leadership can bring people into the call that they think will add value, this could even be an analyst that is working on a particularly sensitive issue that would be able to answer questions or add valuable details. The meeting should last no longer than one hour and in most cases should be less. During times of critical issues the meeting could include individuals internal to the organization that want to keep close tabs on issues but this is not the time to perform incident response (IR), it is a management review and update call.

The format for this call should be very simple, it should be the senior team lead or manager reporting on activity that they deem to be important or what they think will impact performance moving forward, such as an outage. Then SOC management or security management such as a CISO would have an opportunity to comment or weigh in on each of the topics and provide guidance or take action items to resolve problems. This is a great way to ensure that there is good communication throughout the entire SOC organization and that management is properly engaged. Not only is it good to ensure management is engaged but it also gives them a good opportunity to ask questions, make course corrections or provide them with valuable inputs that they need in order to address issues externally. There are two possible times that this call should happen. The first logical time would be after the first shift change, at the start of second shift. This would typically be at the end of the normal workday about 5:00 p.m. Depending on your SOC and if you run a 7×24 or have many SOCs around the world you may also want to consider a morning call as the primary call. By doing this call in the morning at about 8:00 a.m., you can get information at the end of third shift and help set the stage for first shift, but it may also be the start of second or third shifts elsewhere in the world. If the management calls seems to work then do not shy away from using it, there is no reason to not have two calls, one could be in the morning and the other can be in the evening, either way you will be able to capture inputs from all shifts and have good high level discussion, if you place the calls carefully in-between shifts and logically to how you split your shifts then you should be able to keep up to date on all important activity.

## CRITICAL BRIDGES

Because the SOC deals with critical issues that affect the confidentiality, availability, and integrity (CIA) of an organizations data and systems, it is important that when there is an incident that impacts the CIA for an organization that communication be handled quickly, efficiently, and properly. Sometimes depending on how the incident effects an organization or who it affects you will need to swarm the issue. An emergency hotline or critical bridge may be a way to break outside of the normal processes and get the right people to the table to address and resolve issues quickly.

In many cases, escalation to authorities, engineers with different skill sets or to people with different access privileges may be necessary. The SOC is sometimes not in a position to take action all on its own. In some cases, the SOC is only responsible for monitoring a system but cannot make any decisions about it. The analyst needs to know who to call to get approval to remediate a threat or to get someone who can make a needed change that would prevent or fix an issue. The SOC procedures must be documented and have some rules on escalations or when to establish a critical bridge. It should be noted that an analyst should have the power to establish a critical bridge at any time if they deem it necessary, nobody should get in trouble for starting up a critical bridge if it was determined that it was not necessary. You need to make sure that your analysts feel comfortable engaging and asking for help.

Depending on your organization, the critical bridge escalation procedures could be based on the type of system, the type of attack or the business/organizational unit affected. The choice very much depends on how your organization operates, where the risks are, and what works most efficiently for your organization.

Ever wish you had a big red phone that you could just pick up and the right person or people will already be at the other end of the line waiting to help you? Well this is how you can accomplish pretty much the same thing at the time of crisis.

Swarming is not a new concept but using it in a critical operational environment with potential remote or geographically separate resources can be a simple thing to overcome. By swarming an issue, you quickly bring a diverse group of experts together in order to assess and solve complex problems as a team. When you swarm a technical issue like this it could be a quick 5-min call where someone jumps in after hearing the initial problem and then clicks a few buttons and all is good or it could be several hours where multiple people are diligently working to resolve a large problem.

A phone bridge or standard conference call number can be established and all the key people you want to be a part of the critical call or emergency hotline can be given that information to be programed into their phones. Then a webpage can be established that includes the ability to send out a group text/SMS message that notifies everyone that his or her presence is required on the conference call for a critical issue. The text message can either go out to a primary person or if you are able to add logic to your system a secondary or backup person. You also want to ensure you have a paper version that documents this process that details everyone who would need to be on the emergency hotline, their phone numbers and who their backups are in case they are unreachable or on vacation.

In case of a critical or major incident defined by your organization, which could include a system being attacked, a potential compromise, a denial of service attack or even an unplanned outage, an analyst can, as part of or in addition to IR processes initiate a critical bridge. This can happen any time day or night, it does not matter what time it is as long as the bridge is established in a reasonable time after a critical incident is detected and not too long where participants cannot be effective in making positive remediation's or key decisions. If it takes too long to establish the bridge and get all the right people engaged then there may be too much damage for anyone to do any good, so the calls need to be made quickly after incident discovery and classification. Because these calls can happen at any time you may want to develop a process that has different people on an easy to understand call rotation so that the same people are not being woken up every night.

Once the bridge has been opened and all required personnel are present the SOC will brief everyone of the status of the incident. This brief will consist of where the incident is occurring, who is causing it (if known), what the incident consists of, how long the incident has been going on, and what the potential root cause of the incident is. After the briefing, the SOC will give its recommendations for remediation of the incident, and then open the floor for discussion. During this time, the remainder of the SOC team who are involved will continue their investigation of the incident and provide updates to the bridge as necessary. Once an approved remediation step has been decided upon, the SOC or engineering will implement the solution and provide an ongoing status to the bridge. If it is considered necessary by the bridge team to contact the vendor of the system, the owner of the system or anyone else that can provide value to the team, the SOC will initiate the contact with them. The addition of any further resources can be done on an as-needed basis and would depend on the issue. If the initial remediation action fails or is not complete, the SOC may deem it necessary to escalate to a management in order to inform them of any potential impacts or customer issues that may result from the event. This gives management an opportunity to get ahead of the problem and make any arrangement for initiating proper customer communications or may even allow them the chance to authorize a partial disaster recovery plan to get business flowing again if it is impacted. Management may also be needed to approve the removal of systems from service or to rapidly rebuild systems, regardless of action, management should know if there is any impact to business services or any impact to customers.

Additionally if the critical incident is deemed to have a data loss that would be consider a breach or loss of credit and payment card information or a loss of personal health information then other specific groups must be involved as part of the bridge escalation process. The groups that you may want to include are legal or a privacy department but maybe if you are a large retailer you may have a banking department or credit department that has ultimate responsibility for breach notification to the acquiring banks or credit card companies as required by contract. There may be very specific state, federal, or international laws that you will need to follow after detecting a data loss. By including other groups in the call once you have positively determined a data loss then you are going to give those groups the best opportunity to make key decisions and to make notification to the proper authorities in a reasonable amount of time. It is important for effective daily operations that the SOC work with the organization to understand who would need to be contacted and when for various types of incidents and who would need to be engaged on a critical bridge at the time of significant incidents. Depending on the type of incident, its criticality and who needs to be engaged, it would not be uncommon to have two critical bridges going at once. The first bridge can be for technical experts working together to resolve the issues and the second bridge can be for management and other business resources. This way the conversations can be kept separate and will not get people confused or taken off track of their primary focus. The SOC would act at the liaison between the two calls and would provide updates to both bridges on regular intervals or when important information needs to be relayed.

Once remediation is successful, the incident is considered closed. The bridge will be closed and the SOC will begin building a post-mortem briefing that will be delivered to all involved parties and should include any compliance teams in the organization as well, if available. The briefing will include details around the original event, a complete timeline, who participated on the bridge and what remediation actions were taken. It should also include a root cause analysis and a list of action items that would be needed to prevent future occurrences. It is important that when performing root cause analysis and post-mortem briefings that the documents are kept factual and that the process is not used as a weapon against other teams or evidence as to how someone is not doing their job. For example, if the IT department is responsible for security patching on servers and an attacker is able to take advantage of a vulnerability that was not patched, this is not the time to beat up the IT department. Instead, make sure that you detail the vulnerability, the time frame in which the patch for the vulnerability was available and then you can make comments on the need for increased efficiencies in patch management. The post mortem process can quickly turn to finger pointing and will often put people on the defensive, this takes away from the core focus of helping an organization becoming more secure. The SOC should always ensure they take a factual and passive approach to documenting deficiencies and let management and business leaders work through the challenges that may be present in an organization. Do not let passion to be secure or passion to provide the best service possible get in the way of achieving the goals of the SOC.

The following is a flow of how the critical bridge process can work, it is very similar to the overall incident flow but has the deviation of opening the critical bridge and managing the bridge process.

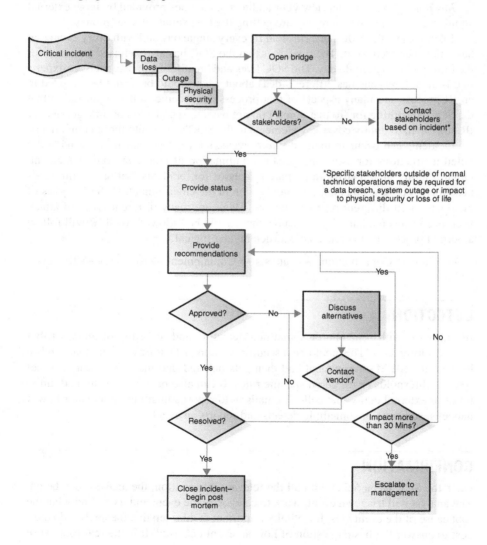

## IR

Auditing to regulations whether it be Sarbanes Oxley (SOX), Payment Card Industry, Health Insurance Portability and Accountability Act (HIPAA), or whatever your industry requires is a necessity. It is a good tool and sometimes is required to get Information Assurance goals moved forward. A security department and especially a SOC need to embrace auditing and work with auditors as best as possible and make things as easy as possible. But it seems that without fail, whenever I have built an enterprise SOC in a regulated environment I seem to always get an auditor from an external company that comes around to ask when the last time the SOC tested and practiced an IR.

*Key point:* You can interview your auditors, even ones provided by large external auditing companies to ensure you are getting the best value for your money.

Joking aside, the SOC performs real IR every single day and with every event that has a ticket created for it. The processes that the SOC has are exercised and used for the most part every single day. The SOC lives and breathes IR and as such are experts in this area. Everyone has different ideas about what should be or not be included in an IR process and many aspects of that process are specific to the organization that the SOC is working for. To that point, I do not want to spend a ton of time going over IR other than to lightly cover key elements in the SOC's view into those components.

Incidents can occur in many different ways, so it is not realistic to provide detailed instructions for every imaginable combination of attack or type of incident. Organizations should strive to prepare processes for incidents that use common attack vectors or cases that are commonly seen in the environment. Different types of incidents merit different response tactics. There are many different types of attack vectors and specific handling measures that should be followed so all IR will follow a normal process that is repeatable, efficient, and logical.

Detection → Confirmation → Analysis → Containment → Recovery → Review

## DETECTION

IR starts off with someone or something detecting and reporting of an event that needs a closer look. This could be a security system or IT infrastructure that sends a log into the SIEM environment and then gets ticketed into the SOC because it met specific thresholds or triggered specific rules. It can also be a user, system administrator or external entity that calls or emails in to report something. No matter how it happens, someone or something detects and reports an event.

## CONFIRMATION

Once the SOC has a ticket with all the relevant information, the analysis can begin. The analyst will triage an event, work to categorize the event and try to find what the root cause of the event was. It is vitally important at this step that the analyst do their best to answer the basic question of how an event occurred. It is the real root cause answer to how it occurred or what impact it caused that sets off other wheels in motion. If an analyst confirms an event that has been ticketed is true and that it is either a threat from a malicious threat source or needs further action, then more processes will take place. If on the other hand if an analyst sees the event as a non-issue and can confidently close the ticket with a reasonable explanation as to why, then the ticket is closed and no further action would be required.

## ANALYSIS

An in-depth investigation must occur by the SOC to know the full scope of what happened. Analysis or IR teams must establish how successful the attack was, all the systems that were compromised and all data that was access or removed from the devices if applicable. The full extent of the incident needs to be well understood and a complete timeline needs to be documented to ensure that all questions about the incident are answered. For example, analysts should not have any network traffic that is unaccounted for or that cannot be explained. Was there privileged access, were all logs collected, how long did the incident takes place, and what was the ultimate method of compromise. If any data was accessed an in-depth review needs to be performed to understand the nature of the data and if it was intellectual property or regulatory protected data. During this analysis phase is when a determination should be made on how to escalate and communicate the incident. As we will discuss later, the communication plan will be a key document to use once analysis has been performed.

## CONTAINMENT

If an event indicates that there is something bad happening or about to happen, then the event can instantly become an incident and the SOC needs to direct activity in order to have the event contained. The primary purpose of containment is to ensure that further negative impact does not occur. This could be the removal or isolation of a system from the rest of the network, enhanced monitoring, rerouting of network traffic or even the blocking or removing of an email now known to contain malicious attachments. There are many different ways to contain an incident and each will depend on the type of threat, devices, or data that is being threatened as what techniques you will use. Also, during the containment phase the SOC should be rapidly collecting information to understand the full scope of the incident. This information should include a list of any compromised systems or accessed systems, data accessed and a timeline should be generated. Additionally, network flows, IDS events, or any other data related to the attackers activities or the particular incident should be captured and stored in the ticketing system.

Just a word of caution, before you perform containment actions ensure you are working with the system owners in your organization or you are very aware of the outcome of any containment actions you take. If you are not careful the actions you perform could cause a worse consequence than the security issue you are trying to protect against.

## RECOVERY

The recovery phase can be as simple as reinstalling a server or workstation from back-up or performing a fresh install all the way to a planned remediation event that includes a complete network shutdown and rebuild. A complete recovery event could include changing everyone's passwords, making significant active directory policy changes to harden the environment, and applying security patches to everything. Depending on the type of event and what you need to do, your actions should not only recover your computing environment back to normal but also keep that type of event happening again. The analysis performed in the previous phase should be detailed enough and clear enough to know exactly what the vector of the incident was and how you would need to prevent it from happening again. The changes needed to be performed could be specific application changes, business processes, or network policy rule changes.

## REVIEW

All incidents should have some form of a review whether it be a quality review, a root cause analysis review or an administrative review by legal, compliance, management or other interested parties depending on the scope and degree of the incident and outcome. The final review and reports that the SOC generates for critical or high priority incidents must be completed in a reasonable amount of time to allow for external notifications within any legally mandated time period, if appropriate.

The review document, or root cause analysis document should answer all the questions anyone would ask. It should at a minimum answer who, what, where, when, how, and the impact of the incident. All of that information must be in the report so that there can be a better understanding of root cause or what deficiencies were present in the network or the individually affected systems to allow the incident. It is also important to understand trends or motives of around the incident. A SOC needs to mature and these types of review documents will help make that happen faster and faster. By doing the reviews of individual tickets or incidents for quality control and getting feedback and questions about the incident and the analysis from different viewpoints is extremely valuable, but also doing larger more visible root cause analysis reports gives a SOC a detailed understanding of how they did and what they could have done better. It is a good learning tool and will help the SOC move from a reactive to proactive mentality and will ultimately lead them to be more predictive.

We spoke about the maturity of the SOC before but this kind of review is a key ingredient to help make that maturity happen. You will know if your SOC is reactive in securing the organization because they will be focused on post incident detection, confirmation, analysis, containment, and recovery as we have just discussed. The SOC should always perform their tasks in the above way but if the focus is on the process and executing the process then they are reactive. Once the SOC starts to grow and mature they will start to be more proactive. This happens when the SOC has the ability to avoid threats against computers and networks through the understanding of the environment, working with different groups or departments in the organization and IT and be able to analyze potential future impacts along with the ability to implement defensive measures. Lastly, the analysis done on incident reviews and understanding trends and motive will allow the SOC to become more predictive. They will be able to anticipate future threats and vulnerabilities based on that strategic analysis along with threat intelligence, and the understanding of how the correlation of the two will impact the organization. The goal of maturing the SOC should not be to move the entire operations into a predictive mode. Instead you need to stay focused in each area while you move toward a predictive security posture. For example, performing forensics and malware analysis is an advanced skill set that you can either have in your SOC or use the services of an external third party or MSSP. The forensics and malware analysis function is reactive in nature but advanced as far as skill sets. The SOC should have advanced skill sets across each of the evolutionary areas in order to provide the best operations to secure an organization.

## COMMUNICATION PLAN

The SOC should have a standard communication plan above and beyond what we have already talked about in daily operational management calls or critical bridges. This communication plan should detail all the different scenarios where distinctive people should be contacted and what their contact information is when specific events or incidents occur. Organizations should work hard to establish the best IR communication plan as possible and it should be reviewed on a regular basis to ensure that lessons learned and organizational changes are accurately reflected.

The communications plan should include an easy to read table of contents that list specific types of incidents and page numbers or tab number. Each incident listed should have a short description of the event along with conditions in which an analyst would execute the communications procedure.

The procedure should be a list of functions or roles of people in the organization or outside the organization that would need to be contacted. Some of the communications would be through email where as more critical notifications would be direct phone call. Each incident would have its own listing of who gets emails versus who would get the phone call. The variation of who gets what would be listed on a case by cases basis based on the incident as different incidents would have different importance's to different departments or groups. The plan may just list the departments or individual roles that an analyst is to call, such as V.P. of IT Infrastructure or Security liaison to Legal, external marketing or communications. The plan should not list individual's names in the description or procedure portion, instead the specific names and contact information should be included as an easy reference in the back of the plan. This way the plan does not need to be updated every time someone changes phone numbers or positions.

Each person assuming a role in the organization that would have incident or breach notifications should have a simple record of contact information in the back of the procedure book. The information to include is basic:

- Name
- Title
- Phone #
- Alternate phone #
- Email address

The number of people that can be included in the communications plan can be extensive, it may be more manageable to split the contacts up into different groups. For example, the first group could just be general SOC and IT management along with other closely interested people. For example, if you had an internal incident that was a violation of policy you may want to include SOC and IT management and also HR, but it may not necessarily be appropriate to contact legal right away. Instead you may want to save notification to legal as a secondary escalation. Then if legal believes that the person should be arrested or if there is going to be an external agency brought in then you may want to include public affairs as a third level of escalation notifications.

Additionally your notifications may not necessarily be just to individuals that are assuming roles in your plan. You may also want to reach out to vendors or third parties that may need to get involved to help or provide services. This could be an IR team as part of your managed security services, or just your Internet provider that can help you block specific types of unwanted traffic. If your SOC has a relationship with local law enforcement you may want to include them as well.

Here are some of the people you may want to consider being part of your communications plan:

- SOC manager
- Incident handler
- Legal affairs
- MSSP
- Privacy officer
- CIO or CISO
- Public affairs
- Internet service provider
- Internal audit local law enforcement
- Local FBI
- Bank
- Human resources

## REGULAR WORKSHOPS

Once you have established your incident processes and communication plans you need to get on a program of continually improving upon the program and making sure everyone is up to date. You cannot just sit back and feel good that it is done because sometimes as soon as it is done you will find its time to update it.

Annual or quarterly workshops are a great way to not only make sure that all the information is correct in the communications plans but that everyone still agrees with the processes. Brining organizational leaders together and the people who are part of the communications plan to discuss the detail of the plan will help to keep everyone knowledgeable and up to date. The workshops can consist of an update of everyone's personal contact information. It should also then talk about any metrics or challenges the SOC has had regarding the execution of the communications plan. Lastly there should be a table top discussion and sample scenarios that are discussed to see how people would respond, who would want to be notified and what details would trigger additional actions. These regular workshops are a great tool to help validate that the SOC processes are not only the right processes but that they are appropriately up to date.

The workshop is also a great training opportunity not only on the process itself but not everyone lives with security everyday like a SOC, so it is a good opportunity to discuss security, its importance, and the value the SOC brings to an organization. Do not miss a great opportunity to market the SOC and help bring the mission of security to the front of people's minds.

## CHECKLISTS

It is important to have some basic checklists that the SOC will use in the daily environment. These checklists can be built into the ticket system that is used in the SOC, be a webpage, word document, or can just be paper copies. Either way, it is important for processes to be consistent and to ensure that analysts and engineers capture the right and complete information that is needed, make sure you have checklists that mimic your important processes.

The example below is an incident report form, this form could be used to document a specific incident and that would be used to distribute information to interested people or management. It should be factual and accurate and should include all the relevant information someone would need to make basic conclusions about the incident. The form should relate to a specific ticket and the ticket would have more detailed information and back-up data to support the completion of this form. A status should be stated on a form like this, an open status would indicate that the form is being worked on and could be waiting for more input. Whereas an in-progress status may indicate that the form is complete but that action items or activities are still pending. Lastly, a closed status would mean that all actions have been take and the issue is now fully resolved.

The type of issue could be related to the category of the threat such as a virus, insider threat or denial of service and the result of the activity would also be detailed to include an indication if there was any outage as a result. To answer the question of who did it, you should try and determine the origin of the attacker. Sometimes it is easy because it could be an insider or unknowing accidental system administrator or it could be an external hacker and even a former employee.

The rest of the form is fairly straightforward and should be self-explanatory. Once complete a copy of the form should be associated or uploaded to the original ticket that was used for the investigation and then it can be emailed or stored in a central location for others to review and comment on. The form can also be established inside of your ticketing system or in an IR portal. Completed form submissions can be automatically emailed out and also have the answers stored in a database. Depending on the criteria you use to complete these types of forms and how frequently you use them, it may not be a bad idea to perform a weekly or monthly review of all incident reports. You could have management representation as well as technical experts review the forms to make sure that needed action items are being taken care of and that if specific trends are emerging then those issues can be bubbled up to a more strategic level to be dealt with. If you have enough of these forms being filled out, you may even want to perform regular metrics and trend analysis on various elements in these forms as well, it may help you get a better idea on some of the organizations weak spots or at least be able to quantify the costs associated with your efforts in dealing with issues that are not getting resolved.

### SOC Incident report form

| Ticket#: | Status: | Date: | Reporter: |
|---|---|---|---|
| Type of issue:<br>Has the problem been experienced before?<br>Yes / No<br>How was this detected? | | Results:<br>Caused outage?<br>Yes/No<br>Attacker? | |

### Target system(s)

| IP/MAC: | Mission critical?<br>Yes/No<br>Yes/No<br>Yes/No<br>Yes/No | System type | Additional info: |
|---|---|---|---|

### Current security measure(s) in place

| ☐ Firewall<br>☐ Antivirus<br>☐ Anti-spyware<br>☐ Secure remote | ☐ HIPS/NIPS<br>☐ Encryption<br>☐ ACL<br>☐ File integrity | ☐ Strong passwords<br>☐ Physical security<br>☐ Warning banners<br>☐ Digital signatures | ☐ Whitelisting<br>☐ Log monitoring |
|---|---|---|---|

### Recommended action

| ☐ Disconnect<br>☐ Validate Permissions<br>☐ BLOCK | ☐ Validate binary's<br>☐ Physically secure<br>☐ Collect logs | ☐ Inform legal<br>☐ Reinstall<br>☐ Vulnerability scan | ☐ Restore<br>☐ Virus scan<br>☐ Forensics |
|---|---|---|---|

☐ Other:

Relevant packet or log data

Comments

Timeline

After action notes

Other types of forms can be useful but as you develop them but do not make them too ridged, allow for modification and alteration. All too often when you put a new form into operation you may quickly discover deficiencies or issues. Allow your forms and checklists to change as you grow, mature, and learn the needs of the organization you are protecting. Sometimes forms and checklists can come from necessity, if there are operational issues where people are not following direction or mistakes are occurring too frequently, enforcing that a checklist be completed can help not only be informative to ensure everyone knows the process and the required steps but will also help resolve any issues with people cutting corners or just not following process.

Other types of forms and checklists you may want to consider using are specific incident forms such as a checklist regarding what to do in the case of a credit card breach or loss of Patient Health Information. If your organization has lots of direct connections to other organizations through VPNs or direct links then you may want to checklist for how to handle incidents regarding third parties. The checklists do not have to be based on incident workflow, it could be for any process, but the primary checklist you will likely have will be based on either incidents or troubleshooting of tools in the SOC.

## SHIFT SCHEDULES

Planning security operation shift schedules can be an art but the goal is very simple right? Just make sure you have the proper coverage during the hours you need it most.

One of the main questions I get asked about running a SOC is what the best schedule is to maintain and how to maintain schedules with SOCs that may be spread out all over the world. SOCs that want to run 24×7 will have its own unique staffing problems and many of these will concern what the right recipe is for staffing levels and who they have to fill needed shifts. The fact that an organization offers security services or wants to monitor its network around the clock does not always mean that the staffing requirement will remain constant. You will need to make sure that the ebb and flow of staffing changes and fluctuations are properly reflected in your scheduling. You will most likely have your workday divided into something that resembles a shift, even if there is only one shift, which is a normal workday or weekend. Each shift will have different requirements in regards to staffing levels, skill mix and the type of role you need to be present in the SOC. For example, the workload in the SOC may require two people during the week but only one during the weekends. You will need to make sure that whoever is responsible for managing the staff schedule is fully aware of what will be needed for each shift and that they have the right reports and metrics to back up the schedule. For large operations, this is not just a case of devising one schedule and using it continuously without regard for changing conditions, you have to be able to adapt. The demands in regard to work will always be changing in most organizations and staffing levels will need to reflect this, especially around the holidays and for international organizations you will need to consider staffing in all your SOC locations based on international holidays, not just the more popular or local holidays. The person looking after scheduling should be able to anticipate what is going to be needed for each shift and should be able to plan accordingly far in advance. Determining and maintaining optimal staffing levels is critical to efficiency of your operation. Overstaffing is costly and you may not have the required resources such as computers and desks to allow everyone to work, this may result in you sending people home so it is not just a cost to payroll, it is also a moral issue. If overstaffing happens to the same person over and over it could cause that person to lose interest in the organization and result in them having poor performance on the job, as they will feel underutilized and not needed. On the flip side, understaffing creates can create stress and pressure on your SOC staff and also can cause excessive overtime. It can also become a safety risks from fatigue, absenteeism, and even cause burnout.

In SOCs that needs to operate 24-h a day will require several shifts filled with different people performing in different roles and who have distinctive skills sets to ensure that all the hours are covered and the right resources are available to deal with any incident or event that occurs during that shift. The first shift or day shift usually would start around 8 a.m. and go until 4:30 p.m. The day shift is a nice shift to have in a SOC because it is the most normal working hours. It would mimic what the rest of the organization and the world work for the most part. Second shift, evening shift or what is also commonly called the swing shift is a shift that starts in the late afternoon at about 4 p.m. and runs into the late evening typically until about 12:30 a.m. Working on the swing shift can be demanding, especially for parents, as it requires unusual sleep schedules and does not work well with school hours for kids who may need daycare. Nevertheless, there are some advantages with being on the second shift for students as it may allow them to take courses in the morning and early afternoon, and then go to work in the evenings.

The third shift is also known as the night shift or graveyard shift. This shift will typically start at 12 a.m. and go to 8:30 a.m. The night shift can be very difficult to adjust to even if it is your permanent shift. A nice benefit to the night shift is that it does give you the day off to do errands, attend to kids or anything else you want because most places will be open for business once you get off work. People who work the night shift will typically stay awake for the day and sleep during swing shift so that their daily routine is the same as most people where they wake up, get dressed, and go to work albeit midnight. There are many different variations of shifts and schedules, and organizations will have to figure out what works best for their organizational goals, the SOC and their people. Typically, the more senior someone is in a SOC, the more he or she will be able to control their own work schedule or choose the shift that works best for them, while less senior people will usually find themselves on graveyard and swing shifts, rather than the usually coveted first shift.

# TYPES OF SHIFT SCHEDULES

8 × 5

| | Weekly SOC schedule | | | | | | |
|---|---|---|---|---|---|---|---|
| | SUN | MON | TUES | WED | THURS | FRI | SAT |
| First shift 9 a.m. to 5 p.m. | | X | X | X | X | X | |

   In smaller organizations, doing a standard workweek where people come in and work in the SOC an average of 8 h a day Monday to Friday may be sufficient. This does not mean that people will only work standard hours. Instead they can be on-call or configure their SIEM to alert them via SMS or email when something passes a threshold and triggers an alert that needs to be addressed. This is a great option for smaller organizations that cannot afford to hire lots of people for round the clock shifts. With a simple schedule like this you could run your SOC with only one or more people. Also, in smaller organizations it is typical to see network traffic be dramatically reduced after the normal workday is over. This is because there are less people on the network generating events, and triggering rules. This means that the rate of incidents will go down that require investigation and the SOC can let the system run on autopilot and just get alerts remotely when something is going bad. If this is a problem and people are not able to sleep at night because they feel nobody is watching the security of the organization then instead of hiring more people you can consider outsourcing to a MSSP. During the day, the internal SOC will handle all the regular Tier-1 events all the way up to the engineering issues but at quitting time the SOC can just turn over the initial triage and Tier-1 analysis to the MSSP. With an MSSP doing the overnight monitoring you can rely on them to analyze events and only call you when needed. Instead of handing off the analysis to an MSSP, you do not have to be an on or off type of relationship, you can keep the MSSP monitoring 24×7 and your internal SOC can just handle escalations by the MSSP around the clock and perform IR as needed. If you only have one person running all of your security then you may also want to look to see if you have anyone in your IT organization that could be a suitable backup resource in case of that one person going on vacation or taking sick time.

8 × 7

| | Weekly SOC schedule | | | | | | |
|---|---|---|---|---|---|---|---|
| | SUN | MON | TUES | WED | THURS | FRI | SAT |
| First shift 8 a.m. to 4:30 p.m. | X | X | X | X | X | | |
| First shift 8 a.m. to 4:30 p.m. | | | X | X | X | X | X |
| First shift 8 a.m. to 4:30 p.m. (*Optional) | | X | X | X | X | X | |

If the SOC needs to cover weekends because the organization is active or there are specific risks that need to be monitored for, then an 8×7 schedule can be used. In this schedule, you can do multiple things and start to get creative but as before the SOC is only staffed during normal business hours. You need at least two people to accomplish this schedule and have your weekends covered. With this schedule you have each person work one weekend day and only four work week days. This way each person still gets two standard days off but each has to work only 1 weekend day. This is also a nice option because they will still be able to work together, train together and advance security together during the 3 days that they are overlapped. Sometimes this schedule can get in the way of peoples personal time or family vacation plans when it is every single week that they need to cover a weekend day. The two people may be able to cover a shift for each other from time to time or a week, and then have it made up to them in a later week. Another option is to bring in a third person assuming the workload warrants it. This third person could work a normal Monday through Friday shift and cover on the weekends when needed. Also, keep in mind that having three people at the same time in the middle of the week may be too much, but it gives you the option of spreading things out and creating an optional rotation.

## 15×7

The next logical step once you need to grow the number of hours people are in the SOC is to move to a 15×7 schedule. This is a great option for an organization that may need to cover hours of operation in multiple time zones. If the SOC is located in the eastern part of the US and business hours need to be maintained in the SOC for the west coast then there are additional hours that need to be covered. Adding a second shift would easily cover the 3-h time zone difference. You can also easily move the two SOC shift hours to start earlier to cover GMT, Eastern, and Pacific Time zones.

| | Weekly SOC schedule | | | | | | |
|---|---|---|---|---|---|---|---|
| | SUN | MON | TUES | WED | THURS | FRI | SAT |
| First shift 8 a.m. to 4:30 p.m. | X | X | X | X | X | | |
| First shift 8 a.m. to 4:30 p.m. | | | X | X | X | X | X |
| First shift 8 a.m. to 4:30 p.m. (*Optional) | | X | X | X | X | X | |
| Second shift 4:30 p.m. to 12:30 a.m. | X | X | X | X | X | | |
| Second shift 4:30 p.m. to 12:30 a.m. | | | X | X | X | X | X |
| Second shift 4:30 p.m. to 12:30 a.m. (*Optional) | | X | X | X | X | X | |

24×7

| | Weekly SOC schedule | | | | | | |
|---|---|---|---|---|---|---|---|
| | SUN | MON | TUES | WED | THURS | FRI | SAT |
| First shift 8 a.m. to 4:30 p.m. | X | X | X | X | X | | |
| First shift 8 a.m. to 4:30 p.m. | | | X | X | X | X | X |
| First shift 8 a.m. to 4:30 p.m. (*Optional) | | X | X | X | X | X | |
| Second shift 4:30 p.m. to 1:30 a.m. | X | X | X | X | X | | |
| Second shift 4:30 p.m. to 1:30 a.m. | | | X | X | X | X | X |
| Second shift 4:30 p.m. to 1:30 a.m. (*Optional) | | X | X | X | X | X | |
| Third shift 1:00 a.m. to 1:00 a.m. | X | X | X | X | X | | |
| Third shift 4:30 p.m. to 1:00 a.m. | | | X | X | X | X | X |
| Third shift 4:30 p.m. to 1:00 a.m. (*Optional) | | X | X | X | X | X | |

When you move to a 24×7 schedule you need at least six people but with only six you leave no room for sick time or vacation time. It would be best to have at a minimum nine people working in your SOC for complete 24×7 coverage. This will allow several overlap opportunities and shift rotations to cover for any absenteeism. Adding in the third shift is an interesting dynamic and you need to pay close attention to how you operate this. The third shift can easily start to feel left out, as there may be less management members on a night shift, fewer opportunities for special projects and less options for training. If most training opportunities happen during the day then your third shift will be left out. Make sure you give them the option to stay late for early morning training or allow them to temporarily switch their shift for the duration of a training program.

As you grow larger you may have several combinations of each of the previous schedules all going on at the same time. You may find that what works best is that the analysts will cover 24×7 monitoring but engineers will only work 8×5. To compensate for not having engineers physically available for every shift, the engineers can work out an on-call rotation. This way the SOC analysts can reach out to an available engineer at any time to assist with issues or problems. These on-call engineers would also be the ones to participate in management calls and critical bridges if needed. Additionally, SOC management may only work normal business hours but can also be on call for any critical problems that arise.

Different roles and responsibilities may be needed in the SOC at different times of the day or night or even weekends. The size of your SOC and the volume of work that your SOC performs will also be a driving factor in how you manage your shift schedule.

# OTHER SHIFT OPTIONS

12's

One popular SOC shift schedule is to run is to have a few people on 12-h shifts. This is a great idea if most of the SOC members are on 8-hour shifts and a few are on 12's. This allows for greater consistency between shifts as you have individuals who overlap and are able to blend information for those two shifts. An individual who is going to work 12 h shifts will typically do 3 days of 12 h shifts in a week with 4 days off and then do 3 days of 12-h shifts with 1 shift of 4 h in a 2 week period. This way the SOC member gets a full 80 h across 2-week schedule. It is not advisable to try and run two 12-h shifts as your only shifts to cover the complete 24-h day. The 12-h shift can be popular with some people but not everyone as it could lead to a drop in productivity and fatigue. But some people will enjoy the extra days off that a 12-h shift will bring them.

4 Tens

Sometimes there are SOCs that will run 4 tens as an optional rotation. This is where people will work four 10-h shifts in a row with a 3-day weekend. You would run this the same as the 8×7 schedule where you will have overlapping days. The one advantage of doing this is you can get greater overlap in the shifts across 24 h and you will also have greater flexibility when looking to provide training to everyone in the SOC. Not everyone is cut out for this type of schedule and this will typically have the highest burnout rate. On the other hand people will enjoy having 3 day weekends every week and that may be a great moral booster.

# FOLLOW THE SUN

I often hear about operations groups doing a follow the sun rotation to manage needed coverage for their SOC. The follow the sun shift rotation is where a SOC located in the Americas, Europe, India, and maybe the Far East have been established. Each SOC will work during normal daytime business hours and hand over tickets and issues to the SOC in the next time zone as the day goes on. This seems to be a popular option and a logical one but I have seen more problems with this model then any problems it was designed to solve. This can be very expensive as you have a duplication of offices and facilities that go unused for 16 h out of 24 when you are only running an 8-h shift. You also loose efficiency and accuracy in shift hand-off because it is not happening face to face unless you use video conferencing. You also have to deal with inconsistency in training, customer service and skill sets. A better practice for the follow the sun shift rotation is to have one primary SOC run 24×7 and have other SOCs around the world take on work as needed. This helps establish a base with core skill sets that will control the flow of work and will stay on top of escalations. The SOCs located in different countries can be established to help with international privacy laws regarding the moving of protected data outside of the country. Having international SOCs around the world can also help with local language support if you have customers or business units in foreign speaking locations. If you do have international or geographically separated SOCs make sure you work to blend them as best as possible. All the SOCs will need to share processes, knowledge and work load. If travel budgets are available, move people around from SOC to SOC, this will give them exposure to coworkers and allow them to build good working relationships with each other. It may also be a nice benefit to allow someone to do international travel for a few weeks, it gets them away from the daily grind and helps expand their experience while building new bridges with coworkers.

## SHIFT ROTATION

Shift rotation is a practice followed by many organizations that work 24×7. Analysts and engineers working in the SOC will do a rotation of nights to days to swing shift and back again on a regular basis. Some people may feel that this is a fairer way of assigning shifts especially when people do not really like working nights. Keep in mind that people will encounter problems with this rotation system as it can be difficult for people to adjust to the time changes. Try to make sure that people have a few days gap to adjust otherwise people can start to have some health problems. Alternatively, it is preferable to have a permanent night shift where people are hired specifically to perform during those times. Keep in mind that for people who work the third or overnight shift you want to work out a way for them to get any training the rest of the SOC may get such as switching their schedules temporarily or trading them temporarily with someone who is on first shift that may already have the training. This training can also be given early in the morning as they are finishing their shift or later in the evening and they can come in earlier to start their shift.

The way you run a shift rotation is based on a 28-day revolution. A slow, forward rotation from day shift to swing shift to night shift will happen across the 28 days. It will take your four teams of people (which could only be 1 person per shift) to accomplish a complete 24×7 rotation and the average hours worked will be about 42. Because this is a shift rotation you provide at least 2 days off after any 7 working days and 3 days off after seven consecutive night shifts. This allows for recovery time and lets people adjust to their next 8-h shift schedule. The down side to doing this is that an individual will only get a free weekend once every 7 weeks and they will have to work one 7 consecutive days stretch and one 7 consecutive night stretch during that 28 day cycle. The good news is that everyone is only working 8-h shifts and the average overtime would only be about 2-h per employee per week unless you can cut people early off of a shift. Here is how it would look:

|  | Days 1–7 | Days 8–14 | Days 15–21 | Days 22–28 |
|---|---|---|---|---|
| Team 1 | DDDDDDD | OOSSSSS | SSOONNN | NNNNOOO |
| Team 2 | OOSSSSS | SSOONNN | NNNNOOO | DDDDDDD |
| Team 3 | SSOONNN | NNNNOOO | DDDDDDD | OOSSSSS |
| Team 4 | NNNNOOO | DDDDDDD | OOSSSSS | SSOONNN |

*D, day shift; S, swing shift; N, night shift; O, day off.*

Deciding on the best shift rotation or schedule for your SOC can be a tough choice but do not do it alone, it is often a good idea to allow the people in the SOC to have some say in what way they would like to approach it or what schedules they would prefer to work. This way the people in the SOC will have more say in their schedule rather than having a certain shift rotation just thrown at them. It will never be possible to please everyone with any type of shift rotation or schedule but a general consensus should be able to be reached. Some SOCs will have less flexibility when it comes to deciding on the form of rotation and schedule because of the organization they work for and the hours that need to be covered, so it may be necessary to assign people purely on the basis of skill mix and availability to a specific shift.

## DEALING WITH ABSENTEEISM

Nobody likes to have to deal with a member of the team that just cannot make it to work. That being said, it is going to happen and you will have to deal with it. The first thing you need to consider is a policy on not coming into work. In a SOC, it is different that working a regular job especially in a SOC that operates 24×7. Typically an individual coming to start a shift in a SOC is going to relieve someone else so they can go home, but if they do not show up and your short-handed what are you going to do. From a policy perspective if a member of the SOC wants to call in sick they should do it at a minimum of 8 h prior to their shift. This gives team leads or management time to find someone who can cover that shift. If the person calling out does so any less than 8 h it should count against them during review time and should affect any raises or promotion opportunities and if continued issues occur they should be terminated. It is just not fair for everyone else when there is a lack of respect by someone who cannot plan far enough in advance as to not negatively impact other people, it does not make a good teammate and will lower moral in the SOC. How should sick calls handled? The shift lead or senior team lead needs to begin calling people who are not schedule to work to see of anyone can cover the shift. Optimum coverage would be the preplaned number of people who were designated to cover the shift but the team lead or shift supervisor may feel that one person will not make a difference and could decide to go without that one person for a day. Typically it would be best to find someone to cover the whole shift but you could also offer overtime to people to work a half shift by asking them to stay late or even ask someone on a later shift to come in early, as this may be a bigger attraction to an individual and it may help you get over a potential busy rush. Another option may be to offer call-back pay and round trip mileage for anyone willing to pick up an extra shift as well to entice people to help cover required shift gaps. This all seems logical when you are paying people hourly but it is also possible to give people additional pay and bonuses when they are salary so get creative, it will work.

There are a ton of sites on the web that can give you different ideas about how to best work your shifts, how to split the shifts and make things as efficient as possible. This brief overview of the different kinds of shifts and patterns that you can use in your SOC should help get you going in the right direction. Knowing where and what time you need the bulk of your SOC to operate is half the battle. Keep a good eye on your staffing levels for each of the different roles and skill sets you need in the SOC. Then make sure you monitor how effective events and incidents are being worked. Based off of those metrics you can add date and time stamps to see when things are falling through the cracks or when you have everything covered, then adjust your staffing levels accordingly.

# Training

Frequently I get questioned on how to train a SOC. The questions are also compounded with issues regarding training across shifts or even how to apply consistent training across multiple SOCs in different geographic locations. These are great questions and it is obvious that no SOC can be effective without the appropriate training of its staff.

With the number of people it takes to staff an operation, it is unlikely you will have the budget and capability to hire fully trained and proven staff that can come into your organization and hit the ground running. There are more things that a person needs to know about security and working inside an operational environment than you can get out of any book. Every operation is different, objectives are different, and processes are different. So although you may be able to find people who know what an IP address is or how to read a packet capture, you are almost always going to have to train people on how to be successful in your organization.

Just a quick warning, you can always train someone who wants to learn and who is new to the career field. If they are hungry for the knowledge and have an aptitude for the technology then you should have no issues growing people in your organization. It will be important for you to work hard to keep them motivated and interested. On the other hand, if you can afford to bring in people to your SOC that are experienced and skilled then you are very lucky but being able to do that brings other challenges. Typically seasoned security professionals will want to make some changes, re-engineer how operations work, or make modifications to the way they like to do things. This may not be a bad thing if that is what you are after but if not then you may have a challenging time ahead trying to teach an old dog new tricks.

Luckily, there are very good options for building an effective training program both free and at a cost but you will have to devote time to any program that you develop. The good news is that costs can be controlled and easily budgeted for but at the same time you need to allow for ample training time for each and every employee. At the time of writing this, there can be found no real formal educational or training path specifically for security operations staff and there is limited documentation available, almost all the written material found comes from white papers, workshops, or internal slide presentations. Most of all training documentation is on specific technical tasks and skills, and while that is all very important, it is not specifically about job training in a SOC or how to apply those technical skills to a SOC environment. Organizations should use a wide variety of training programs, tools, and resources to train their staff. Training should be performed to bring new employees up to speed and help them quickly become proficient in their required job functions. The training should also help keep staff sharp and up to date with emerging technology or adversarial trends.

A good training plan will be well rounded and should include items such as:

- Internal functional training
- Internal skill set training
- Job task qualification training
- Tools and product training
- Formal training and certifications
- On-the-job training (OJT)
- Communication training
- Management training

## INTERNAL FUNCTIONAL TRAINING

You have to give people a leg up when starting a new job; do not assume they automatically know where all the light switches are or where the bathrooms are. You should ensure you welcome your new people into your operation properly by giving them a few days if not a few weeks of new hire training. In many companies, a brand new employee may go through basic HR training to learn about the company, its health plan options, and other benefits but that is about it. Think about taking this a step further, ensure that your new employee gets a tour of the place and they know where all the important things are in the facility. Show them where important people sit and introduce them around to help them get acclimated to their new environment.

Continue this training by teaching them how to do basic tasks like how to use the phone system, especially if you have a complex automated call distribution (ACD) system. Teach them about the computing environment that they are going to work in, ensure they know how to access all the tools and that they have all the internal company links that they will need, access to SharePoint or wiki or whatever.

Specifically, you need to focus on internal functional training that includes how to use the phones, access the building, where important documentation is stored or anything else that is very specific to your organization or your site that someone may need to know. This information is typically what is known as viral or tribal knowledge and is often never written down or documented. You may have internal resources such as websites, databases, or information stores that are built and managed by employees and are extremely valuable resources. But they only get announced (maybe via a group wide email) to the people who need to use them once and if you hire a new person after the announcement of the availability of the tool then the only way they will find out about that resource is if someone thinks to tell them about it. This significantly reduces overall effectiveness of an organization and should be prevented. Make sure that as you mature your operation center that you document any internal controls, tools and especially policies so that anyone new walking through the door can take advantage of all of it and be "in the know".

As an example of what not to do, one organization I worked with was very proud of how they handled internal resources and believed that everyone had access to the tools they needed to be successful. Not only did they push out browser bookmarks to their SOC computers but they also had a resource page on their internal SharePoint site that listed all the links to their tools. Unfortunately new employees did not automatically get access to the SharePoint site and each of the 50+ links required a user account to be set up and all were completely different access accounts from their network login, additionally there was no indication of whom to request access from or what even the resource was there to do. So they had a ton of great stuff but no documentation as to what it was or how to get access to it. Most people will take the approach that if I need something then it will be given to me instead of them asking for a resource that they think will help them or they may even be shy to ask for access to something they know exists. In most cases, people do not even know what to ask for because they do not know what is available. Spending time ensuring that internal knowledge and functions are documented and passed on to everyone in the organization is an invaluable activity that should not be overlooked.

Due to its extreme importance, as part of internal functional training, data handling and classification should be fully reviewed on a regular basis. As your SOC is most likely responsible for breach and IR due to loss of data or compromise to a system potentially containing protected data, its vital that all members of your SOC fully understand and be trained on how your organization views the importance of data, what data is important from not only an internal intellectual property perspective but also a customer, regulatory, or government perspective. During an incident even the most experienced staff members can feel a high level of stress, this is when mistakes can happen, repetitive training on how to deal with sensitive information will help prevent what may already be a bad situation from getting worse. Unfortunately, some of that stress results from the potential consequences of handling information inappropriately.

Regular refresher courses should be conducted, as they are necessary to maintain a firm awareness as to why it is important to follow the established policies and procedures. But, by also performing repetitive training and even exercising some of that training you create muscle memory in the hopes that when something bad does happen your people will execute their duties properly, effectively, and professionally. It is also important to emphasize people's responsibility to actually execute those procedures and enforce those policies.

## INTERNAL SKILL SET TRAINING

Your employees need to know their job, this seems like an obvious statement but in an operations center it is more of a true statement than anywhere else. By the very nature of how the operation center is supposed to function, a tier 1 analyst has a very specific role and must be able to perform that role as flawlessly and as efficiently as possible. Later we will talk more about some of the specifics but as an example, for a tier 1-analyst function, the tasks they perform must be more prescriptive with very clearly defined outcomes or escalations. As you move up the tiers, you will move your tasks from being rigid and prescriptive to being more investigative tasks that require more thought in the process. The more you can document and train your staff to ensure repeatable outcome, the more consistent your SOC will be and the easier it will be to control. Some SOC's management has even spent the time and effort to create an IR "runbook" or "playbook". This is a very descriptive and prescriptive step-by-step process or checklist for different tasks that must be followed verbatim. This can even become part of an audit process by organizations outside the SOC. This way you can further help ensure expected results with specific and important types of tasks.

## PLAYBOOKS AND RUNBOOKS

There is a reason why professional sports teams create binders of documentation detailing their plays and executions of specific offense or defenses. This is because they train to those exact specifications and details in order to help predict or guarantee an outcome. When you have very specific steps that you can train people to, you are giving them a process that not only can be followed but also can more importantly be memorized. Memorization can make an individual more efficient in performing tasks and achieve predictable and desired results. If every time we did something it was new and we had to learn it from scratch then we would almost never get anything done and never have processes that we can repeat. As you look around your organization you will find many different things you can document into your play/runbook. But if you are looking around scratching your head because you just cannot find anything that would fit then you really need to look at your processes and review how productive your operation center really is.

Here is a basic idea of what some positions should be like in regards to training and documentation and in most cases playbooks can be created for each role or level in your operation.

| Level | Training objective | Documentation needs |
|-------|--------------------|--------------------|
| Tier 1 | Quick, rigid analytical triage | Heavy and specific in processes, procedures |
| Tier 2 | Deep analytical triage | Heavy and specific, room for some variance in analysis |
| Tier 3 | Investigative, deep look | Resource refiner, trainer, documentation specialist |
| Engineer | Implement, repair | Vendor or outside resources, documentation creator |
| Management | Efficiency, reliable, and repeatable response | Heavy and specific, processes, procedures |

## JOB TASK QUALIFICATION TRAINING

As an extension of the skill set training, task qualification training is the next logical step in learning. This is not specific to just internal skill. Once someone reads about a function they are to perform and receives instruction on that function or even has it shown to them then they should demonstrate that they could do it. If the person is successful in performing a task and it is reviewed by an instructor or supervisor then they can be considered qualified. I know that this sounds very basic and maybe a bit of a pain but imagine the alternative. Suppose your internal or external customer satisfaction was being reduced because your level of communication has dropped off and after investigation you find that a few new employees were not comfortable with operating the phone system so they stayed away from using it. Once your employee has successfully demonstrated they can perform a function is a good idea to maintain a training record that specifies what the task functions are and a date when they demonstrated they could perform it along with a signature of the person who witnessed it. This is extremely helpful not only to management who need to ensure they have properly training people working but also to the analyst or engineer who may want to know what they need to learn to better perform their job. Not all tasks are going to be able to be identified or built into a training plan or even tested as part of a qualification but the more you can formalize the closer you can guarantee outcomes in your SOC as well as when you perform critical functions such as IR.

## TOOLS AND PRODUCT TRAINING

Training your staff on the specific operation of the tools and products in use at your operations center is essential. You may hire specific individuals to perform various functions in your organization but it would be very rare to find someone who knows how to use all the systems deployed in your organization. Even if you could find someone who knows most of the products they will not know how you have them configured, deployed, or the processes you use to maintain them on a regular basis. Additionally, depending on the position of the person they may only need a basic understanding of the tool where others may need a more in-depth education on it.

Specific tool and product training does not have to be something that you pay for or that the vendor needs to provide for your organization but it can be if you want it to be. Instead you could easily have a SOC engineer or an internal security engineer develop specific training for the team. This does not have to be formal training where you have a professional set of slides, no need to boil the ocean here. Just focus on specific topics, it may be a good idea to use this type of training to address common mistakes or issues that you find happening in your SOC. To address those issues, reduce errors and make the team more efficient, run a training class on a specific tool or product and then focus on the problem areas. Show people the "right" way to do things and the way to drive better results. These focused trainings only need to be an hour long and will have an extremely positive impact on your team and their moral. It will help promote the individual who puts the training together and teaches the class to a team mentor as it helps expand the knowledge of the entire team. Some of the topics you could train on:

- New product management processes
- New futures coming out
- User interface tips and tricks
- General "How to"
- Advanced operations, hidden functionality or secretes
- Integration aspects with other tools or products

Typically tool and product training in your SOC would not cover topics such as setup and deployment of technology but rather the operation of the items as it is currently used in the environment. It should cover special configurations, rules, purpose, and any restrictions on use such as any adherence to audit requirements, change management, Privacy or data handling issues. You may also want to consider performing training on escalation procedures, fault or failure resolution of any tools, and even current known issues or problems. Product and tool training should be included in your regular refresher-training program. This way you can continue to build on previous trainings and advance the SOC together on specific topics. For these training sessions, it is best to keep the material very focused, short, and sweet; it should be a short session (1 h or less), do not try and teach an entire weeklong course in just an hour. People will be able to better grasp the materials and absorb the information you are trying to present when you bite it off in small chunks for them.

## FORMAL TRAINING AND CERTIFICATIONS

If you asked me several years ago about formal training and certifications I would have dismissed them as a waste of time and money. I would have even gone as far as to tell you that a college degree is not a requirement to be successful in a SOC and that real world experience beats everything else. You might have guessed from my tone of the last two sentences that I have changed my view, but that would only be partially correct. As Information Assurance and network security has grown due to large public breaches and news stories about government sponsored cyber attacks there has been a focus by training organizations to produce content and programs designed around the skill sets needed for various positions in cyber security. Several organizations have really stepped up and are now providing real and valuable training that all security organizations should look into and be investing in their people to take some of the training. But like all training courses and programs in any industry you have to ensure that what they say they are going to teach in the brochure is really what you want your people to learn. So, before you spend around $5,000 dollars and lose a person for a weeklong training course you need to read through sample course documents to ensure you are going to get the best value for your money.

A word about certifications, although certification training just prepares you for the certification exam and not necessarily gives you any ability to perform a job function. It does certify that the individual has been exposed to specific information and has retained that information to certification standards. This is not necessarily a bad thing but be warned that just because someone has heard about a concept, application, or process does not mean they can execute in that space.

I do not want to recommend one specific training company, program, or course over another simply due to the fact that this changes so frequently. Courses are constantly being developed, improved, redesigned, and recreated. The security industry is moving fast as well. Something that may be a hot topic today may not be tomorrow. Instead I would like to point you in the direction of a few organizations that have programs worth looking into and should be on your list of potential training options.

www.opensecuritytraining.info

There are a lot of open or free courses out there on the Internet and even universities that are out there that offer free courses. Performing a basic search for cyber security training or open training will yield a long list of options and opportunities. Specifically opensecuritytraining.info helps us in security by not only offering course material for free but also collecting materials that can be used as formal training. This training can be used by an individual to teach an entire class or can be used by the individual as a self-study guide. Currently there is great content on the basics of information required to reverse engineer applications specifically related to malware.

www.Sans.org

Starting off as a simple organization designed to teach topics of security by security practitioners, it has grown to an international training and certification organization that offers a wide variety of course topics and training paths for individuals and companies. Recently, Sans has opened their Sans university which offers accredited courses to its students. This is a great resource and a win/win for organizations and their employees. Not only do organizations get to send their people to good quality training but the employee gets to use the credits toward degree awarding programs.

## SCHOOLS AND UNIVERSITIES

Over the last few years, schools and universities have really caught up and have developed great programs that focus on cyber security, Information Assurance or even specializations such as computer forensics. Some leaders in this area include:

- Maryland Cybersecurity Center (http://www.cyber.umd.edu)
- Regis Universities Information Assurance Masters program (http://www.regis.edu)
- University of Rhode Islands digital forensics and Cyber Security Center (http://www.dfcsc.uri.edu/academics/)
- Carnegie Mellon University (http://www.cmu.edu)
- Norwich University (norwich.edu)

This by far is not an exhaustive list of schools and universities offering programs and there are more and more everyday. Many of these schools also offer online programs and degrees in areas that people who are working in a SOC can take advantage of. The online options also allow people working odd shifts in the SOC to take advantage of the great educational opportunities now available.

Some other commercial training and certification programs worth looking into:

CEH (Certified Ethical Hacker), CCNA/CCNP (Cisco Certified Network Associate/Professional), CGIH (Certified GIAC Incident Handler), GCFA (GIAC Certified Forensic Analyst), GCIH (GIAC Certified Incident Handler), OSCP (Offensive Security Certified Professional), CISM (Certified Information Security Manager), CISSP (Certified Information Systems Security Professional), and CISA (Certified Information System Auditor)

Other nonsecurity related but important certifications may be:

ISO27001 Lead Auditor Exam PMP (Project Manager Professional)* ITIL v3 foundations

Never underestimate the power of skills that can support effective process, help define common language, and work to blend security personnel with other professionals in the technology field.

## VENDOR TRAINING

It seems like common sense but vendors that have supplied your tools are an excellent source of training for your SOC. Most often vendors can bring people into your organization and provide focused or custom training and more often than not this can be FREE training. The vendors have a vested interest in your continued use and satisfaction with their product, so depending on what you need they may be more

---

*Typically you would not think of project management as a certification or desired skill but much of security is about implementing the right equipment in the right places. Having project management skills and training helps ensure that there is structure, communication, and proven processes that can be applied in a project team that may have been assembled from various departments in a larger organization.

than happy to provide you with some real training. Additionally, vendors should be more than willing to come in and speak with your SOC about new and upcoming product enhancements, features and capabilities. Larger vendors have offices and resources around the United States and even around the world, so vendor training that you want to get for one SOC site you may be able to arrange at multiple SOC sites if you have them. This way you are helping to maintain constant training for all your SOC locations. Also, if you feel like your SOC or specific team members need enhanced or in-depth training, most vendors will also provide extensive or weeklong training courses but these typically do have a cost associated with them. Make sure you maintain a good working relationship with your vendors, as it will always pay dividends in the long run.

## OJT

The positive impact that this type of training gives cannot be under estimated. OJT can give people one on one time with senior people who can show them step by step how to perform specific tasks. It is a very cost effective training tool as it is given by existing people in the SOC and can be almost any topic. It is also a great way to ensure that material is consistently taught as the materials such as tools and documentation are your own.

The process of OJT is to help build up a new person and make them proficient in specific tasks. This typically starts off with a senior or more experienced person in the SOC showing the new person how to perform a task. The observation of the task being performed should be discussed in detail and the new person would have an opportunity to ask questions during each step. As the new person becomes more comfortable with the task being trained they can "drive" and perform the task with the senior SOC member looking on and correcting any issues they see. As the new person performs the task better and more confidently, then they become proficient enough to handle that task without any additional assistance. Keep in mind that some tasks are easier than other and therefore will require different levels of effort on the part of the student and the trainer. Specific task training may take minutes, hours or even days and weeks before someone is really proficient. If your SOC is responsible for breach and IR or if your SOC is a managed operations center servicing many clients then there will no doubt be some very stressful situations where SOC team members need to be able to stay calm, ensure they are using the correct words in their communications, and they know who to call, what to say, and what to do. The best way to ensure all of this gets done right is through OJT and by running several training scenarios and exercises. Training through repetition along with easily accessible and clear documentation is the best way to ensure that SOC staff will execute properly during extremely stressful times. OJT does not always have to be for new staff, it is also important that existing staff and even your senior or more experienced staff maintain their proficiency on specific tasks in your organization. This is a great way to ensure that highly important tasks but infrequently used skills can remain sharp in your operations.

The more tasks you can identify the more you can standardize and train people with the OJT process. Keep in mind that this does not take place of properly documented processes and procedures. In fact you should have all of these tasks documented and a proficiency checklist should be created that you can have the senior SOC member performing the OJT sign and document that the training was accomplished to proficiency. Training checklists and documentation are a critical component to any training program, an example checklist is provided later in this chapter for your reference.

Because OJT is such an effective training tool, I want to further this discussion with some specific examples of how OJT could be beneficial above and beyond the basic SOC analyst core functions. Having the skills and technically knowing how to analyze security information is extremely important for an analyst in a SOC but being training on communication is vital to everyone's success. Through OJT an analyst can be taught valuable skills on interpersonal communication as well as customer service. It is one thing to be able to spot a security incident but it is completely another thing to be able to effectively communicate that issue to the right people with the right tone using the right words. Although you should have specific documented processes and procedures on when to contact people via email or who to call or who to assign tickets to, it is vital that the correct information be placed into those communication methods to ensure the correct message is received. Interpersonal and customer service training is vital to ensure the SOC's message is received appropriately, at the right level and does not cause any undo pain and suffering to the recipient of an escalated event.

## TRAINING PLANS

I have worked at several large security operation centers and inside these operations centers people are performing multiple functions and multiple jobs and one of the key elements of success is having a training plan suitable for your organization and for the positions that people are holding. Without a proper training plan it is hard to ensure that all of your employees in your security operation center are meeting expectations and are capable of doing the job that you expect. Additionally without a documented training plan, it is very difficult to communicate to your employees what the expectations are for them to advance their career and move on to higher positions inside your organization.

It is important to develop not only a training plan but also a checklist that help ensure that each person going through the training plan documents the training they are doing and each task gets signed off by a more senior person in the SOC. Additionally, when they do OJT alongside other analysts or engineers that work with them or trains them there is a sign-off for those tasks as well. The Military and U.S. Government organizations do this very well. If you want to see very detailed and robust training plans look at some of the U.S. Air Force Career Field Education and Training Plan (CFETP) documents which are mostly available on the web. These documents detail all the skills, tasks and training that are required for an individual to progress over a 20 year career. The one CFETP that is most related to the content of this book is for the Air Force career field number 1B4x1. That training plan should be located on www.e-publishing.af.mil or more specifically, http://static.e-publishing.af.mil/production/1/saf_cio_a6/publication/cfetp1b4x1/cfetp1b4x1.pdf

You may not want to lay out a 20 year career for your SOC but a good explanation of this in a simple organization that has a tier one, two, and three security analyst position structure where each had a different role or more advanced function than the other. You can build a similar document that helps people progress from day one of a new analyst coming on board to the organization where they would be handed a new hire checklist, and a training book with a training checklist all the way to completion of their tier 1 training. The new hire checklist would include certain things that are important for SOC management to keep track of, like issuing of their badges, issuing of a token for VPN access, and issuing of their network credentials. It also included checklist items for a laptop, cell phone or any other items they might need in order to do their job. All of these items also had a name or department associated with them so the new employee knew a direction or someone they needed to speak to in order to get the items. After each item was issued the respective department or responsible person would check off and sign that the items was indeed issued. In addition to this list, the training checklist detailed all the various elements of a documented training plan and materials that they need to go through and one by one get signed off on. The analysts would go through an on the job-training program augmented by technical reading and computer based training where possible.

New hire SOC documentation is always an important document to generate and give to employees. This is in addition to the documentation your Human Resources department may distribute, because a SOC can play by different rules and have very different procedures than what you would find in the rest of an organization.

An Administrative SOC book can be created and issued to include items like:

## SOC SHIFT OPERATIONS

Shift responsibilities may seem like common sense type items that you should not have to tell a reasonable adult about and if you have ever worked in an operation center or have done any kind of shift work these type of things will be fairly common but in a SOC or any other type of operation center you have to ensure that everyone is operating with the same set of rules. For example, when arriving to work all analysts must be ready to begin work at the start of their shift (i.e., login to their computers, access the phone queue, and read up on all their email). Then all analysts would be required to ask the previous shift for updates about any recurring issues (these issues should also be documented on a SOC SharePoint site, or portal system.) Departing at the end of the shift is also something that should be documented; your expectations for the analysts to close out their work and any preparation items you need for them to complete for the next shift should be documented. For example, maintenance tasks, systems updates, that is, change management items. A lot of these items were reviewed in the daily operations chapter but keep in mind that simple training documentation becomes reference information for people to use later. Train people on these basic operational items now and save many problems in the future. One essential rule you may need to communicate and train people on is if you require all tickets to either be closed or passed on to the next shift. This helps in ensuring that tickets do not get orphaned and remain open in the system forever.

General responsibilities are items you need to train people so that there is common set of practices on how you want everyone to act and interact with each other and with your customers. For example, you may want to train people on the precise procedure of securely dispose of any paper that has customer names, IP addresses, IDS or firewall rules or any other sensitive information. It is also important for new staff to review internal documents, such as policies and procedures, case studies, or past incidents that have been documented by the team or information in past tickets.

## LEADERS

It is also very important to know who is in charge in the SOC and to make sure that there is someone in charge at any given time so you may need some training on what it means to be in charge. You may want to designate the most senior analyst to be acting as the team/shift lead if no actual lead or manager is around. In this case that senior person will assume the duties and responsibilities of the team lead and therefore will be granted the same respect from the SOC staff as they perform leadership duties.

Train your staff to take charge. Give them the right process to perform IR, or give them a calling tree so that when something goes wrong they have the right phone numbers for the right people they can call. Train them to reach out properly to customers or internal departments, and as discussed previously, ensure they understand how to appropriately communicate. If you are running multiple shifts, you may need aids to help communicate issues across different shift, do this you may need a shift log, well then you need to train your people on how to complete a proper shift Log report at the end of every shift.

Leaders in your SOC need to know how to monitor the workflow, ensuring that tickets and appropriate email accounts are worked on in conformance with any of the SLA or internal SLO you have signed up to support. Also, leaders need to be trained to review representative sample of tickets for accuracy and content and produce reports on procedure discrepancies, anomalies, or good samples. They also need to know how to review tickets to ensure that your SLAs are being met. If they are not being met, what type of course corrections can they take to get back on track. A leader in a SOC may have to make constant changes to get the right tickets moving in order to keep up with the SLAs. Teaching them how to do this is critical in ensuring you are successfully meeting your obligations. Your leaders are responsible to take escalations from the SOC floor and do something with them. They need to be able to either technically handle all escalations or know who to reach out to. In many organizations, this information is never written down. Do not be like that: train your staff to handle issues appropriately, effectively, and efficiently. Ensure you document everything for training purposes as well.

## CUSTOMER NOTIFICATIONS

We discussed this before, but it is worth mentioning in more detail. It is very important to train your SOC how to properly communicate. The SOC is dealing with what could be very critical information and incident details. If you do not train your SOC to handle this information accordingly then nobody else will. What this means is that sometimes security professionals can become complacent with incidents as we may see them all the time. It is not always up to the SOC to decide how to react or respond to an incident, which may be up to some other department or a Computer Emergence Response Team (CERT). Regardless how your organization handles an incident you need to respond appropriately and that usually entails a notification to an internal or external customer. If all you do is call someone but do not leave a message, was the information important? Your SOC needs to be trained on who to call and the proper frequency and escalation of those calls. This may be different based on the customer, type of incident, severity of the incident, or even the time of day. These notification details may change as people leave the company, go on vacation or move positions within a company. Not only do you need to train your SOC on these notification procedures but you also need to keep your documentation up to date so that your analysis will always call the correct point of contacts. Lastly, when communicating with customers a SOC needs to be trained in customer service, they need to know what to say and how to say it. Often you may hear the story about someone getting a security alert for something and then immediately shutting down a company's critical server, which in turn shuts the company down. The analysts need to be trained to be calm, to help customers understand the criticality of a situation but without rising any unneeded alarms or panic. They also need to understand that their customer may not be an IT person; therefore, they need to be able to communicate in ways so the customer understands what just occurred and how it needs to be handled and/or resolved.

## SOC PHONES

It is kind of weird that culturally we are such technically minded people but I cannot believe how many times I see several very smart IT people struggle to get a video projector to work. There are just some technologies that happen to evade our ability to command that will always frustrate us the most. The phone and connected phone systems you may typically see in a SOC environment may be quite complex and may be worth some training.

Many operations centers use ACD systems. These systems allow an incoming call to be routed to an appropriate analyst in the SOC who is available and ready to take the call. This requires an analyst to log into the phone queue using a unique code or agent identification number. This allows the tracking of calls, call times, call frequency, and so on. This is definitely a great tool for getting metrics. It is also something you want to think about when reading the SOC metrics chapter. Due to some of the complexities of these systems it is important that you train your SOC on its proper use. For example, when you step away from your desk usually there will be an away button that needs to be pressed, this helps pull you out of the call queue so that someone calling in does not waste time ringing your phone. Also, to ensure basic customer service and as to not upset anyone calling into the SOC, everyone should be trained on basic call set up like, transferring calls, creating a conference call or answering voicemail.

Here is a quick list of items you may want to have in a communications document that you want to train people on.

- Inbound call handling procedures
  - What you say when you pick up the phone
  - Caller authentication (optional depending on your organization)
- Incident notification procedures
  - Outbound call handling
    - What to say during an incident escalation
  - Email handling
    - What to write
- Group email handling
  - If you SOC shares a single group email box, how do you handle ensuring all emails are acknowledged and handled, what do you do with the email once it is been addressed

It is not just about communications, it is also important for an analyst to know about the organizations they work for. It is the core reason you are there; therefore, you need to train your SOC on who you are, what your mission is, and who your customers are. If you have external stakeholders or customers then your SOC needs to know who they are and what specifics are important about them. It is not enough for you to just give your SOC a phone number to call your customers, you need to train them in the right way to deal with those customers regardless if they are internal or external to your organization. They need to know that if they call Bob between the hours of 2 a.m. and 6 a.m. they better have a damn good reason or they will make a very powerful and influential customer very upset, but calling him any other time for even a minor issue is required. Customers have specific expectations and your SOC needs to do its best to meet those needs, spending time training your staff on how to deal with them will pay huge dividends.

An administrative SOC checklist can include items like:

| SOC general tasks | | | | | |
|---|---|---|---|---|---|
| | **Certification for OJT** | | | | |
| **Tasks, knowledge and technical references** | **A Start date** | **B Completion date** | **C Trainee initials** | **D Trainer initials** | **E Certifying official** |
| **General Tasks** | | | | | |
| Lights after hours | | | | | |
| Phone use | | | | | |
| SOC voice mail | | | | | |
| After hours on call procedures Time off notifications Building and SOC access procedures Facility maps Dress code Shift schedules Calling out sick or late procedures Emergency SOC procedures (not IR) Instructions on how to use the telephone system Locker or personal space usage information Special computer system use procedures Physical security of the SOC Items allowed or not allowed in the SOC (cameras, personal phones, etc.) Data protection Video wall management Temperature and environment controls rules and procedures | | | | | |

| Required tools and access for daily duties | Date granted | Granted by | Trainee initials | Date revoked | Revoked by |
|---|---|---|---|---|---|
| LAN access | | | | | |
| Email | | | | | |
| Log management | | | | | |
| Anomaly detection | | | | | |
| IDS system | | | | | |
| IP Management | | | | | |
| ticketing system | | | | | |
| Antivirus console | | | | | |
| Web proxy console | | | | | |
| SOC SharePoint | | | | | |
| VPN | | | | | |
| Patch management reporting system | | | | | |
| Domain admin | | | | | |

| Equipment issue | Date issued | Serial# | Associate initials | Date returned | Returned to: |
|---|---|---|---|---|---|
| Laptop | | | | | |
| Docking station | | | | | |
| One time token | | | | | |
| Cell phone | | | | | |

During initial OJT, the new analysis should sit with various analysts. The more experienced analysts or engineers should work through the training manual with the new person. They should be taught all the various sections and then they would have to demonstrate proficiency in that section before they could get that section signed off. This always seems to be the most effective way because in busy SOC environments there are no guarantees that a single senior analyst would be able to be dedicated to train new employees. With the checklist and training documentation, a new analyst can bounce around from person to person getting the required training without having to explain where they are, what they have done and what they feel they need to know. Everything gets documented and signed off before it is reviewed by management. Once the training plan is completely signed off then that was the indication the new employee could begin to work on his or her own. Ensure they retain all their training materials to be used as a guide and reference.

The signoff sheet should be filed away in a personnel folder where you could track any annual refresher training, certifications they may get or other various items you wanted to track for either your own use or for compliance needs.

## PROGRESSION AND VISIBILITY

If after, let us say six months, a new tier one analyst may be looking for a promotion to a tier 2 analysts. If they are doing a good job, you can give them the training documentation and materials to learn and study for what is required for a tier two analyst. (I am not saying 6 months is the right amount of time to start progressing your people, which is something that you have to decide on your own in your own SOC based on the person, on your needs and the needs of your organization.) Every organization is different and progression will happen in different ways at different times for different people working in different organizations. You figure out what the right balance is best for you. It is not uncommon to see organizations that will not even begin to think about advancing someone to the next level for 2 years. Again your organization might be different and 2 years might be too long and in other organizations that might not be long enough, 2 years, 6 months, whatever works for you is the best thing.

Of course this does not mean that your analysts cannot work to train themselves to get better and advance themselves. When it comes time for them to step up, they are already prepared. I would highly encourage you to allow your analysts to progress and learn as much as they possibly can whenever you can. Never prevent them from growing. Growing is a vital and important part of your organization, the more they learn the better they are going to be and the better security they can provide for your organization. You need to embrace training and you need to embrace the people who are willing to go out on their own and learn. There is nothing more valuable than an employee that goes out on their own and brings knowledge into the organization. It helps rejuvenate the organization, and helps advance the entire organization's body of knowledge.

In the best SOC I have ever worked, training was a daily occurrence. An environment where you come to work every single day with the objective to either learn one new thing or impart some knowledge on someone else is truly a magical place to work. In these lucky environments, people feed off of each other and learned collectively. People would come in to work and talk about new vulnerabilities, mitigation strategies, news stories or experiences they had with some tool or program. Sharing is caring, and in an organization that values open sharing of information, skills and knowledge will become a world-class operation.

Some organizations worry that they train their employees at a high cost. They even invest in getting them professional certifications but then their employees become more valuable and eventually leave the organization. The concerns is that the organization invested lots of money training people when all they are going to do is leave once they are trained for bigger and better jobs. Although this is true, you are making your employees more valuable but you also need to value them more as well. The more time and dedication you provide to your employees, the more time and dedication they will have in return. Making your organization a place where people want to work, enjoy working and a place people feel they get benefit from is a great way to retain your people and ensure they will not leave as soon as they are trained.

I assure you that if you put no value into training and advancing your staff they will leave you anyway and go work for company that does value them and does want to advance them personally and professionally.

Some ways to help retain your people once they are trained is to not just promote them but promote their knowledge. Make sure you have open forums with your SOC to discuss operational challenges. As people progress in you SOC environment they will absolutely find ways to improve processes, documentation or technical controls. By listening and implementing these improvements, you not only build a better SOC but you also give your people a sense of accomplishment and pride in what they are doing in their job. This is a great way to retain people, they want to part of the solution and if you do not give them a way then they will just go away. You may even want to try and build a continuous improvement program. This program may require annual documentation reviews, tool configuration audits or whatever you need. The bottom line is do not just audit your SOC, have your SOC perform audits on themselves, have them be part of the solution, and get them working together as a team that can better themselves. It will help keep them current on training, documentation, and ensure integration of new information back into your tools.

Employees, especially new ones can easily be overwhelmed with the sheer volume of information, policies, and procedures that you may have in your company but especially in your SOC. You should be careful and take precaution on exposing staff to tasks where they might not be fully trained especially when there is a possibility of inadvertently disclosing sensitive information. By focusing efforts on training, you not only invest in your employees by helping them learn their profession but you also help prevent costly mistakes.

## TRAINING EXERCISES

Learning out of a book or classroom or even in the SOC working along side other more seasoned people may not ever be enough to prepare someone for that big event. It is not just that large breach you need to be worried about it is also the smaller successful attacks or the activities of real advanced persistent threats that you need to worry about. These are hopefully not things you see every day, so in order to be best prepared for those types of events are to exercise your SOC. Applying your knowledge in scenario-based training such as an exercise is a great way to not only stress test your staff but give them ultimate on the job training and the ability to test out their skill sets without having to worry about a real negative impact to a customer or the organization.

To perform a simple training exercise you can have internal members of your team try to stage an attack by tripping signatures on sensors or generate logs that should create an event into your SOC. This is a good way to ensure that your SOC is paying attention and that they handle the event appropriately if they even see the event in the first place. This simple exercise ensures tools, processes and procedures are working the way they are supposed to and that people know how to access them and use them all to be successful. After the event is over and the SOC has completed its process everyone should get together and discuss what happened, what went wrong, and how to improve it for the future. This is a very effective way to test your SOC and make sure everything is working as expected. Do not get this type of exercise mixed up with other types of testing. This is not a penetration test. It is not a vulnerability test of the network. This is purely a controlled test to ensure the SOC is operating properly and to train staff on proper operations.

For a more advanced test, you can setup something like a network war game where with a controlled set of rules you can have a team be "red players" that are going to safely attack the network. Then you will have "blue players" that are protecting the network. A lot of companies, as well as governments, use this type of exercise to not only find weaknesses in network infrastructure or other security vulnerabilities but also to help train security and information technology personnel and their management. To start with, I would not recommend you hire an external company to bring in penetration testers to beat up your network. Instead, bring your management and security experts to a room with a whiteboard and do a series of tabletop exercises. In this format, you can have lively discussion on different attack or defend scenarios. You may find that just through exercises like this you will find issues with your SOC processes or even weaknesses in your organizations network that the SOC is not prepared to defend against. In these cases you can bring your results to the attention of the appropriate management to have them look into it for further resolution. This whiteboard approach is great for organizations that have never done any real exercises before and gives you great opportunities to learn and talk about risks, weaknesses or items to improve upon. If you involve business leaders in the exercise they can also help you with your hypothetical discussion as to what impact specific events would have on the operation of the company. It is good to do these types of exercises at a technical level but do not be afraid to expand upon it and get your business, finance, legal department, HR, or even customers involved in the discussion.

Once you are ready and you feel that you have worked out all the kinks and issues you can from your whiteboard discussion you can then start to think about taking it to the next step. This is where you do have people actually perform live attacks on the network, these could be either internal resources or you can hire an external company to come do this for you. The red team in this case would actually attack either the entire network or just specific parts while the blue team detects, responds, and defends the network.

I will strongly caution you that you need to make sure you bring a wide audience into the planning part of this type of exercise. One of the first things you should decide on is what you want to test. The SOC is obviously going to be tested but what part of the network do you want to test is what you need to decide. You need to figure out if it is the organization's externally facing systems and DMZ or internal database system that you want to test. Either way, you do not want to put any real production equipment in jeopardy by performing any unsafe vulnerability exploits. It is always best, but not always possible to launch real live attacks against test or development systems. Do what you can to make the exercise as real as possible but without causing any real impact to the organization. In some cases, controlled red team activity can be performed on production systems as long as the testes and attacks have been previously validated to not cause and production performance issues. A test can even be as simple as placing a desktop computer on a server network and see if detection tools or your SOC is able to see that change. Another simple test may be the performing of a simple vulnerability scan that does not change, alter or damage the network in any way but would look like a potential attack to the security operation center. Keep in mind that depending on what your organization does there may be systems you never want to subject to live attacks even if performed by skilled and trustworthy people. These may be isolated systems running critical infrastructure or supervisory control and data acquisition (SCADA) systems that manage power, gas or other dangerous systems. In these cases, it is not that you do not want to discover vulnerabilities or security issues, you just do not want to find those issues on production systems actually performing critical functions.

When you feel confident in your SOC's abilities to detect, protect, and defend the network appropriately and you have a consistent set of policies and procedures that your SOC is following then you may want to consider bringing in an external team to perform red team functions. By bringing in an external company, you can really begin to test the effectiveness of all of your security equipment and your SOC by allowing the extra company to utilize known emerging threats, new threats, or even threats your security team has not seen before. This is a great way to help improve your security operations and start to introduce security skill sets and intelligence from outside sources to better your infrastructure, better your security operations performance and increase your overall protections for the organization. Some government regulations or industry regulations such as PCI may require your organization have a vulnerability scan performed by an authorized scanning vendor. The vulnerability results would be reviewed by your organization and ultimately be part of your regulatory compliance documentation. It is great to be able to utilize these required vulnerability scans to test the effectiveness of your security operation center. Essentially you are able to kill two birds with one stone, comply with your regulatory requirements for also using the same money to test yourself. Most external security scanning vendors will be more than happy to work with you to create this type of training environments while providing necessary documentation for compliance. In some cases, your regulatory compliance activities may dictate that a test of your SOC or IR is performed on a regular basis, by integrating all these activities, you are reducing the workload burden on all of your participating organizations while reducing costs.

This type of exercises can be a huge learning environment for everyone involved. Not only will it help your SOC learn and improve processes but it will also help them learn about your company or the network they are charged in protecting. Further, you can even find competitions that mimic the same kind of exercises. These are typically called cyber capture the flag exercises and competitions. They are run on networks built just for this type of activity and some have very well defined and mature rules and scoring systems for participating teams to follow. These events are usually run by universities or sponsored by vendors and you can also find one at the Defcon (www. defcon.org) conference in Las Vegas every year.

This does not always have to be training for the SOC personnel participating on the red or blue team but this can also be training for the company and its users. In today's modern threats, the weakest links are typically the non-IT users. By performing red team tactics on your users, you can effectively help train them on how not to click on suspicious links, open email attachments from people they do not know or give out their passwords to anyone who asks. Your red team can be the ones to send out phishing email to employees and provide immediate positive feedback or training opportunities to the people that perform specific actions.

There are many different options and scenarios you can play out with exercises and it can be free or as expensive and elaborate as you want it to be. But in the end the training everyone can gain from this type of event can be invaluable to everyone involved.

## SUMMARY

In looking at all the different training options, scenarios, and programs that are available out there, there is really no reason an organization could not provide ongoing and continuing education to its SOC while maintaining consistent training across shifts or sites. The extent of free training and online resources these days is nothing short of massive. All it takes is for one person in your organization to seek out the effective resources you need and assemble it into a cohesive program that can be tracked and monitored. Although there is plenty of free training, you should set aside a training budget and get enough funds yearly to expand the proficiency of your SOC in technical areas and new disciplines or even legal aspects of security. Funds can also be spent on bringing training in-house for everyone or rewarding individuals that stand out by sending them to popular conferences. You should also have a library setup where people can access either physically or digitally books, magazines, and other technical references that will not only help encourage learning and expanding of knowledge but also help in keeping people up to date with emerging trends in the security space.

Ask someone in the SOC to build a 1-h training presentation. It does not need to be a seasoned professional; it could even be someone new who is seeing things through a fresh pair of eyes. Then when he is ready to teach the lesson, buy the SOC lunch, it will get everyone there and help them pay attention.

As I mentioned before, do not boil the ocean. There are many different ways to train your SOC. Be creative, be focused, and make sure you carve out the time for training as it will only benefit the entire organization in the long run.

# Metrics

# 8

## CHAPTER CONTENTS

*To know that we know what we know, and to know that we do not know what we do not know, that is true knowledge.*
**Copernicus**

Information is the key to success in anything that you do and knowing that you are on the right track and you are being successful is a great feeling. Without metrics we are just guessing that we are doing the right thing. We need numbers in our jobs to track what we are doing, to show we are being successful, or that we are failing for some defined reason that can be shown through metrics. In security and especially in security operations, we collect a lot of data, a huge amount of data and for some people too much data. But, data are an invaluable raw material that must be harvested. Once you have data, you can turn it into information. The information tells you something, it has structure and tells you a story, and allows you to organize into meaningful metrics. You need to analyze metrics, it causes you to think and evaluate. In order to understand what the metrics tell you, you need to question it. The analysis of those metrics gives you what you need so that you can act. Metrics are a product of that process where you take data, turn it into information, and analyze that information in order to take action.

Data > Information > Metrics > Analysis > Action

Metrics for the sake of metrics does nobody any good. I have spent a great deal of time creating metrics out of ticketing systems, security devices, end point devices and a combination of devices, you name it. I have created some of the most visually appealing, interactive charts, images, and dashboards that you have ever seen and that nobody will absolutely ever use because the data are completely worthless to anyone. You can get lost in metrics for years and make some of the most complicated and complex data sets that even you will not be able to figure out what you did a week later. Once I sat down to make some metrics and focused on nothing else for a week to generate some useful data. At the end of the week I had just over 100 different data sets and metrics. All individual reports, charts, graphs, and spreadsheets that were easy to update and were all interlinked to each other. I presented my weeks' worth of hard work to my leadership team and I got looks like I had three heads. They all had the same question, what do you want us to do with all this?

I realized one critical value that I was missing from all my cool wizardry, the user! I did not think about the practical application of any of the metrics I had created. Instead I just created some very powerful and visually appealing junk. This does not mean that the data were bad but once I put the reports into context of who could use it and why then the reports took on a life of their own and became one of the most powerful tools an operation center could ever utilize.

In the next few sections I am going to discuss metrics as it relates to various people and positions. The idea is not to give you a prescriptive metrics list of who needs what, but instead to help you put valuable data sets in focus of the user who needs it most. It is very important that you have accurate representation of metrics in a SOC. You may not have all of these positions in your SOC or you may call them something different or may even combine some of these into one, it does not matter how you break it up or combine them. Take the concepts and apply it appropriately to your situation as you desire.

What are the types of metrics to use and how you use them are almost as important as the information they represent. Simple visualizations may include a table showing the metric result for the organization whereas graphical visualizations where the metric result is plotted on the graph. Additionally you can use complex visualizations for displaying the metric result for cross-sections by organization or ticket type, incident classification, or incident priority. Additionally your metrics may indicate threats to high valued assets (targets) in your organization. This could include assets that contain valuable data but are vulnerable due to missing patches or updates. Later in the chapter we will talk about using metrics to prioritize assets in order to gain a clear vision of how critical an incident is to your organization, which will ultimately help you communicate the criticality of an event to your senior leadership or it may help you highlight the fact that there are a large number of assets that are largely un-managed or owned in your organization which could quickly become targets for attackers.

## HEADS UP DISPLAY

If you have ever seen an operation center, the first thing you may notice are the large monitors, projectors, or video walls of what seems like really cool graphics, moving charts, TV channels, and so on. It is the one major impressive thing that an operation center has for eye candy. All too often I have been in an operation center and have seen tons of money spent on these large walls of impressive multimedia but when the work begins nobody really uses it. Nobody looks up at them and the screens just blink away silently. Seems like such a waste of money and energy powering all that eye candy.

It is such a shame when that happens because these massive video walls can be an operation centers must valuable asset. Take a good look at what you display on your wall, if something is not useful in keeping analysts informed or updated about important events then get rid of it. These large video walls are large for a reason, they are needed to help convey important information and there is what seems like never enough real estate to display it all. If you do not believe this is true, turn all your monitors off for a day, does your operation still run? Did things still go as they should? If so, you may need to rethink what you are displaying and evaluate the metrics that you cannot live without.

## SUPERVISOR METRICS

Let us take a look the purpose of your supervisor or shift lead you may have at your SOC. They may be there to ensure people show up on time, take escalations from more junior analysts or help to resolve unforeseen problems, customer issues, or begin the incident response and communication process. Additionally supervisors may be ultimately responsible to ensure that organizational service level agreements are consistently met. Metrics for this position is your first line of defense to combat any issues and to keep everyone focused. It is important to give them real-time metrics so that they can make on the spot course corrections as needed.

If you have priority ticket types or priority customers how do you know that those tickets are actually being worked in a priority manor or are given the special attention they deserve. One key metric would be a simple visual or heads up display that would alert the supervisor to the presence of a ticket or issues that meets those criteria. Your ticketing system may be able to do this for you or maybe you can develop a way to make this a visual or noticeable item that would attract some attention on a video wall or projector screen. Once a supervisor sees that something like this exists they can then evaluate what work is being performed currently in the SOC and assign the priority event to the next best analyst to work on or even handle it themselves.

A supervisor needs to be aware of all the work that is going on during a shift, knowing who is working on what and for how long is critical to keeping things moving. Sometimes analysts can get hung up on a specific problem or issue and dive into it for extensive periods of time. When dealing with technical issues it is hard to ask for help, technical people typically want to be the problem solver, there is an ego and pride to it all. At the same time, there is a business to run or company to protect and other issues to solve. A supervisor needs to know what analysts are working on and how long they have been working it. In a small operation, this is easy because you can verbally check-in with people on a regular basis, there is conversation going on and everyone may be in-tune. In larger organizations, a more technical approach is needed and a metric should be developed to track this.

Time-based service level agreements or objectives are also a metric that is vitally important to a supervisor. Knowing how many tickets are in a queue that are untouched or unresolved or how far an operation is getting behind on issues will allow supervisors to evaluate the work and see where they can apply additional resources or maybe even the supervisor can jump in to help out the queue for a bit to elevate a backlog. Sometimes analysts working tickets will not always take tickets in priority order, instead they may be more selective and only take tickets for issues they feel more confident in handling sometimes called "Cherry Picking". This is not necessarily a problem but a supervisor needs to be able spot when this becomes an issue because select tickets may be in the queue for too long, they can then direct people to take specific tickets to keep things moving. A simple metric showing analysts the top 10 oldest tickets in the queue may help motivate them to resolve those issues first, or they may just get sick of seeing them and want to close them out the best they can. No matter how you make these metrics work they are a key component to allowing your supervisors to make course corrections to help the entire operation stay on track and meet obligations. Supervisors also need to know how the people on their shift are doing, what their skill levels are and be able to rate the quality of work people are doing. This is because we want to provide the best possible service to our organization and the supervisor needs to know where problem areas are.

To evaluate analysts, one type of metric that can be useful is a ticket type metric. This is where you look at the types of tickets being worked by each of the analysts on shift. For example, if you notice that a specific analyst is working mostly IDS generated tickets but not working any virus issues then there may be a problem here. This may indicate that the analyst does not feel strongly enough in the skills that it takes to properly analyze and investigate those types of tickets. A supervisor needs to evaluate his staff to ensure everyone has the right training to be able to appropriately respond to potential incidents. A metric like this could be a good indication of a problem where someone needs additional focus, training, or mentorship.

Time based metrics can also be very valuable for a supervisor but are also very hard to create. Your ticketing systems need to have a time tracking function build in and then you can begin to track all kinds of interesting things. For example, imagine a report that tells you the average time a new ticket has to wait before being taken out of the queue and worked on by an analyst.

So for your supervisors as well as the managers it would be important to know the number of tickets per analyst that has been opened as well as closed. This will help you understand the number of tickets that your operation is actually dealing with on a regular basis. By looking at the same information by day as well as by week and month will also help you in understanding what your maximum load may be as well. You should also look at the number of individual closed versus open instead of a total SOC average. I would not use this metric to see how Bob is doing compared with Charlie but instead see who is doing what and like what was discussed previously who may need training.

Average time from ticket creation to ticket closure is a another nice ticket based metric, depending on how detailed you can get you will be able to find out not only how long it takes each ticket or ticket type to be worked to completion but you will also be able to spot problem areas that can be addressed to help you close tickets faster. You may even find that you need to work on your communication skills or relationships outside the SOC as the longest time to resolve tickets may be getting action or information from other departments.

Average time worked on the ticket is always good to try and figure out. Unfortunately time is not always an exact value to measure. Depending on how you implement the time tracking your results will vary. If you ask analysts to enter time values for each work log entry into the ticketing system, you may find that they are not very accurate as sometimes when people get heavily involved in technical issues, time escapes them and 3 h may seem like 30 min. When a ticketing system tracks time the system can only do so much. If an analyst opens a work log entry and the system starts to track time based on the fact the log is open you might think that is a nice automation until the analyst goes to lunch and forgets the clock is ticking in the ticket. Another issue regarding this is when an analyst does the majority of the work outside the ticketing system and then just copy and pastes their work into the ticket. Then 45 min of work could look like 4 or 5 s of logged work. Sometimes to most basic of time based measurements are the best like total average time/days open or a weekly metric to show how many tickets are open, closed, or currently open but neither closed or opened that week.

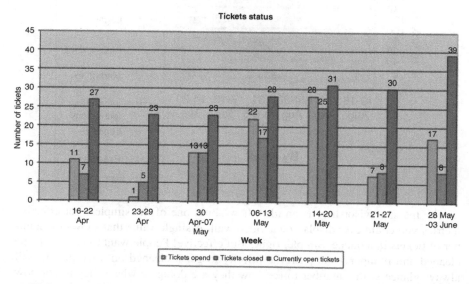

Ticket type is another interesting ticket based metric that can be interesting and fun to look at. I typically design my tickets systems to have tickets be categorized based on the US-CERT incident categories as we detailed in Chapter 3.

Once you have all your ticket categorized properly you can start to track what tickets are being opened for and really get a sense of what your SOC is doing.

**Current week Incident breakout**

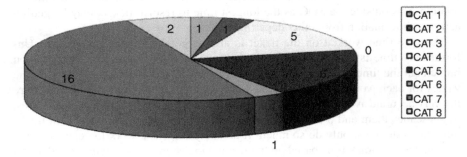

Number of tickets by division, location, or industry is also helpful so that you can easily identify where problem areas may be.

**Resolved ticket trend**

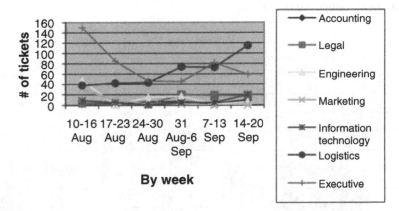

For the supervisor here is an idea, how about one of the simplest yet effective metrics you could ever display on a video wall. A single value that shows the number of tickets in a queue. Simple, right? But effective! People want to get the queue cleaned and if supervisors push the priority to get it cleaned out then people will always glance at this number to see how they are doing or where they are or how they are doing.

Got a problem with missing SLAs on tickets? How about a simple metric that shows how many ticket SLAs have been missed. Of course these are all metrics about tickets but there are plenty of other metrics that are important like if your network is up, are your devices up, web sites alive, and so on.

In one SOC, we had a 15-min service level agreement to acknowledge all new tickets. Using the time based functions of the ticketing system we were able to project on our video screen ticket numbers that were in jeopardy of missing the SLA because nobody has touched them. This quickly became known as the jeopardy queue and when things were busy, this is where everyone would go to get their next ticket to work on. You can even take the approach of changing the visualization of a ticket based on time. For example, if your ticketing system displays tickets with a ticket number and short description and date/time created then you should be able to display the oldest ticket first at the top of the list. To go a step further, taking the 15-min example, if all your tickets are displayed in black text maybe you can get your ticketing system to display all new tickets 5 min old as red text to visually separate them from the rest of the tickets, then you may even be able to get tickets 10 min old to not only be red but blink. These are good examples of how to get your SOC to take notice of priority work through visual metrics.

Time based metrics can also help you maximize your staffing efforts and make you more efficient. By looking at how many tickets are in the queue when you most frequently miss your SLAs for new tickets can help you determine the backlog levels. After you obtain your backlog levels, you can then map that against the time of day and the number of analysts you have on shift. Depending on the frequency of missed SLAs and the volume of tickets you may discover that you have too many people on one shift and not enough on another and therefore need to make some shift staffing changes. Depending on your SOC and the volume this metric may just tell you that you are getting overwhelmed. Your next step would be to look at the ticket types and how long it takes each of them to get resolved. If you find that there are always the same ticket types that take the longest maybe you can look into the processes and procedure the analysts are performing to see if there are any efficiencies that can be gained to improve the time it takes to resolve the tickets. In some cases, this time to close metric can mean two different things. First you can look at the overall time it takes from when a ticket is open to when it is completely closed. The other way to look at it is how much time was actually spent working on the issue the ticket was opened for. In other words, a ticket may be open for 5 days but only 10 min of actual work was performed to close it out. The two metrics mean very different things and actions you would take to reduce the time of each are very different. Continuing to make efficiency changes in your processes or apply automation will help you resolve tickets faster but it will also help your increase your ticket to analyst ratio. You need to maximize the number of quality tickets your SOC analysts work on and resolve, that is a lot to say in one simple sentence. What is a quality ticket how do you find out the analyst to ticket ration and how do you know when you are maximized. All good questions can be answered by looking at very simple metrics.

The total number of resolved tickets divided by the total number of analysts obviously would show you the average number of tickets an individual analyst resolves. For many reason this is not a fair average. For example, one analyst may be very fast at investigating and resolving tickets where another is slower but maybe more methodical. Another reason this metric can get thrown off is if there are a few particularly hard tickets to resolve that take long amounts of time and work. In order to help offset these issues are to look at types of tickets resolved divided by the total number of analysts. This way you can dissect the information in a bit more granular way and address specific issues with ticket types. You may find that virus events take longer to resolve but there are more virus tickets the second week of the month compared with any other week, whereas IDS generated tickets occur more frequently on Wednesdays but are relatively quick to resolve. Further investigation of these occurrence may help you realize that Wednesdays are the day the IT department typically patches systems which set off the IDS systems and generate a ton of false positive events. Similarly you may find that the second week of the month is more frequent for antivirus events because that is when patches are typically announced and when zero-day exploits are attempted more frequently.

If your SOC is receiving 5000 or whatever number of tickets per week or per month, take a regular look at those tickets. See what they are and how the staff is handling them, are they resolved, are they remaining open for long periods of time, ask some hard questions about the tickets and the associated events. This may sound silly but ask why the tickets are open in the first place.

Let us say that IDS devices generate a majority of your tickets. Which is not uncommon, many companies like to constantly keep their IDS devices up to date with the latest and greatest signatures treating them like some kind of antivirus update. So they just add signatures as they come from the vendor and take little regard for what the impact or need is to the organization. Take a good look at the top three events that open tickets. There are a lot of questions that need to be asked about these three events. One easy question could be regarding the percentages of false positives each of the three events are generating. If your staff is spending an average of 5 min per event investigating and working an IDS ticket and there are a total of 600 of these three events combined per week then you are spending 50 h of your staff's time on these, is that worth it?

Efficiencies can be gained by performing regular reviews of work being performed and ask the basic questions such as do we need to be doing this? Is there a better way?

Depending on how your SOC is setup, you may want to set a threshold of a false positive rate on IDS signatures if you can quickly determine that more than 90% of a single signature generating tickets is false positive then take it out of rotation and let someone evaluate it. Can you make the signature better and less false positive? Is it something that the organization can live without? Maybe the signature does not need to be on all devices and only on some that it matters more to. After asking the right questions and reviewing the information take these signatures out of production if you can, let your engineer fine tune them to reduce the false positives or even evaluate whether or not the IDS event is even worthwhile to the organization it is protecting.

Imagine the engineer who on a Friday evening and has been working on a new IDS signature all day. In his rush to get out the door, he installs the signature on 30 production devices and leaves for the weekend. The signature is not too bad but maybe not fully tested and it starts to fire once every other hour, so each hour 15 tickets are generated from the 30 devices. In a small SOC with only one or 2 weekend analysts, this may be obvious but in a larger organization with 10+ analysts it may not be noticed because everyone is grabbing tickets and doing their work. At the end of the weekend, 24 h later using the same 5 min per ticket average you would have wasted 30 h of your analysts time working a bad signature. $15 \times 24 = 360$ tickets at 5 min each

There are many built in tools from the vendor to help with this problem but it is not always possible to get it right. A good solid process to evaluate, test and install new things that trigger tickets for analysts to work on will pay huge dividends in the long run. One way that I like to measure my engineering staff is by false positive rate. Since the engineering staff can have a dramatic positive or negative effect on SOC analysts performance I will typically make a line item in every engineer's yearly review regarding false positive rates. Installing a bad IDS signature can open thousands of tickets in an automated system and waste a huge amount of time cleaning up unless you have an automated way to do the clean up. There should be a fair amount of testing before putting anything new into the SOC for analysts to react to. A simple metric to use would be percentage of overall tickets closed by the SOC analysts as false positive. This also has another advantage, in several organizations I have been at there is a divide between the annalists and the engineers, this metric gives the SOC back some power and creates a feedback look to measure how well the engineers are doing their job. Do not wait until the end of the year to pull this metric, evaluate every week and see where the problems are, make quick course corrections, and that ensure your annalists are able to focus on the tickets that matter the most.

Getting into more specific security metrics you may want to calculate the number of detected security events the SOC has experienced during a specific time period such as a shift, a day, a week, a quarter, and so on. This metric can further be split by business division or customer type or even by region. You can also define the metric by event type such as policy violation opposed to attempted exploit. In combination with other metrics, this can indicate the level of threats, the effectiveness of a specific security controls, or your incident detection capabilities. Additionally this could also help you see if changes to the environment are positively or negatively affecting your security posture. It will help you to strike the right balance, to find what is too many incidents and what is not enough, this is a good way to see some of that.

# VULNERABILITIES

Vulnerability management is a vital part of keeping an organization's assets safe; identifying and mitigating weaknesses found on systems especially priority or critical systems and applications reduces the risk of negatively impacting the business should these vulnerabilities be exploited. It is worth mentioning that it is impossible to predict or anticipate what vulnerability is going to be exploited. Because of this it is imperative that IT organizations and individual system, administrators work hard to get as close to 100% vulnerability free as possible. The SOC plays a key role in this area on several levels and can become a great partner in this effort. The primary question this activity is concerned with is: "Are my systems safe?" In vulnerability management terms, this question can be decomposed to: "Are there vulnerable systems? Have systems been checked, and if so, what was found?" and additionally how soon after a vulnerability was found did it get fixed. Finally, the last question is how well are system administrators managing and maintaining systems in the environment? Vulnerability assessment is the process of scanning networked devices and discovering vulnerabilities before hackers can exploit them, which is a perfect task for a SOC. Whereas vulnerability management is the process of evaluating vulnerabilities, communicating required patches, escalating missing patches and vulnerabilities to the right teams as well as approving exceptions and then overall reporting of open vulnerabilities in the environment.

An organizations network relies on accurate and timely exchange of information. Due to the increase of threats and well-known vulnerabilities, an organization must have a vulnerability Management system or process that provides the latest vulnerability fixes and security updates to the organizational network. The SOC can provide analysis on the latest vulnerability information, fixes, and security updates to all divisions responsible for maintaining network and computing assets. The purpose of the SOC engaging in this effort is to monitor and identify new threats and new vulnerabilities (hardware and software) that might affect the confidentiality, integrity or availability of the organizational IT assets. Also, these SOC services should be designed to aid system administrators in identifying existing and known vulnerabilities as they emerge and to look for the successful application of security updates and configuration as recommended by the vendor. Additionally the SOC should be the point of contact to support IT system administrators in the correct application or support of applying patches.

The SOC can also be a focal point for collecting and approving exceptions to patching and vulnerabilities. If a vulnerable system cannot be patched due to operational constraints, the patch breaks core functionality or a system administrator is just too scared to apply a patch, the SOC can help. I say this last sentence partially joking, sometimes system administrators maintain legacy systems that are so old and have been so problematic that they are afraid to touch it because something always goes wrong. The bottom line is that you are only as strong as your weakest link and the process of approving exceptions in a vulnerability management process is one that should not be taken lightly. System/network administrators in cooperation with the SOC should put a mitigation plan in place of each vulnerability that cannot be properly patched in a production environment. Mitigation plans could consist of IDS block rules for the specific attempted exploit for the vulnerability, Removal of the system from a production VLAN, significantly limiting or blocking of the effected ports on the firewall to the vulnerable system or even removing the system from the network till a fix, security update or some kind of mitigation can be applied. I am sure there are many other mitigations you can apply and your organization may even have some unique mitigations. As always it is up to your organizations practice on how you want to apply mitigations as part of the exception process but it should be a joint process between the SOC, your system administration team and your risk or compliance departments if you have them.

Typically the SOC team is responsible for keeping up to date with the latest threats and vulnerabilities and recommending mitigating strategies, solutions or fixes to System Administrators to be pushed to systems connected to the organizations network. The SOC can receive notifications/security alerts of new vulnerabilities and exploits related to security bugs or issues that may affect the network from places such as, US-CERT; full-disclosure; and Bugtraq. Any vendor's technology that you have widely deployed in your environment will likely have a mailing list, twitter account or some kind of news announcement related to vulnerabilities that your SOC can subscribe to and upon receiving an alert of a new vulnerability, the SOC perform vulnerability management processes to determine the vulnerability criticality as it relates to your organization. For example, if your SOC receives a notification that there is a critical vulnerability effecting Firefox on Linux but your organization does not use Linux then the SOC can downgrade the alert from its original critical to something that does not affect the organization and therefore would ignore. Conversely if that same alert effected Firefox in Windows and your organization heavily uses Firefox then the SOC could make the vulnerability widely known throughout the organization that it needs to be patched. There is also a large amount of data that can be obtained from intelligence sources and industry organizations sharing intelligence information but more of that is covered separately in chapter 9.

As part of the vulnerability assessment process I like as a best practice to ensure that every IP address in an organization is tested for vulnerabilities every 30 days. If you want to go back and read the last sentence that is ok because I did say "Every IP!". I typically do not believe in scanning known assets because a network can be a living-breathing thing and as the network gets larger the movement and changes of the network happen faster so you are more likely to miss assets. By scanning IP address ranges you are scanning all possible locations for a device to exist regardless of where it is, how it got there or where it came from. Even in a very strict IT change management program things can take a long time to get updated or can be temporarily missed. By scanning all available IP addresses you can feel confident that you are going to get a large percentage of devices on the network at the time of the scan. The SOC can have another critical role in this area by reviewing scanning results and performing a comparison to an asset management tool to obtain a total percentage of devices scanned. In almost every environment there is a likelihood of having devices off, not connected to the network during the scan or that are transient such as laptops that do not get scanned on regular schedule because they are not always on the network. Keep in mind that various mandatory regulations may have an opinion in this area, which is something the SOC can help ensure compliance with. For example, the Payment Card Industry—Data Security Standard (PCI-DSS) states "all devices that store, processed, or transmit Primary Account Numbers" are in scope for PCI audits and as such must be scanned quarterly for vulnerabilities and have 4 quarterly clean reports. Something like the PCI-DSS limits your tolerance for devices not being scanned on a regular basis especially if it is in scope for the audit. Ultimately, you will have to figure out what is acceptable percentage for your organization. As I stated before, I like as a best practice in your vulnerability management program to scan IP on a 30 day rotation, this is typically due to the fact that new vulnerabilities are released every month and systems should be patched within 30 days of a patch being announced and available from a vendor. Again, for organizations complying with PCI, the PCI-DSS states that you have to have document quarterly clean scans, but if you only scan once a quarter it is not likely you are going to be successful in producing clean reports. By scanning every 30 days you give system administrators or your patch team three shots at getting a clean scan. This cycle is long enough to not to cause undue network bandwidth or impact performance of servers and desktops but quick enough to be able to see improvement metrics. The SOC has another important role here as vulnerabilities and patches are announced. The SOC should have the ability to pull in patch compliance of something that is deemed highly critical to an organization. This would require all system administrators (assuming system patching is not a responsibility of the SOC) to patch in some time frame less than 30 days. In my experience, there seems to be one or two times a year where a SOC I was building would require quick compliance for patching in 7 days. This is because the vulnerability the patch protected against was severe and that the risk of exploitation was so great that waiting 30 days would be too risky for the organization. Typically in those situations I recommend the SOC hold a conference call or meeting and invite all of IT or all interested parties to join together where the technical implications of the vulnerability and impact to the organization can be discussed. This will allow for clear communication regarding the time compliance expectations and what the requirements are to resolve the issue. It also affords the IT organization to ask questions, raise concerns or offer up ideas on how to move the process faster.

So what is a vulnerability and why does all this stuff matter?

Vulnerabilities are security holes and bugs that are typically defects, or errors in software such as operating systems, drivers, and software applications. Unauthorized users and/or malware can use vulnerabilities to access desktops, laptops, servers or computer networks to steal data, degrade performance or disrupt services, and so on. As these vulnerabilities become known, software publishers develop patches, fixes, or updates that can be downloaded to fix the problem.

A good resource for vulnerability information can be found here → http://nvd.nist.gov/.

## VULNERABILITY PRIORITIZING

There are many different ways to score vulnerabilities but the principles are the same, the highest score equals the most critical vulnerability. An organization needs to have a fair and easily understandable way to score vulnerabilities and different methods mean different things for different people. What is right for your organization is up to you and there are many tools for you to use to help you in this area.

For example here are some ways to score vulnerabilities:

| Simple | PCI | Vulnerability vendor | CVSS |
|---|---|---|---|
| Low = 1–4 | Level 1 | Low | 0–10 |
| Medium = 4.1–7 | Level 2 | Important | |
| High = 7.1–10 | Level 3 | Medium | |
| | Level 4 | Severe | |
| | Level 5 | Critical | |

CVSS2

CVSS2 provides a universal open and standardized method for rating IT vulnerabilities and scores range from 0 to 10.0. The scoring system is fully documented and available for use by the public.

## BASE CVSS2 THRESHOLD

The base equation evaluates the access vector, the complexity involved to exploit a vulnerability and the level of authentication required to perform the exploit as well as the impact of a successful exploit on the confidentiality, integrity, and availability of data. So an exploit of a vulnerability that can be performed over a network connection is easy to perform and requires little or no authentication receives a high score for exploitability. An exploit that reveals confidential information, damages or modifies the information in some way, or makes information unavailable to those who need it receives a high score for impact. The calculated values for exploitability and Impact are used in the base formula to determine the CVSS2 score. The base score is a value ranging from 0 to 10.

More information about CVSS2 Base scoring is available here → http://www.first.org/cvss/cvss-guide.html.

Calculations to establish base score can be found → http://www.first.org/cvss/cvss-guide.html#i3.2.1.

## TEMPORAL CVSS2 THRESHOLD

The temporal equation produces a score based on the base score as well as the current exploitation, remediation, and validity ratings of the reported vulnerability. A confirmed vulnerability for which a highly effective exploit is available, and for which no fix is available, will have a high temporal score. Temporal scores range from 0 to 10 can be no higher than the base score and no more than 33% lower than the base score.

More information about CVSS2 Temporal scoring is available here → http://www.first.org/cvss/cvss-guide.html.

Calculations to establish base score can be found → http://www.first.org/cvss/cvss-guide.html#i3.2.2.

If you are required to comply with PCI then you have to use an authorized scanning vendor/product to perform your scans and as a scoring system PCI uses the CVSS2 system but puts things into their own categories for compliance purposes. For example, scores range from 0 to 10.0, with 4.0 or higher will indicate a failure to comply with PCI standards and must be patched or an exception must filed and approved. There is also the legacy PCI scoring system that can still be used, as sanctioned by the PCI DSS. This system ranks vulnerabilities on a severity scale from 1 to 5. Any vulnerability ranking above 2 indicates failure to comply with PCI standards.

Level 5 vulnerabilities permit attacks with remote root or remote administrator capabilities that can compromise an entire host.

Level 4 vulnerabilities permit attacks with remote user capabilities and partial file system access.

Level 3 vulnerabilities permit access to specific stored information, such as security settings.

Level 2 vulnerabilities expose some sensitive host information, such as precise versions of services.

Level 1 vulnerabilities expose information such as open ports.

Also with PCI, any vulnerability leading to a cross-site scripting (XSS) or SQL injection will indicate failure, regardless of CVSS score.

## ASSET PRIORITIZING AS A PART OF METRICS

Now that we have reviewed how to categorized vulnerabilities, we need to do the same with assets. Just as a reminder from above, the idea with vulnerabilities is to shut the door on hackers and malware as quick as possible. You want to be 100% patched across your entire organization but need to make sure you compliant as efficiently and as effectively as possible. Prioritizing assets are a great way to measure your overall risk exposure and give the senior leadership a level of comfort that risk is always being reduced in priority order. If you have a system that uniformly applies patches across your organization regardless of criticality I would still perform this exercise. Focused metrics and performance statistics on key or critical assets are extremely valuable and if you are always patched then that is a great metric to produce. This also allows you to measure the effectiveness of risk mitigation by setting goals of reduced vulnerability exposure and speedier mitigation. As you look at these valuable assets in your organization you can use them to audit the performance of security and IT teams performance, and implement process improvements to build a culture of refining your security operations.

Defining the relative criticality of assets is an essential step in your disaster recovery and business continuity planning process; as such this is a great opportunity for you SOC to get involved in detester recovery (DR)/business continuity (BC). In addition, the contingency plan standard in the HIPAA security regulation calls for organizations to "Assess the relative criticality of specific applications and data....". If you do this right it will save you a significant amount of time because the information is reusable in many different areas. Here are some things to consider before embarking on your asset prioritizing effort.

Keep in mind that the criticality of your information assets is nothing more than a business decision about what systems or applications are more important than others. You should work to get a varying degree of opinions on each system or application. The more views the better. Chances are that an engineering team will have a very different viewpoint than a finance department. The relative criticality analysis is a team effort.

In managing critical assets, many organizations fail to fully understand the meaning behind a criticality ranking of systems. A "critical" asset may have the greatest impact on the organizations function, be it production rate, quality of product produced, cost per product produced, core network functionality or key financial system. Through proper construction of criteria and analysis of systems against that criteria will result in an analysis model that an organization can live by to determine what their critical assets are.

Here are some of the things you may want to consider:

- Business or customer impact
- Financial impact due to downtime
- High availability/uptime requirement (e.g., 7 × 24 availability)
- Safety or environmental impact
- Preventive maintenance history
- Mean time between failures (MTBF) or "reliability"
- Probability of failure
- Replacement or parts lead time
- Asset replacement value
- Planned utilization rate
- Number of users (i.e., large number of users)
- Stores critical information (e.g., grades, social security number)
- Impacts to reputation of the organization due to downtime

Also keep in mind that systems may be a critical part of your organization according to legislation, regulation, policy, contractual, or other predetermined means. There are many books and documents out there to help you in this process, I am merely using these points to show how a SOC can provide value in this area as part of the overall vulnerability management program.

The most common examples of critical servers are departmental file servers, web servers, mail servers, and database servers. A "critical" server can be classified as such by being important to accomplishing organizational missions or one that stores legally protected or other important non-public data. Here are some examples of what you may find as critical servers in your organization:

- Enterprise level services that is used by all employees or significant to one or more lines of business.
- Servers storing significant amount of legally protected data

- Availability is critical or important
- Servers hosting key financial applications
- Servers running or hosting applications for industrial control systems
- Credit card processing servers
- Servers on disaster recovery plans
- Core routers

Now that we have an idea about vulnerabilities, ways to prioritize them as well as assets, we need to put it all together to demonstrate some useful metrics. These metrics are key to how your SOC is viewed outside of its area. It can very quickly become a critical product that becomes one of the key faces of the SOC.

Scanning metrics can be tricky and time consuming to produce, you have to be careful that you represent what is truly happening in an environment. Good vulnerability metrics can be vital to an organization and a key product of your SOC. Vulnerabilities are very dynamic in any environment and it is not always easy to get a handle on it in a consistent way. Creating metrics in this area is highly valuable in order to continually improve your security risk posture, you must measure it using common metrics and compare it to past measurements in some meaningful way.

Some of the challenges come from how often new vulnerabilities are announce or the frequency of when patches become available. Additionally, vulnerability-scanning vendors regularly update how they detect vulnerabilities by changing specific methods to verify or discover that a system is indeed vulnerable to an issue they were checking for. For example, this means that in some cases if you have a system where 10 vulnerabilities are detected today and report it as such and then next week you detect that there are 12, did you increase by 2? In fact, all 10 of the previously detected vulnerabilities may have been resolved but 12 new ones were detected. In this case if you reported the metric of 12 you are going to upset the system administrator or the person in charge of patching systems unless you can accurately reflect the previously accomplished work.

For another example to help understand the complexities, let us say that you decide to only report on newly detected vulnerabilities 30 days or older. As scanning vendors update their detection engine you may find that a system was vulnerable to something several months old but not detected until now due to the updated detection method. This is because the scanning vendor constantly tries to improve its product and customers constantly provide feedback and various false negatives get fixed. This does not mean that the system was not vulnerable until it was just detected but it could be that nobody knew about it until it showed up in the scan results. So let us say that this occurs and the newly detected vulnerability was actually announced by the vendor a year ago. This vulnerability has affected the system for a year but it was just detected, so do you beat up the system administrator for having an un-patched vulnerability on their system for a year or do you expect them to patch during their normal cycle now that they know about it and you can hold them accountable to the results? Some would say that administrators should patch their systems regularly and should be fully aware of any vulnerability that affects the systems that they manage regardless of scanning and reporting. Unfortunately this is not always reasonable in large organizations so be aware of this pit fall and make sure when you report your metrics that you are not alienating your IT staff, you need their help.

Now that we have discussed some pitfalls of vulnerability metrics, let us look at some other more specific metrics you may want to consider. This is where a SOC can provide some great benefit. As security professionals the SOC should be able to look at the results of a scan and be able to quickly determine the validity of the results, rule out any obvious false positive items and craft meaningful reports for the various levels of people in the company who need them.

A simple metric is the number of current vulnerabilities detected in an organization. This metric can be shown against the total number of devices in the organization by region if you want.

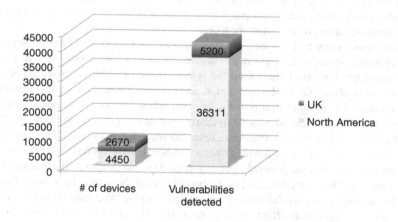

Sources of vulnerabilities could include new un-patched systems or applications introduced to the organization's environment or the discovery of new vulnerabilities on existing systems and applications. Unfortunately this can be a fairly large number and a bit scary if you are just starting out. As we previously discussed, one of the very first things you can do is work to classify vulnerabilities and your assets into priorities to help make the process more efficient. If you have a high priority system with a high priority vulnerability then it is obvious you need to fix this first. Then a simple report can be generated to show the top 10 vulnerabilities that exist on the top 10 critical assets. Seems like an ideal punch list for someone to focus on if you ask me!

Let us break this down further and see if there are other interesting metrics that can be produced.

The vulnerabilities can be breakdown by operating system, application, or organization division. The intent is for the metric to show the number of high, medium, and low vulnerabilities that exist in a specific area in the company. Again, as discussed before, you may use a different breakdown of vulnerabilities other than high, medium, or low. This metric provides a high level measurement of how the organization is doing, cut across several dimensions. You can break it up as much as you need to in order to fit your organizational requirements.

A nice example of this metric may be the following:

| # Critical vulnerabilities detected | # Devices | Operating system | Department |
|---|---|---|---|
| 3474 | 247 | Windows 7 | Finance |

Another important metric is the most vulnerable applications, with a breakdown into vulnerability score by application version—this metric helps highlight old, vulnerable versions of software that should be upgraded or eliminated. This also demonstrates the risk to an organization associated by a specific piece of software that is not being managed or updated properly. There are many ways to show this and depending on your organizations patch management practices this could be very useful to highlight areas that need more focus.

How about unowned devices and unapproved applications? Vulnerability scanning systems typically do a good job at enumerating device names and if you are performing authenticated scans then the system should be able to provide you a list of installed applications by devices and as an entire list. Assuming your organization uses a standard naming convention for devices, when you look through a sorted list of device names you should be able to easily spot devices that do not belong. If you are able to filter out devices that were detected on guest networks then you should have a fairly good listing of devices that are either misconfigured or just do not belong on your production network. Having your SOC track down these devices and determine why they are connected and who connected them may be a smart thing to do. This metric is very useful to track "unowned" devices that may be rogue devices or simply contractor/consultant systems, as well as the trend of applications that are not specifically allowed on the network.

## HISTORICAL MONITORING OF PATCHES

If your SOC announces patches to the organization and tracks those announcements then you can chart metrics based on those previously announced patches between specific dates. Take a look at the announced patches against the number of assets detected to be missing those patches. This will help you determine the number of patches still not installed. This could indicate entire software updates that have not begun to be installed by system administrators or by patch management tools. As a result this can easily tell you the number of open vulnerabilities due to the missing patches that currently exist on your network. Although this is a risk metric it is also a good metric to give your system administrators as they can use it as a priority list of patches to be installed if you assume the highest number should be patched first.

After the fact metrics are also vitally important, you need to know how long patches are an open issue. This will tell you how long your systems are vulnerable for but will also tell you what the average time to remediate systems needed patches take. Like some of the other metrics you can slice and dice this up by device group, by category or by patch type. From a compliance perspective, this metric also tells you how many patches are behind per your organization policy that has a dictated deadline. Additionally this metric can be further expanded and compared with other metrics such as what vulnerabilities are currently being exploited in the wild, are currently not patched in your organization but are also being taken advantage of by malware that AV may not be catching.

Finally your SOC can track how many systems are being compromised due the malware and exploits taking advantage of known missing patches on systems that have been reported to be out of compliance. Depending on how bad this situation is in your organization it would also be important to create a metric show how much time it takes for the SOC to go through this entire process of announcing patches, scanning for vulnerabilities, remediating systems, and providing metrics.

Putting this all together, you can create what I consider a metric of the window of opportunity. This is the time from when patch is available until there is 100% application of that patch is the "window of opportunity" to have that vulnerability exploited and leaves the enterprise at risk. Although you may think there are other items that can be in this list, the basic concept is the same no matter how you want to slice it up. The order usually looks like this.

1. Vulnerability discovery

   a. This is a "negative day" event; this is where an attacker discovers a vulnerability and creates to software needed to take advantage of the hole. The attacker will then devise a mechanism to deliver and properly exploit that vulnerability. This could typically happen several days or months before the next step of zero day.

2. Zero day

   a. Typically zero day refers to an attack that exploits a previously publically unknown vulnerability in a computer application. This also means that there is no patch to address the vulnerability and close the security hole.

3. Public exploit code available

   a. In this stage, the code needed to exploit a vulnerability is no longer in the hands of the select few. It is either published by the original creators or someone else and is now freely available to the general public who are interested in using it.

4. Mitigations deployed

   a. Depending on how much you know about a particular vulnerability you may be able to perform several actions to reduce your risk and exposure without actually patching. This could be closing off or restricting firewall rules, deploying intrusion detection signatures for the type of activity that might occur, and so on.

**5.** Patches available

    **a.** This is the day the vendor publishes the required software patch and procedure to fix the hole.

**6.** Patches deployed

    **a.** This is the day your organization deploys the required patch.

There are many metrics you can make if you track any of the above information for an individual vulnerability and its specific patch. Select metrics could consist of the mean time to risk reduced. This is great to show how proactive your SOC is and the steps you take to protect the company. A residual risk metric could be a tail value, which would be calculated after your set policy deadline for patching, the number of devices where the vulnerability still exists and the criticality of the vulnerability associated with the effectiveness of the mitigations you deployed. It will also help to demonstrate the current state of risk your organization is in when the vulnerability begins to be exploited and malware begins to arrive targeting the issue.

The numbers should help drive the point home that patching in the first place is cheaper, more efficient and just better for everyone involved. Otherwise you are demonstrating through metrics all the hard work of your SOC, which is not a bad thing at all.

Keeping on the trend of incident based metrics, and using them for security analysis, threat based metrics can have some very interesting results and can also help tell you and your organization how well you are doing in specific areas.

Have you ever wondered how many viruses were blocked by the antivirus system? As a security practitioner this is not a value that is very important to you but if your antivirus (AV) systems are doing a good job then people may forget how important the tool is in protecting the computers they are installed on. Your management and leadership may not realize that the care and feeding your SOC puts into making sure systems are kept up to date with AV and how that pays off. Of course the number of viruses AV let through and how many systems get infected on a regular basis is also an important metric and one that should be tracked on a much closer basis.

Sticking with the malware theme, understanding the types of malware encountered (i.e., virus, worm, Trojan) and how this compares to other similar organizations or the universe as reported by an authoritative source is very important. There are a few magazines and websites that publish weekly or monthly virus metrics, you can use these sources to compare what you are seeing on your network. You want to make sure you are seeing and catching the right things or you may find that you are missing something. If possible you also want to find out how the threat penetrated the organization in the first place (i.e., email attachment, website visits, hacking). This information is vital when you look to see how you can improve the overall security of an organization. It will also help you evaluate the need for additional purchases of threat mitigation solutions. It should also help you understand how you should prioritize different threats and which ones you may need to monitor more closely or even which assets you should monitor closer.

Overall metrics are also important to calculate and use especially if the metrics show the effectiveness and efficiency of the SOC. The SOC needs positive press to ensure that people can appreciate the hard work they do. A great way to present the efforts of a SOC into an easy to understand metric is a funnel chart. The funnel chart can show all the data feeds the SOC is currently collecting, such as Firewall data, VPN, IDS, and so on. There is a raw number of events that are generated by all these devices and fed into a log collector or SIEM tool. Based on rules, correlation, and aggregation of these events only a few incidents are generated into tickets that the SOC actually has to analyze. Then there is a false positive rate that can also be calculated based off of ticket information. To build this chart you need to look at every aspect of the SOC.

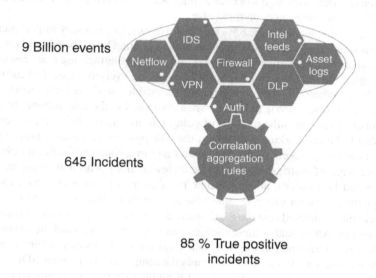

We start off looking at every single individual event that was either collected or generated into the SOC tools inside of a single month. In the case above, we are looking at 9 Billion events total for the month, this can be broken out by device type or what device generated the event if you want that level of detail. Next, all the events go through a SIEM tool or some kind of collection point that is able to look at the events and determine their validity for a SOC review and analyze. There are many ways that events can be condensed down. First you can have an aggregation process, this is where you take multiple events that are the same, count them up and produce only a single incident representative of all the others. So for example, does a SOC need to see 10,000 deny logs from a firewall or just a single event that states there were 10,000. Aggregation saves a ton of time and dramatically reduces the number of investigations a SOC needs to perform. Multiple events that are generated by the same session or packet, same host or destination or that has similar attack attributes can all be condensed into smaller or single events opposed to sending the raw information to an analyst.

Rules and correlation are a way to take events that mean almost nothing and join them together to mean something that is worth an investigation. For example, one user visiting a website is not necessarily bad unless there is a rule that states the website is bad and an incident gets created for the SOC to investigate.

The reduction of raw events by aggregation and the creating of new events with rules and correlation in the above chart shows that 645 incidents were generated in total for the month out of the 9 Billion presented. This is a good metric to look at and can help you understand many different aspects of your SOC. For example, if the total time it takes to address an incident ticket, analyze, and escalate if needed is appropriately 15 min, then this translates to approximately 161 h of work for the month by an analyst. That is enough work for a single analyst working a 40-h workweek and they will have no time to do anything else.

The next value we see is the 85% true positive rate, this is a very important metric because it shows the overall effectiveness of the system. Out of the 645 tickets generated less than 100 were created falsely. If you have an engineering team responsible for tuning all the devices, creating rules and making everything work then this is a great tribute to their efforts or whoever is responsible for all that hard work. It also gives the team a nice metric to look at when compared to the total number of events, the number of rules and the total effort going into managing the entire system. The focus should be on working hard to get the true positive percentage higher so that nobody is working tickets that do not matter and everyone can work on tickets that do. These types of metrics should also be reviewed along with how many new rules were created in a month, alongside new rules created in security devices such as IDS signatures or data loss rules and how those new additions effected the overall total incidents generated into the SOC and if the overall true positive rate rose or fell for the month. Additionally, these metrics can help you understand the overall level of work being performed in the SOC and what the total capacity is for the SOC to perform its function. If you use the graphed example above in your SOC and you had two analysts then you can deduce that if all the tickets were evenly worked than each analyst worked 20 h a week on incident tickets. Knowing that the average ticket takes 15 min then each analyst has the capacity to work an approximate additional 80 tickets per week, assuming that analysts do nothing else but work tickets. This is important as you look to put more security tools in place and increase the workload in the SOC. This metric allows you to see how efficient the SOC is running and what your overall capacity may be to perform incidents. Obviously there are many other factors that need to be reviewed and a single significant incident that takes all day to resolve or many days or weeks to resolve may cause these numbers to change dramatically.

Lastly you can break down what type of incidents occurred in what parts of the organization against what assets or types of assets. This will help you evaluate repeat issues or targets that may be too soft and needs some hardening or even users that may needs some extra security awareness training. Additionally, by looking at these types of metrics you may even be able to understand better who are our attackers and specifically what are they targeting or possibly trying to steal from you.

As you progress in building your operations, the metrics will help you evaluate your response to security threats. You can ask important questions like how many incidents are you tracking and how long did it take to investigate and remediate incidents or even how effective the security systems are that you have in place. Are your resources allocated appropriately? Do you have the right number of people reacting to issues? Only your metrics can tell you. Your operations center will have largely different metrics than others, that mean something to you and that help identify how well or how bad your tools are behaving for you. Different security suites of tools will lend its self to different metrics that you will want to track. Do not worry about having too much, or metrics that are not good enough, metrics that work and that tell the right story will be asked for by others. Try making metrics, use spreadsheets or pull them from your tools directly, not matter how you get them just get them and try to use them, try to make sense out of them and try to see if others would benefit from them as well.

Every SOC should see themselves as a service organization. Even if you are an internal operations center or especially if you are an outsourced security provider you need to define and identify who your customers are and make sure you are continually providing value to them. Keep your customers engaged, show off your value, produce quality metrics that mean something to them and that is as actionable as possible. Engage with them and ask if there are more metrics you can provide or work with them to define better metrics. The SOC is on the front like every day battling the cyber war, unfortunately there are no physical wounds or physical costs associated with this as it is all virtual. You need to demonstrate your strength, efforts and communicate your weaknesses effectively so that others easily see your value and understand your struggles.

Provide daily metrics to your SOC to keep them on task but do not overload them with meaningless information. Keep it simple, useful and easy to understand. Provide supervisors with a nice mix of daily, weekly and monthly information to help them ensure they are steering the ship in the right direction and have enough real-time data to make immediate course corrections. Provide management with weekly, monthly and yearly metrics to help educate them on trends and ensure they are kept up to date on trends, issues and of course successes. If at all possible, ensure that senior leadership also gets metrics specifically designed to keep them updated on what is going on and things that may be important to them. The SOC may never get a seat at the table with senior leadership but that does not mean you should not provide regular information and updates to the best of your ability. It will go a long way when problems do arise and you can be assured that they will. Do not forget that data become information that can be turned into metrics. It is those metrics that you must analyze in order to take the right actions.

# Intelligence

# 9

## CHAPTER CONTENTS

> "If you know the enemy and know yourself, you need not fear the result of a hundred battles. If you know yourself but not your enemy, for every victory gained you will also suffer a defeat. If you know neither the enemy nor yourself, you will succumb in every battle."
>
> **Sun Tzu**

Security intelligence is critical for a SOC to have in place. It is the single greatest tool that is used to help protect an organization's network. What is security intelligence as it relates to the protection of information technology and why do you need it?

Intelligence information can come from many different sources and is the process of gathering information, evaluating it, correlating and interpreting, and then disseminating it to decision makers or, in the case of the SOC, applying it to rules and tools that make it valuable.

There are arguably more than two types of intelligence, but I want here to break intelligence down into two simple types based on ultimate source.

First, you have reactive information gathered internally by fully evaluating system compromises, forensic examinations, malware analysis, and also by asking key questions and building metrics to explain an increase in successful security incidents or if there is some kind of trend underway. This information is typically more in line with traditional security and is a trailing or lagging indicator of something gone wrong. An absolute critical component to your intelligence program is that once you know something bad about one system, you can then go look for that same bad thing on all your other systems to see if there is more out there. You can "wash, rinse, repeat" this information over and over again and every time you find something new on your network you can go over it again and again.

Next you have proactive threat information or leading indicators. These typically are gained from external sources. This is information that is open source (OSINT), purchased information, or information gained by being a part of an organization that shares threat data. This is information that is gained from other organizations that may have already seen this activity but is advanced knowledge to you because you may not have known about it previously. These proactive methods employ the use of information from partners, suppliers, reputation, and trust databases. The intelligence information can be extracted from web pages, blogs, wikis, IRC chat sessions, search engines, phishing emails, open FTP sites and file sharing networks, P2P networks, newsgroups, online auctions, and many others. It is a move from a more tactical approach to a more strategic focus.

This is an approach that integrates intelligence analysis methods, tools, and processes proactively to address security risk in today's highly threatened environment. This is an equal part practical application of traditional Internet and network monitoring with applied intelligence analysis. Your SOC will need to perform advanced search strategies and pattern recognition techniques to identify, detect, and analyze actual and potential threats to your organization. The use of intelligence is uniquely able to protect an organization or enterprise as well as individuals and their identities. By identifying threats generated by criminals, predators, extremists, activists, insiders, and other blackhats, information can be collected and analyzed and actions can be taken toward the prevention and mitigation of security risks.

By using these two types of intelligence, you can create a new form of warning system or warning intelligence. This is collective information that can alert you to emerging threats and can be inputs to your risk management system. For example, if you know of a piece of malware that is taking advantage of an exploitable bug in software you run on a critical system, but were not able to patch previously, you may be able to do something about it now knowing your risk may be increased. Some of the warning intelligence is a bit of a no brainer. For example, if you are seeing nine out of 10 of the latest malware variants taking advantage of holes in Adobe Flash, then perhaps you should make sure that all Adobe Flash players on your network are up to date to mitigate that threat. Other times it may not be so obvious, but knowing how a specific malware family works may help you dial-in to effective mitigations. A good example is how the Blackhole exploit kit works. I don't want to get into too many technical details here, but it's worth a quick look.

A user who visits a web page hosting the Blackhole exploit kit becomes compromised. How this works is simply that JavaScript quickly determines via a vulnerability scan what applications and versions of those applications, such as Adobe Flash or Acrobat, Microsoft Office, or Internet Explorer are on the user's computers and loads exploits to which it thinks the computer is vulnerable to and tries to exploit those applications. Once the computer is compromised, it will download further malware. Your intelligence research may yield you two things: first is a list of known domains and links that are hosting the exploit kit. If you are able to load up those domains into a SIEM or other log management system or build rules around the domains in other tools, then anyone on your monitored network going to those domains will be spotted and you can react appropriately. Second, you may discover that there is a loose pattern around how the domain names are built or what the links are and you can build a regular expression rule to catch anyone going to a URL matching that pattern. In this case, you may have a high degree of false positives; but, if you correlate that information with antivirus logs, you may be able to detect the exploit activity to some degree of success. Short of having a rock solid intrusion detection rule built and deployed on your network, this is a great example of how multiple pieces of intelligence can be used to build an effective warning system. Getting this information, digesting it, and being able to use it in an innovative way to protect your organization is just another way your SOC will provide continuing value and remain relevant.

The previous example seems fairly straightforward. You can argue the effectiveness or the accuracy and by the time this book is printed, the exploit example may be old news, but the point remains the same. Your effective use of intelligence information will go a long way to protect your organization. In that pursuit, you also always need to keep in mind the quality of the intelligence you receive from outside sources and ensure that the information is accurate and as complete as possible. You also should make sure that the information you are getting is timely and that it's real. Timely may not be that big of a deal if it's ongoing and valid data, but depending on what you are dealing with you need to make sure your information is as accurate as possible. A good example of this is in one SOC where I worked. The thinking at the time was that creating a massive MD5 database of all known good and bad files would help to make things much more secure. You can block the known bad or only let the known good execute or both. There are plenty of tools and hash databases out there to help you with this as well. The National Software Reference Library is a good example of where you can get this type of data (http://www.nsrl.nist.gov/). I am not going to tell you that MD5 hashing is good or bad, but as an example of inaccurate intelligence, this MD5 system will choke you. You see, the SOC was putting so much time and effort into creating MD5 hash databases that a good hash got into the bad hash system. There obviously was a process step missing to validate information and the quality of the intelligence that was being fed into the database. Unfortunately, the bad hash database was preventing any files from executing on participating systems that matched the bad hash list, essentially creating an execution black list. The hash that was incorrectly inserted into the database was a key file needed to run the endpoint antivirus software, which essentially caused a shutdown of antivirus on all the workstations and laptop systems on the network. HaHaHa, very funny, well let your imagination run wild a bit and see how badly this error could have impacted an organization's operation such as a hospital or power plant. Again, I am not saying that MD5 hashing is a bad idea, but this example shows you how bad intelligence fed into the wrong system can have very negative impacts. Make sure you have high quality of data and that you have the right processes and procedures to validate and test that data.

You need to know the quality of the intelligence you are receiving and also need to do some evaluation of that information as you apply it to your tools. Change management in this case becomes a very important function that your SOC needs to engage not only internally but also with the remainder of the IT organization on an ongoing and regular basis.

When one of your SOC analysts or engineers generates intelligence information internally, using your tools, that information should be considered both highly reliable and trusted, especially if they are following internal SOC processes to develop that information. If you get some intelligence from a magazine, newspaper, TV, or some random blog site, then its source and reliability may not be of such high quality. Information Security Intelligence is very fast moving, and can change in seconds. You are not always able to get verification of information from multiple sources, thus you have to trust the original source as much as possible and do the right thing with the information. Good intelligence information can include IP addresses, domain names, strings found inside an executable, and file hashes but these elements can be highly volatile or they may stick around for a while. Whether you generate your own intelligence information, purchase it, or get it for free, keep in mind that the more generic your information, the more false positives you likely will have; but, at the same time, intelligence that is too specific will not be agile enough to spot minor variations in your applied data.

Security intelligence is a constantly growing collection of information from outside sources (know thy enemy) and from within your own organization (know thyself).

## KNOW THYSELF

Adversaries are constantly changing their tactics, techniques and procedures (TTP). SOCs need information related to these new TTPs to ensure their tools are configured properly to see and/or stop the attacks the adversaries are making or be able to detect malware coming into the environment. By collecting all usable information from every incident, performing forensics, network analysis, malware analysis, and discovering new ways to better detect those events is intelligence you build yourself. They all are part of the "know yourself" side of the equation. But that is only part of the battle, you need to know how your network is configured, how your desktops and servers are hardened and protected, what active directory group policies are applied, and how your networking infrastructure—such as routers and switches—are managed. As stated before, if your organization has a mature IT department, your SOC also need to be a part of change management and have access to asset management tools. SOCs need to know what systems are doing on the network, what is their purpose, who put them there, and who must be contacted if there are questions or issues. This may appear like a lot, but it is basic information that helps the SOC determine if there are issues or if they are just chasing ghosts. It also helps the remainder of the IT organization because the SOC is not typically involved in building infrastructure. Thus, when there is an issue, the SOC will need to call people from IT to get answers instead of being able to help themselves. For example, just knowing that a specific server is a database server such as MySQL may be very helpful to a SOC instead … of guessing it is a web server that an attacker just compromised.

Having access to an asset management system goes a long way for an organization like a SOC in the "know thyself" part of the equation.

There are several places from which an organization can obtain intelligence. The type of information you can use depends on the level of sophistication in your SOC and the tools you have deployed. Information such as honey-pot-captured payloads may be used to create your own IDS or you can even find already-built signatures to try. Sometimes you can find IDS or scan logs of large sensor networks that can indicate trends you may want to search for on your network. Intelligence related to denial of service attacks (DoS) statistics may prove helpful if you can translate the information into something with which you can tune your devices to protect against or detect. Of course, there is also a wealth of information out there regarding general security news and vulnerability reports. These are helpful for noting how your organization is effected or protected and can even help prioritize needed upgrades or remediation issues. Captured malware samples are good to see trends and test your anti-virus tools to ensure you are properly protected. Phishing infrastructure and sample data is good to use to help tune your spam filters and prevent these types of email messages from getting to you users. Also botnet command and control data are fantastic intelligence data that you can use to check if systems on your network are talking to known bad servers.

Let us get into a bit more detail and describe what you can do with this information, how you can benefit, and perhaps even spark some ideas for you. Getting information and finding good sources of information are the first steps. But, be sure you evaluate the information you find and ensure you can build a valuable use case for that information. Being an intelligence hoarder does not sound like a bad idea, but collecting information for the sake of having it will only overwhelm you and your tools. You need to make sure you have the right information to achieve your goals.

The information you collect should all be actionable; then your actionable threat intelligence must be optimized for collection, analysis, and delivery.

When building an intelligence component of your SOC, you must gather, correlate, and aggregate events from across many different threat vectors and then apply them appropriately to the tools you have. Then you need to focus on how to present the information in a way that provides context and relevance. The intelligence information will then provide you situational awareness and actionable data and give you the visibility you need to protect your organization or begin your incident response and notification processes. In order to make this work in your SOC environment, you need to ensure your events are properly correlated and aggregated into incidents that matter to your organization and to organize the threat landscape to provide situational awareness. Then, as discussed in other chapters, your incidents will then be prioritized by relevance and severity for incident response actions and remediation efforts.

*Key point*: Sometimes intelligence information can come in the form of a single string or thousands of IP addresses. Your SOC should work to automate as much as possible: automate the collecting of the information and the application of the data. Scripts can update different tools or software and in some cases can be created by the SOC team.

The following are examples of current intelligence feeds that your SOC can use in its tools arsenal to help combat such things as advance persistence threat and common botnets, but also the more common financial cybercrime and identity theft.

## KNOWN IP SPACE, KNOW THY ENEMY

A quick search on the Internet can get you lists of IP addresses by country. This information may not appear like very useful cyber intelligence, but blocking as much IP space as possible is always a good way to start protecting your network. The SOC should always be aware of what IP space an organization does not need to allow access. If there are specific countries with which you do not work, then shut out their IPs from connecting to your network. There may be IP addresses from countries or locations you are unsure of and can't block, by identifying these IPs you can put them on watch lists and see what they do. There are also lists of other classifications of IP addresses you may be interested in watching. Known proxy IPs, VPN networks, and transient DHCP networks may also be of interest to you. By classifying these external IP addresses, you can categorize the connection information and begin to build some intelligence from them.

There are also many other types of bad-IP lists that your SOC can use to give you greater fidelity into what may be going on with your network or hosts in your organization. Known spamming IPs … botnet network IPs … there are also many different block lists of IP addresses that have done various bad things for which you may want to be on the alert. These lists can get more and more fine-tuned as you get into it and as you find them. There are also various intelligence exchange networks that you can become join. These exchanges can offer you IP reputational databases that are updated in real time and tell you of bad-acting addresses. This can help you find internal IP addresses that may be communicating with known Command and Control (C&C or C2) servers. These C2 servers may be master consoles of botnet or zombie networks and if you discover internal systems communicating with them, you have some incident response and possible forensic work to do. The exchange also may be able to give you information that will help you spot peer to peer (P2P) botnet activity. P2P activity can be very difficult to spot on your network and any information or intelligence about the different botnets out there can only help.

Various companies and the open source community have installed several honey-pot networks. These honey pots collect information about attacks and probes and then publishes that information for you to consume and use to help protect your network. One such honey pot watches and monitors how data is stolen or exfiltrated from a network. This server network allows an attacker to compromise the server systems and then watches what the attackers do to remove data from the network. The attackers are observed using the normal web protocols of HTTP, FTP, SSH, or they even just email the information to themselves. An attacker will use these methods as well as more covert data transfers like DNS or ICMP. This by no means covers all the ways an attacker can steal data, but the important thing is that this information can be observed and valuable intelligence can be gained from watching the actions of the attackers. This information can then be shared in the cyber defense community and be used by your SOC further to advance the capabilities of the tools deployed in your organization's network to detect this type of activity.

Another such intelligence database focuses on malware. I am not talking about an antivirus database or how antivirus software detects malware but something even more. This database catalogs the network exploit packets, which are the actual packets that are seen on the network that indicate a system has been compromised. These packets are sometimes too sophisticated for intrusion detection and need advanced correlation between DNS requests and web proxy URL requests to be seen properly. Additionally, this database can be used to help spot how the C2 connection appears on the network. Sometimes a system will only send one packet or beacon of information to a peer or central server to register itself to the botnet network. This is like looking for a needle in a haystack. If you employ the information from the malware database properly, however, then you ultimately will be more successful and prepared when that one packet of information gets transferred. You may think this information is fairly static, but if you look at the statistics from any of the major antivirus vendors regarding the number of new malware entered into the wild every day, you easily will realize that this is a large set of information with which to deal. Over the last year or so I have seen this information grow and change to the point where there are 400 new communication strings and hosts a day that a SOC needs to be aware of and track.

# BLACKLISTS

A few years back, a new tool in the network defense arsenal started popping up. Blacklists containing information about IP addresses that exhibited poor behavior started growing. Each blacklist created focused on a different thing in an effort to differentiate themselves. These lists ranged from spamming IP addresses to websites hosting malware. Many lists were created to track spammers and some lists have not survived over the years, but there are a few out there that are worth a look.

Most commercial vendors, spam filters, and web proxy companies will use these blacklists as well. It is important for a SOC to be aware of them in case they need to further apply specific lists that their tools may not be utilizing or if there are technical reasons why they want to apply the information in a different way or with different tools.

As with what I mentioned before, the biggest lists contain IP addresses of systems that have been seen sending various types of spam. But others also include information on universal resource identifiers (URI) that are typically seen inside of phishing emails that entice a user to click a link. Email can easily be spoofed so the true sender may never be known and mail servers from which the messages are sent can change rapidly, but the link the attacker wants a user to visit will change less frequently. By adding this type of intelligence to your tool set, you will be adding one more piece of information that will help you see when something bad goes wrong on your organizations network.

As mentioned before, knowing what IP addresses are operating as a proxy can be an important piece of intelligence information. There are free and open public block lists that are dedicated to tracking IP addresses that are being used for this purpose. Some lists track IP addresses that are purposefully operating as a proxy such as IPs that are on the onion routing (TOR) network, but there are also lists that actively go out and scan systems looking for those that are open proxies where the owner may not know they are being used to proxy network traffic. The use of this information can be invaluable, for example, knowing that an IDS attack is coming from a proxy's IP address helps you validate the malicious intent of the traffic.

Phishing has become one of the most effective vectors for attackers these days. The way the attackers can entice a user to click a link to open an email attachment is nothing short of genius. We as security professionals have to hand it to our advisories, they really do their homework and have studied our users, their habits, and what will get unsuspecting users to click on something. I mean, why play the lottery when there is a general in Nigeria hiding from political prosecution that we can help out for a few million bucks, that is worth it, do not you think? Or how about those loveable cats, who can resist a few pictures of a few cute cats, I know I cannot. What about when our bank emails us to tell us there has been fraud on our account, are not we concerned about that? When I get those emails I click the link right away! But I am not looking to get what they want to give me, instead I want their malware, their domains, their IP addresses and everything and anything I can get from their miserable attempt to compromise our organization's users. There are several phishing databases and working groups that can help you spot when a user is in trouble. But first you have to understand the problem we want to solve. Phishing is a simple-to-understand concept, but at the same time takes a complex technical execution to make it work. Phishing attacks use both social engineering and technical knowhow to achieve the attackers goals. Social-engineering schemes use "spoofed" e-mails to lead users to counterfeit websites designed to trick people into giving out information that they should not, such as company financial data, credit card numbers, account usernames, passwords, and social security numbers. You need to keep in mind that phishing is always a multi-stage attack. What I mean is that it does not stop with an email, it only starts with the email and then further advances via malware and then unfortunately attacker activity on the compromised system.

This is not your regular run of the mill spam. Phishing or even spear phishing (the practice of sending malicious emails to senior executives) takes finesse, skill, and a command of the language of the people that may be targeted. I say language because this is not specifically an American or English problem, instead, depending on who you are and where you are this may be a criminal problem, advanced persistent threat, or a money-making venture for the attackers. So whether or not you are in the United States, United Kingdom, Australia, Germany, Japan, Italy, or somewhere else that has money, you are a target. Years ago it was easy to spot spam or emails that contained viruses because the spelling of the worlds in the email was so horribly wrong that you would just delete it without a second thought. These days' emails are "spoofed" to look like they are from people you know, they are written in the same voice or tone that you would expect and contain information in which you may be interested. In some cases, the email accounts of your friends, coworkers, colleagues, or associates are compromised and used further to send out malicious emails to you as well as others. This is not like the viruses of old either where the virus automatically would send or email itself to the first 50 people in your contact list, but instead the attackers would handcraft these emails to users you may typically email but include malicious attachments of documents in which they may also be interested. This all makes spotting the bad messages much harder for the end users. So knowing all, this how would you stop it, slow it down, or detect when it is going on? That is something for your SOC to work on and is an invaluable service that you can offer the organization that you serve.

Because email addresses can be changed and spoofed, the addresses themselves are not reliable … so blocking will not work. Even if you are sure that bad emails are coming from a specific address, that address is easily changed. Not only are these attributes easily changed, but they can be changed as frequently as each email so that you cannot spot a common pattern of these messages so you would be able to add to a rule to block them. But there is still hope, as we have discussed before, there is intelligence to which you can subscribe that may help open up a wealth of information that will help you spot this activity without using email attributes.

Going back to the example we had before, what if we knew the links that were bad and were being included in the emails that were being sent out? We can protect our users in several ways with this information. First we can block those domains and make sure that if a user goes to that URL or domain that it's blocked. Second, when a user does go to that URL it sets off an alarm that the SOC can respond to and ensure that not only the access was blocked but that no harm came to the computer or the network. Then an investigation can take place to see what emails were sent that got the user to click and some internal intelligence can be gained and used to further strengthen the SOC's tool sets.

Several open source intelligence databases are available to aid in this effort and can be used as real-time sources of information to either block users from accessing or to import into other tools such as your log management system to detect when a user clicks a link. But again, when you use this as a detection method it's a lagging indicator, meaning the event already happened by the time the SOC gets to it so you are in reactive mode. You job is then to only ensure that no harm came to the end user and that there are no other emails or events of significance for which you need to search. As stated before, the phishing is only the first part of the attack; if successful, then you may see password dumping, privilege escalation, and eventually data exfiltration. Ultimately, your SOC has many opportunities to detect and prevent this type of activity and protect the network.

As a side note, this may differ from your experiences but as a rule you may want to use the number five as a magic number. What I mean is that when you are investigating attacks such as this, they rarely ever happen as a single instance. When you spot something, use the Rule of Five, which means that when one thing happens look for at least four more. You may find that with specific malicious emails they operate in campaigns of multiple victims of either a specific group of employees, all the people in one specific department, or several people who are part of a project team but otherwise are not associated inside a company. Once you are able to discover who, if any, are the other people in your organization receiving the same malicious email, then you may be able to draw a conclusion as to how the attacker got those email addresses. This information can then lead you to a completely different compromise of another system or data. Further, this also can help you develop some great indicators or internally generated intelligence information. For example, your SOC may be able to create a rule that when the same five people get the same email, send an alert for an analyst to investigate to see if it is indeed legitimate or another attack.

Certainly to fight this battle there is nothing more powerful, more effective and beneficial in the field of information security then user-based security awareness. Security professionals have fought this battle with users time and time, again but organizations struggle to secure their computers and networks while users fall prey to these phishing tactics. So, while technology and intelligence plays an important role in doing so, end user education is vital to securing your organization and you need to make sure your SOC is educating users at every opportunity it can.

I know that this is a chapter on intelligence, but this seems like a good time to mention user intelligence, meaning how do we make the user smarter. We have to face it at some point, because it's not a matter of if we will be compromised by a phishing email, but rather when. When we talk about educating our users, we should not just focus on one specific area such as phishing, but rather give them a broad range of topics to think about that can help the organization become more secure. Topics that you may want to include are things like password safety and security, how to store passwords, not sharing passwords, and that tech support will never ask you for your password. Remember that social engineering does not always come in the form of email, but may be a phone call. Users are accustomed to multitasking, so you need to hammer in the concept that they are not to give out their password under any circumstance. Additionally, you obviously want to focus on email safety and giving them the tools to be able to detect current trends in phishing, scams, spam, abuse, and harassment types of email messages. You also may want to educate your users consistently on your organization's acceptable use policy. This will help users to understand better the dos and don'ts of the organization and how to steer clear of trouble.

You can have too many resources in your SOC, but chances are that you will never have enough. In order to increase your effectiveness as a security organization, not only do you need to use effective intelligence as we are describing here, but also you need to employ your users to be an extension of your SOC and educate them on what to look for and how to properly escalate and report malicious behavior so that you can engage effectively and efficiently to prevent any damage to the organization.

Phishing intelligence is very broad and there are many lists to which you can subscribe that will give you very good information. There are even a few lists out there that are actually master lists that they include information from several lists in one easily formatted location. But, again, you have to think about how you are going to use these lists and what they means to you. In some cases, these lists will include the domain or the IP address where the hosted phishing site is located, but your web proxy vendor may already know that information and will very quickly block access to that site before your users go to that link. Is it enough for you silently to block that nugget of information? If it were my organization's network, I would want to know that a user clicked on a bad link so that I can investigate how and why and if there are any other systemic issues I may need to address or remediate. So, your tools may be configured properly to block the link in a phishing email and your alert system may be configured properly to notify you when a link is clicked, but what you do next is really up to you. In the case of an efficient and mature SOC, I usually will want to run this to the ground, meaning that I will investigate it until I find the original email or website that was sent or viewed and all the users to whom the phishing email was sent. I say this is for mature a SOC only because new security organizations typically will not have time to chase down failed or blocked incidents and should focus on more specific threats that require immediate attention. If possible, I will work to get the offending email, extract all the attributes from the email, and create new rules that in the future may help me detect this same activity or block it from happening again.

With a bit of focus back on open source intelligence, there are a few lists that you can find out there that give you a lot of the information in an easily formatted way that includes multiple data sources combined into a single list. What this means is that there may be several lists out there, but some are masters that deduplicate entries, domains, or subnets to give you a clean and efficient list that you can use for your tools.

Again, you do not want information just for the sake of information. You want to be efficient in the data that you collect and apply to your tools. As you collect more and more intelligence data, you will have to be very mindful not only of the false positive rate but also the sheer volume of information because your tools may not be able to handle the load. Ensuring you are not duplicating information or crating rules that max out your processing power will be a key to your success. As you look at generating lists that include phishing links you want to use, be certain you know what sub-lists they include and how they are gathering the information.

Although phishing may be your number one attack vector, it may not be your number one intelligence source or intelligence-based information to include in your tools. For years, we security practitioners have known some very obvious facts.

These are facts that are not able to change in the world of networking or the Internet. There are just some things that will always stay the same and the knowledge of these things can help us apply intelligence to our network defense systems and spot problem areas before they actually become a real problems. Sounds like something will really want to do right? Is it magic or is it reality?

## BLACK LISTING PROJECTS

To further the discussion on open source intelligence, we can review a few more focused projects that collect IP address, domain names, or URLs of known bad actors. Some of these also are lists you may want to generate yourself, as well. What I mean is that if you can see this type of activity on your own organization's network, then you can apply real-time actions in response to the activity and be proactive in your response, but also have it automated.

One such list that you may find out there captures and logs IP addresses that are seen performing brute force attacks. With the correct configuration and collection of logs, this is also a list you may be able to create for yourself. If an IP address somewhere on the Internet is tying administrative SSH logins and you can learn that information before that IP address tries it on your network, then that list may be of value to you. A simple tool that you may use to see if this happens on your devices is Logwatch. This tool reviews all your local logs and generates an email that summarizes activity on the devices. The tool is also able to store that information locally as well, if you want to parse the data further and script it into something that you can use elsewhere, such as block rules for your firewall.

These logs may look something like this:

(As is in common practice the "x" in the IP addresses are to obfuscate the real IPs because this is for example purposes only)

SSHD authentication failures:

root (182.62.x.x) 1388 Time(s)
root (80.91.x.x) 965 Time(s)
root (121.8.x.x) 220 Time(s)
root (203.122.x.x) 180 Time(s)

If Logwatch is not something you wish to deploy or you would like to have a sampling of IP addresses that are broader than what you are seeing on your network, then you can find SSH blacklists that include this information. You may also find blacklists of IP addresses that are trying administrative windows logins as well. The honeypot network is once such place where you can find this information. An attacking IP gets published on a blacklist, which is updated every few minutes and contains IP addresses of hosts that tried to brute force into any of the honeypots hosts. The honeypot hosts are located all around the world and are setup to report and log those attempts to a central database.

Again, if you are able to automate blocking of these IP addresses on your network, then this may be an extremely valuable exercise to try. In some cases, your organization's SOC may not have permission to implement automated IP blocking or even have access to modify firewalls. In this case, correlating logs from multiple sources may be very important.

If you are have firewall logs and are able to detect these IP addresses making a successful connection to your organizations network and are able to match that attempt up against a device log in your DMZ, then that may be something you want to know if the authentication is successful. A nice metric for later review may be a report showing the number of IP addresses from your list that attempted but failed to login, but also the total number of failed vs. successful (there should be none) login attempts. As mentioned in the metric chapter, this is a really valuable way to show how your SOC is implementing effective monitoring. Once the automation is in place, there should be no real effort to alert on successes and report on success and failure attempts on a regular basis.

By way of comparison to similar things that you may implement, typical installations of this type of list could see up to 7000 new IP addresses per hour become added. Because the number of IP addresses is so high, you may want to implement an expiration period where the IP address would automatically fall off of your list. I do not believe there is any hard and fast rule as to what is typical for how long you would want to keep using this data. Then, again, you will need to determine what the odds are that an IP address once seen performing a brute force attack of an administrative account across the Internet would no longer be a threat.

## OTHER TYPES OF LISTS

If you believed that an IP address had done something bad in the past, maybe even the most recent past such as just a few seconds ago, would not you want to know about it? This is where intelligence can play a key role in your overall security strategy. If you could have a lists of IP addresses that are likely to perform malicious behavior or have recently even been detected attempting SQL-injections attacks, DOS attacks, or any other confirmed type of behavior on someone else's network, what would you do with that information? I know that if I have that information, I can monitor it, respond to it, and most importantly prevent it from causing a problem on my system. The information is out there and available and open to the public, all you have to do is search for it.

Those are just a few examples, and I bet you would love for me to call out a few specific examples and give you a few types of places that you can get a lot of this intelligence information from. I do not like to endorse a product, website, or tool, but also want to be as helpful and complete as possible. Because these sites are providing free open source intelligence information, mentioning them here is a simple way of saying "Thank You." Again, as mentioned many times before, please evaluate this information for you own use. You may find it a great starting point, invaluable data, or not for you. Any or all of the possibilities are fine because this includes free publicly available websites that regularly publish trends and emerging threat information. Organizations freely publish information for several reasons: For one, vendors publish security relevant information from their own products to help protect their customers, but also to help market the power of their products. This information includes announcements of security relevant patches or bugs and how to resolve those issues. Additionally, there are several organizations that like to publish limited general security intelligence to show off how their products work. Even though these are just small samples of intelligence, they can be incredible resources. There are many sites available with free IT security intelligence and here are a few examples to get you started:

- Atlas.arbor.com: Arbor has a product suite that actively monitors a customer's network and can identify many different types of security related traffic. The Atlas site is a public resource that provides intelligence derived from its own sensor network, as well as opt-in customer networks that provide data on host/port scanning activity, zero-day exploits and worm propagation, security events, vulnerability disclosures, and dynamic botnet and phishing infrastructures.
- Senderbase.org: SenderBase is a website with data from Cisco's IronPorts network that collects information on email traffic and gives a view into email-based security threats. Organizations can use this site to research reputation scores on specific domains or IP addresses or even use the top 100 spammers report to block or report on spam email for their own organization.
- securityfocus.com: A community driven website that contains information on vulnerabilities, exploits, and emerging threats. It is also the home for BugTraq, where typically all new vulnerabilities are announced and discussed. There are also several mailing lists that you can join that contain a wide array of security topics to keep your SOC up to date on security issues.
- ThreatExpert.com: This site gives you the ability to post suspicious files and have them analyzed to obtain a report if the files are a computer viruses, worm, trojan, adware, spyware, and other security-related risks in a fully automated way. The site also provides interesting reports on other samples and is a good resource when looking for intelligence to add to your systems.
- Spamhaus.org: Spamhaus is a non-profit organization that has been around for many years and includes several spam lists and blacklists. I highly recommend you visit this site and review the many lists it has to determine how you may benefit from its information. Specifically, its XBL list contains good information on known IP addresses performing exploits in real-time.

## ORGANIZATIONS AND INDUSTRY PARTNERS

Paid-for and purchased intelligence services can be a bit more focused and tailored to your organization and even provide you relevant information regarding security issues and attacks across your industry. More specifically, these types of services can help you monitor your name and brand on the Internet. If your organization is worried about unauthorized use of your brand in domain names or phishing emails, paid-for intelligence services can help by monitoring for this type of activity and alerting you to any issues. They also can watch for unauthorized disclosures of corporate information in blogs, message boards, social networking, and other online areas and alert you before any damage can occur. Additionally, some of the paid-for intelligence services, like the open source services, can provide advanced information regarding IP addresses of known bad servers, websites, or where malware is being stored on the Internet so that you can configure your tools to keep users away from those places.

Other paid-for services may give you much more details that just IP addresses. Depending on the intelligence you are looking for, these services can provide you in-depth analysis on attacker groups and help you understand who these people are that are attacking your networks and what they seek. By understanding a bit about these groups, you can further asses the risk you have, ensure your security systems are deployed in the right place to protect against the areas they want to attack, and, if their habits change, your paid-for intelligence service may be able to provide you with that information as well.

These services also work very hard to provide real value in the intelligence they are selling. Some companies perform reverse engineering on malware and gain very detailed understandings of what the malware is designed to do, how it's doing it, and in some cases who programed it. This detailed intelligence information is key to finding and remediating threats such as the advanced persistent threat (APT). APT is the name typically given to very skillful, well-funded, and sometimes nation-state supported attackers. The groups that make up APT understand technology very well, they understand their target very well, and they also understand how to circumvent security controls and avoid detection. This is largely due to the fact that APT uses all the same tools your organization uses, except instead of using all those security tools to protect their network, they use them to test out all their attack tools and ensure they can sneak in to your network undetected. Furthermore, they know how to beat most all antivirus tools. Because of this, it is very important that when you find any evidence of APT activity or APT malware that you analyze it as fully as possible. These paid-for intelligence services can do that for you, but can also share information with you regarding other types of APT attacks and malware they have seen. They can provide you information that not only contains MD5 hashes of files, but what windows registry keys typically get changed or added. They may be able to tell you what to look for in running memory of a system that is exhibiting odd behavior. Other valuable information they may be able to provide include services, ports that may be running on a compromised systems, or even what special strings in packets a system may be sending to remote C2 servers. So, for example, an intelligence service may be able to give you all the relevant components of a post-attack analysis and attribution information. This could be explained through a series of indications that match up to a certain group.

So, if a particular registry key is changed while at the same time a new service is running on a precise port number and is sending a string of "A(j@@7" to what would seem like random IP addresses or domains on the Internet, then this is known as an "xyz attack" and is attributable to "xyz gang." Make sure that if you subscribe to any of these services, your SOC has the right tools in place to use the information and find the bad guys on your organization's infrastructure.

Industry organizations are arguably one of the best places for security intelligence. It has been shown repeatedly that security attacks across an industry usually have the same or very similar characteristics. By sharing security information with partners and competitors, you can see very quickly who or what is targeting your industry and use that information to see if you have also been targeted and use that information to configure your tools to prevent those attacks from being successful. An organization such as an Information Sharing and Analysis Centers (ISAC) is a great place to participate and share. A review of the National Council of ISAC[1] will help you learn if there is an organization out there for you and should help to put you in touch with the right people to begin. Constant participation by industry organizations allows for the gathering of reliable and timely security intelligence information from industry partners, but also other organizations that may have been invited to join the community such as commercial security firms, government agencies, law enforcement, and other trusted resources. Typically in these types of organizations, information is not just one way; they operate quickly to disseminate threat alerts and other critical information to you as a member. The information often not only includes IP addresses and malware analysis, but can also include recommended solutions and protections from leading security experts in your industry. These organizations are built on trust and are very careful to not expose individual organizations information publicly or attribute information to a single entity in any way. The generic sharing of information is based on trust. Normally, industry members of these information-sharing organizations will sign non-disclosure agreements (NDA) with each other. The NDAs help to enforce rules, such as all sharing by default is non-attribution and cannot be shared outside of the sharing organization without permission from the original data owner. These organizations also will have standardized and reliable procedures for submitting and distributing information and will even regularly exercise critical notification processes to ensure everything is working.

If there are no industry groups that appear to match up with your business, you can also look at participating with a local chapter of ISACA. These are local groups usually sponsored by or run by the local or regional branch of the FBI. Depending on your area, you will see different levels of value in this group, but it can never hurt to partner with a law enforcement agency that thrives on the collection and analysis of intelligence data.

---

[1]http://www.isaccouncil.org

# PROACTIVE ACTIVITY MONITORING

Security intelligence information is a critical ingredient to the SOC and invaluable in the efforts to protect your organization's network. The SOC needs to work hard to know what is "normal," whether network traffic is normal or not, and what the "normal" processes and files are on an end-user computer. A network, its configuration, traffic patterns, and the hosts that reside on it need to be as quiet and stable as possible. Similar to how ballistic gel works, when something goes wrong, the SOC needs to be able to see clearly into what happened and determine all the attributes necessary to make an assessment on its threat and risk to the organization. Although user monitoring does not appear like intelligence, information it can be the most effective key to alerting your SOC that something just went horribly wrong. Similar to the lists of IP addresses discussed previously, a list of system administrators or privileged accounts on your organization's network is critical. If you are able to use that information against administrative functions being performed on the network, you will be able quickly to see problems. For example, when a user with administrative permissions logs into a system that houses users account information, that occurrence can be matched up with your administrative user account list to ensure that user is on the administrative-permissions list. If they are not on the list, then either an attacker got onto a system and was able to elevate the user permissions or someone else gave an employee administrative permissions when they should not have. Of course, if it is a legitimate employee then it is less of an issue, but can still be a violation of security procedures or policy and in any case would be important to detect.

I bring these examples up now because all along we have been discussing the type of intelligence you can get from outside sources that are in the form of distinct data elements that you can use to find indications of malicious activity. But that does not always need to be the case. In many instances, intelligence can be in the form of logical rules that help detect behavior indicative of malicious behavior. Building intelligent rules may be your best defense; nobody is going to give you a list of 900,000 IP addresses that just participated in the last distributed denial of service attack (DDOS). Instead, an intelligence rule that can detect what a DDOS looks like on the firewall allows you to spot trouble the second it happens and respond to appropriately. In the SOC world, or security world, for that matter, real-time detection and appropriate response are activities we live by. It is impossible to think that the SOC can stop all attacks or even stop all successful attacks. Sometimes the best we can hope for is to see a successful attack and be able to respond to it quickly and avoid any residual negative effect of the attack such as data loss.

If you are at the phase of maturity in building your SOC where you are active in these intelligence organizations and are leveraging the information you are receiving, you should have a realization that you will never build a big enough SOC to combat the enemy. By participating in consistent collection of reliable intelligence from a range of free and paid subscriptions; and government, industry, and internal sources will allow you effectively to create a force multiplier for your organization. It will give you a more complete picture of what your advisories are doing, what their motivations may be and you will be able to categorize their activities. Focusing on these areas will allow you to fuse the information together in order to develop actionable intelligence from all these sources and then feed it back into your tools. This will keep you focused, fresh, and make you as proactive as you can be and allow you to be more precise in your defense in depth strategies against any evolving threats. Lastly, you will see your overall security improve at a more cost-effective rate.

# Outsourcing

# 10

## CHAPTER CONTENTS

Outsourcing is an interesting discussion topic as there are many different aspects and opinions on it. Certainly contracting to a third party to perform some business function is not new and neither is IT outsourcing, and outsourcing security has been around for a little while as well but that does not mean outsourcing vendors have worked out all the kinks to be able to support all the businesses of the world. For people that have never outsourced, there can be a huge barrier to trying it and an even bigger challenge trying it with their IT security. For those that are more comfortable with outsourcing and have had success with it before will ultimately find it easier to transition security functions to an outsourcer but that does not ensure success. In this chapter, we are going to discuss what outsourcing security operations looks like, its challenges as well as its benefits but we are also going to make comparisons with building it on your own and keeping the functions in-house and what the success factors are of each. Although it may seem that when you outsource you are relinquishing the burden of security to a third party but keep in mind that if there is a significant compromise or a material breach the impact is not at the third party, it is still at your organization and you will be effected. Therefore, you really need to think about what you are doing and what your goals are. Whether or not you are building a SOC internally, going to outsource or some hybrid variation, you should make sure you are comfortable with your goals and the success criteria you are going to use for either situation.

First, let us define what outsourcing security operations mean so that we are on the same page because there are a lot of different names and understandings. We have to make sure that when we look at outsourcing operations we are not mixing it up with other functions.

A company that offers security services may also offer what is called MSS, this makes that company a provider of MSS or what is known as a MSSP. Security operations outsourcing is not the management of a device or specific consulting services. So, for example, although a company may offer MSS, if all you purchase from them is an external penetration or vulnerability test then you are not outsourcing your operations, you are just purchasing a single service or what is sometimes called a professional service. In the definition of outsourcing operations that we use here, to an MSSP you must contract with the company to provide at a minimum, ongoing operational functions such as tier 1 or 2 security analysis along with the additional possibility for management of your internal IDS, firewalls, antivirus or any other security relevant devices in an operational function. There are a lot of ways to slice and dice operations and you can contract with an MSSP for almost any portion of your operations. From remote perimeter management and security monitoring with incident response to penetration testing and ongoing vulnerability management with system patching. This can also include added value services like fraud detection, intelligence services and more.

There are a number of very significant advantages to outsourcing your security to an MSSP. The advantages are so significant that you really need to think twice about building a SOC yourself. But of course if it were so easy to just outsource all this security stuff I would not have too much to write about in this book. After being on both sides of the equation, meaning running large MSSPs and buying services from them, I can tell you that in order for you and the MSSP to be successful you have to have some level of responsibility for security inside your own organization and be a good partner with the MSSP all at the same time. It is not realistic to think you can turn all security functions over to an external company and be done with it unless you are going to contract for services to be internal to your organization as well. That does not mean you still need to have a full blown internal SOC but you still will need some level of internal security functions and the balance of what you need will be dependent on what you outsource, how secure your organization needs to be and how sensitive you are to combating security treats.

# TYPES OF MSSPs

There are several types of MSSPs that you can choose from and the specific kind will depend on your overall technology strategy, your financial situation, and your tolerance for risk. Because there are different types of MSSPs, there may be significant advantages of one over the other just in how they deliver their services. For example, some communications providers may be able to provide managed security in the cloud before issues even get to your network. Need more visibility then you may want a more hands on approach using your own equipment but want external experts to manage them.

## STRATEGIC PARTNERS

In the case of strategic partners, your organization may already have an established relationship with an outsourcer or provider of professional services in the IT industry. This provider may already have a good working relationship with your company or organization and can provided some of the managed security services you are looking for. This can make things really easy since you are already using their services and have experience with them then it is just a matter of adding to what is already there. Keep in mind that since this type of MSSP is involved in other areas, their security service may not be as strong as other services they provide. They may employ some key experts and do a great job but their breadth of services and capabilities may not fully match with what you need. This does not mean you should shy away from using them, just make sure you understand what you need opposed to what they can provide.

## PURE PLAY PROVIDERS

For a pure play provider, security is all they do. They live and breathe security services and are constantly looking for new and innovative ways to provide their services or enhance their capabilities. Security is definitely their core competency and the price of their service may reflect that. If you are looking for a complete turnkey solution to manage your security and reduce your risk, then look at these types of providers. Chances are they will provide much more than you could over hope for to protect your interests.

## BOUTIQUE PROVIDERS

Smaller MSSPs that look to fill very special market gaps are great to look at if you are concerned with very specific issues. You could find MSSPs for example that just manage endpoint security, this is especially useful if you have having problems with data loss, users and overall patching of systems. Use these types of providers as strategic tools to solve a specific problem but do not be upset when they will not scale as you grow or be able to provide other services you may need or want.

Later we will discuss other factors that differentiate different MSSPs that you will have to choose from. Ultimately you need to make sure that the provider you pick will perform the services you want, the way you want them, and that they are a good cultural fit for your organization.

Here is a quick chart detailing some of the services you may be able to contract with an MSSP for, these are a security focus as there may be many other services that are offered but may be more IT specific:

| Service | Quick Description |
| --- | --- |
| Security monitoring | Monitoring of security relevant logs from devices such as IDS and firewall. Analyze system logs to detect anomalies, detect attacks and escalate issues. |
| Compliance auditing | Ongoing auditing of an organizations security policy, PCI controls or SOX, HIPPA, GLB, or other industry or government regulatory control. |
| Vulnerability assessment | Scanning of the internal network on a regular basis and provide reports on known vulnerabilities. May include a patch service to address all security relevant or application required software updates. |
| Managed network services | Monitoring of network performance and responding to outages or denial of service attacks. May also include management of organizations VPN, backups, web hosting, or other core networking services. |
| Managed email | Management of email specifically to reduce junk messages and malware. |
| Managed antivirus/malware protection | Management of antivirus infrastructure and endpoint systems to ensure clients stay up to date and detected issues are escalated properly. |
| Anti-botnet | Specific services to detect internal or remote endpoints that may be participating in botnets. |
| Managed storage/log collection | The collection of logs from specific systems as required by regulatory controls and made availablezfor specific periods of time. May also include off site data back-up and disaster recovery (DR) storage. |
| Denial of service identification and remediation | Quick detection and rerouting of network resources to eliminate impact of attacks. |

| Service | Quick Description |
|---|---|
| Threat intelligence | Advanced analysis and distribution of relevant and emerging threat information. Can include information derived from "Zero day" attack detection, proof of concepts and forensic analysis. |
| Web application scanning/ monitoring | Ongoing scanning and analysis of application to detect flaws before they become vulnerabilities that someone could take advantage of. |
| Identity management | Managing an identity management system that provisions or de-provisions user accounts from needed resources. |

# ADVANTAGES OF MSSP OUTSOURCING

## MSSP SOC in action

7:35 p.m. EST, all is quiet. The only sounds are the whirls of computer fans, a faint hum of a video projector, and someone quietly tapping on a keyboard. The blue glow of computer screens in contrast to the backdrop of 8-ft video walls displayed up and down rows of the security operations center is the only real lighting in the room. It is peaceful and quite, almost makes you want to put your feet up and take a nap.

7:36 p.m. EST, an event comes in to the SOC ticketing system labeled critical. A tier-1 analyst looks at the event and sees that it is an alarm from a customer's firewall that was correlated by the SOC's threat engine and details a security event that shows the device just processed 10,000 drops. Subsequent events start to come in, all with the same information, 10,000 then 50,000, then 100,000 and more.

The tier-1 analyst quickly notifies the senior engineer on duty that a potential denial of service is taking place on a customer's network. The engineer then looks at the data the analyst provided and immediately confirms the findings. The engineer then engages a SOC communication analyst to notify the customer and open a critical phone bridge. The communication analyst then sends out the details of the phone bridge to the customer, SOC management and the security intelligence engineers on staff. Meanwhile, details of the event are passed on to all the rest of the tier-1 analysts in the SOC to be on the lookout for similar activity at other customers and an immediate performance impact assessment is taken.

Security engineers analyze network traffic and with the help of a security intelligence engineer they apply signatures down to the customers network to block the known attack vectors. As the actions are being performed the communication analyst verbalizes the actions on the phone bridge and relays any customer-determined impact to the SOC team.

Then on behalf of the customer, the SOC engineer engages the customers Internet provider and alerts their network operations center of the ongoing activity. The SOC and the provider monitor the attack and any changes due to the mitigations the SOC put in place. Noticing changes in the behavior of the attack, the provider works to reroute the customer network traffic while the SOC deploys new signatures to block the changes in attack patterns.

7:42 p.m. EST, No additional events populating into the SOC ticketing system regarding this event.

Monitoring statistics, visual charts and graphs detailing the health of the customers network returns to normal.

Customer confirmed that no service impact or outage was detected onsite. Communication analyst updated ticket entries on the customer's portal.

SOC management reviewed all the details of the events, actions performed and issued a general watch alert to all analysts for increased attack activity.

7:43 p.m. EST, all is quiet

The above was a simple review of what happens over and over again inside an MSSP's SOC. This type of activity usually can happen very quickly and depending on how large the MSSP is and how many services and customers they manage, this can happen not only several times an hour but multiple events like this can be, and typically do happen at the same time. An MSSP is designed to deal with these types of events on a regular basis and it is the norm for them. They are staffed with fully trained and qualified people who can react properly under stressful situations and have a great deal of experience in handling all types of security events effectively and efficiently.

## COST

Building a SOC can be expensive and if your organization does not have the capability or capacity to make capital expenses or to hire new resources then cost becomes a significant factor in deciding to outsource to an MSSP. Depending on the services that you are going to outsource, the MSSP may come with their own equipment so you will not have to purchase anything. All the software licensing, equipment costs, and even most if not all the setup and configuration of everything may be included in the monthly charge of the service you are contracting for. Additionally, as we previously discussed, the need for investment in a SIEM system is critical for a successful operation. These systems most often do not come cheap and typically require significant hardware, software and specialized skill sets to manage and maintain. Outsourcing to an MSSP may elevate the need for the purchase of an internal infrastructure of SIEM as the MSSP can collect your logs and do it all for you as part of the service.

If your organization is not IT centric then you will need to hire new people to setup, manage, maintain and monitor in your internal SOC if you do not outsource. Depending on the goals of your security and risk program this can be a significant number of new hires. Not only do you need to hire new people but you will also need to keep them trained like we spoke about in the chapter on training. An MSSP brings an established core of people to the table, most all of them will have or will be in the process of getting professional security industry certifications. They have established training programs for their staff and they have programs to keep their people up to date and current on emerging threat trends. In some cases, the staff at an MSSP can be so good at managing equipment that product vendors look to hire them away from MSSPs due to not only their knowledge of the equipment but also their practical experience of managing large volumes of devices in enterprise production environments.

Do not forget that when you are looking at security monitoring and management that it is a 24/7 job. Not only do you have to have the right resources, tools, and staff but you need to have them available and engaged around the clock to support your operation. Failures in IT infrastructure can happen at any time and security tools and technology are no different. In the case of your security tools, if they go down you may lose significant visibility into what is going on in your network and be blind to a potential breach.

## ORGANIZATIONAL

Internal IT departments and SOCs inside large enterprises may not play well together. This is important when you are looking at trying to perform security analysis across multiple technologies that may be managed by different departments in your organization. In order to get a clear picture of security, you need to be able to combine all your security relevant technology into a security event management ecosystem as we previously discussed. This system will normalize, aggregate, and correlate information to produce the essential security information and operation needs to effectively monitor a network. If your organization has one team supporting firewalls, another supporting network IDS and yet another supporting application or host based security tools then your monitoring may be fractured. Not only is it fractured but also piecing it all together to investigate an attack or even monitor a potential event in real time will be an incredibly difficult task. An MSSP can help break down certain barriers in this situation by working with the various groups, teams, and departments to collect the needed security relevant information and bring it all back to their analysis tools for processing. Additionally an MSSP may be able to break down political barriers by providing services not just for the security department but for other IT groups as well. They may be able to provide professional services and consulting work in many different technical areas. This becomes a winning situation for all concerned where everyone can benefit from the relationship in one way or another.

## ENHANCED CAPABILITIES

MSSPs work with many customers, some of the customers may even be in the same industry as yours. This can be a significant advantage for outsourcing your security, as the MSSP should be able to leverage security intelligence knowledge across the same or similar industries to yours. So, if there are specific attacks targeting one company in your industry it stands to reason that the attacks may be seen at other companies as well. If the MSSP is postured properly and have mature intelligence services then they should be able to spot these emerging trends and apply detection or protection mechanisms for your company ahead of the threat or extremely quickly in response. Not only should an MSSP be able to leverage industry threat information but if they have enough customers in a specific industry they can participate in industry information sharing programs which enable them to apply protections in your outsourced services even more often and with greater efficiency. This does not have to be just and industry specific focus, in that if there is a threat no matter where it is discovered the MSSP services should be able to apply some kind of detection or protections to your network for that specific discovered threat. This can help an MSSP leverage the intelligence information for vertical markets and make them experts in that specific industry.

These vertical specialties could range from government, energy, and critical infrastructure, to pharmaceutical, healthcare, retail, finance, or more. An MSSP may be able to specialize in several industries at once depending on their operational size, focus and their ability to gather intelligence to learn what is important to each.

## SLA

Properly responding to an alarm and deciding that a specific even warrants a deeper analysis is extremely time sensitive. It is so time sensitive that it could make the difference between one system infected with malware opposed to 300 systems compromised with APT tool sets and potential data loss. Because of this time sensitivity MSSPs can offer you SLA that dictate how they are going to provide the service to you. Initially you should see some SLAs around the provisioning of services, deployment of any equipment and documentation. Next you should see SLAs around how they are going to perform the service and around how they will respond to events and what the level of effort they are going to put forward to get resolution to those events. Depending on the level and type of service you subscribe to there can be many different types of SLAs offered by your MSSP.

SLAs are a nice benefit to outsourcing your security to an MSSP, again, it is not a consolation prize if something goes wrong but it is nice to know the company is on the hook to perform at a level you are comfortable with. SLAs do not all have to be time based, they can also dictate a specific process that they need to follow such as an escalation process or it could be the frequency of updates they will apply to a system.

When you begin working with an MSSP, ensure you establish well-defined and understood SLAs. These SLAs should be understood from a contracted perspective as well as realistic perspective. What I mean by that is if you are told that all incidents will be responded to in 4 h be aware that this may not be an SLA. The contracted SLA may be that they will respond in 24 h but will make a best effort to try and respond in the first 4. You should also know what "responding" means, I know that sounds silly but responding could be an automated response or a human analyst response. Another ambiguous example of where you may need to further define or understand an SLA is one that states a "100%" guarantee, so if your MSSP is patching your systems, they may say that they guarantee 100% compliance with patching for all managed systems within 30 days of patch availability. But, reading the fine print you may find that 100% accounts for unreachable systems, failed patching systems or systems in some funky state. So 100% may really be 70% with justifications up to 100%. Make sure your expectations are being met and that you are going to get what you think you are paying for.

Once you fully understand the SLAs and you are comfortable with all of them, the next step for you to do is to figure out how all the SLAs are going to be measured. Some MSSPs may have this all done already for you when it comes to their standard SLAs but if you agree to establish anything custom then you need to make sure you and the MSSP also agree on how to measure the SLA compliance. Last but not least, you should know what the process is when SLAs are missed, meaning what the escalation plans and paths are for you to take action and enforce compliance with the SLAs. When dealing with your security being outsourced do not let them off the hook, they need to be responsive because that is what you are paying them for, hold them accountable to the SLA.

This is not really like a company's internal SLA, these agreements are hard parameters that could have serious consequences for being missed. Although it is not consolation prize if something bad happens, the SLAs contracted in your relationship with an MSSP may provide you with service credits or even significant monetary fines for the MSSP failing to meet those agreements. What I mean is that it is not great to have an MSSP refund you a measly $10 or event $1000 for being late in responding to an alert that unauthorized data was potentially leaving your network. I personally would just rather have them be responsive and meet all their contracted obligations. To add a bit more teeth, SLAs could even include additional monetary penalties above service credits for the MSSP in that they could have to pay recover fees for any losses as a result their missing of the SLA, this could be a situation that is similar to cyber insurance.

## DOCUMENTATION

Since MSSPs are typically mature operations with large numbers of customers, there are a few things you should expect when working with them. These are not necessarily things that you cannot get from your own internal SOC but an MSSP should be able to start giving them to you day one of your service whereas your internal SOC may not see these as priorities and may take a long time to develop.

First, a MSSPs service is usually designed with an outward interface to interact intelligently with their customers. A web portal provided by your MSSP is a great resource for you and for the MSSP. Your account should give you visibility into all your services and let you interact with the company on various levels. For example, if you are using an MSSP for log management services then you should be able to access your logs and have a robust interface for searching those logs and generating reports. Additionally you should be able to see all your MSSP generated tickets and inside those tickets you should be able to see the log entries that not only you have made but all the entries of the analysts in the MSSP's SOC that include their analysis and conclusions of the event that generated the ticket.

All of this information should be documented and the MSSP should even provide your organization training on how to use their tools, work their processes and get the best possible service.

MSSPs will typically have a very well established run book that includes all the steps they go through in responding to a wide variety of different events. These processes are typically well thought out, tested and executed with relative ease by the MSSP. Additionally, since MSSPs do typically have larger numbers of skilled security resources then most enterprises, it puts them in a good position to work with your organization in either developing your internal security policies or revising your existing ones to match your security needs and goals. Do not be afraid to ask your MSSP to review internal processes with you and to help educate you on how they do things. The more you know about how they do things and what they do the more you will be able to take better advantage of the services they offer and you will build a better relationship.

MSSPs will also have a good documentation regarding their security policies and procedures. These will be comprehensive documents that are periodically reviewed and updated as well as enforced. You should be able to review this information to make sure they are compatible or exceed your own.

## DISADVANTAGES TO MSSP OUTSOURCING

As much as MSSPs hate to admit it, there are a number of disadvantages to outsourcing and you will need to carefully consider the importance of each one to your organization. Of course there are pros and cons to everything but when you are looking to trust such a sensitive and important function to your organization to a third party you should not go into the relationship lightly. As I stated before, you need to make sure you understand the goals and requirements of your security program well in order to evaluate if an MSSP relationship is right for you.

## LARGE NUMBERS OF CUSTOMERS

As was discussed before, it makes sense that an MSSP would have a large customer base. Some MSSPs have more customers than others and some have larger enterprises than others. An organization benefits from having an MSSP with a strong customer base with its ability to leverage intelligence from that customer base but at the same time there comes a strong disadvantage. Because MSSPs do have many customers it is very difficult for the MSSP to have intimate knowledge of a single customer's network and infrastructure. This is a significant disadvantage because without that knowledge it is difficult for an MSSP to perform effective analysis of events. For example, if there was an attack and the log of the event had an internal IP address on your network an MSSP SOC may deem the event a false positive because that type of attack is only effective on the external side of an organizations network.

An analyst at an MSSP may fail to properly analyze this event because of their inability to know how every customers network is built. In the case of an internal IP, although the MSSP SOC is correct in their analysis of the event being only effective externally, because they are not as intimately familiar with each organizations network they may overlook the fact that the target system in this scenario is on the external side of the network but has network address translation on the inside and it was the inside intrusion detection system that kicked off the initial alarm. MSSPs have worked hard to resolve these issues by making sure they have good knowledge bases and ticketing systems to help their analysts but the reality is that on average an analyst in the SOC of an MSSP may work 50 tickets a shift and each one may be from a different company. That type of volume is just going to make it very hard for analyst to get real familiar with any customers network.

## LACK OF DEDICATED RESOURCES

You may be a small fish in a big pond, meaning that you are using shared resources when working with an MSSP. So, in the case of a crisis where multiple customers in an industry, region or with a specific technology are affected, you may not get the attention you want when the company that has a contract worth 100 times what yours is wants something first. Although MSSPs work hard to provide personal service to each and every customer, unless you are large enough or pay enough, you are not going to get dedicated support when those issues occur. On that note, you have to remember that MSSPs are a business so they are going to do things as profitable and as efficient as possible. What this means is that their services may not be flexible enough to match your exact needs or may not be able to scale up enough to meet your demands at your time of critical need. You have to make sure that the service you are going to get from them will meet your expectations. MSSPs will try to present a custom tailored service as much as possible but in the end they need to stack their service high and deep and have as much of a repetitive service as possible to be profitable. If you have a clear goal in mind and you select the right MSSP who understand the detailed specifics your goals and can they accommodate your needs contractually then you will have a winning relationship. Draw too far outside the lines of their service offerings and you are going to have some trouble. MSSPs are great for providing standard security services but providing custom security solutions to just your business will not scale properly in most organizations. So, in order to effectively use an MSSP, make sure that you are purchasing standard services with realistic expectations and then look to perform more of your custom programs either in-house with your own SOC or security team or with other consulting firms and/or contractors.

## DATA STORAGE ISSUES

When we typically think about data storage, most of us can recall how limited storage was in the past and how large and inexpensive storage media has become. But when looking at large enterprise data storage systems that collect millions of events per day and need to be online and available for audit purposed typically for a year or more the storage requirements start to become massive in size. Then add in the fact that MSSPs need to store all this data for possibly hundreds of clients the issues become as large as the data itself, and the when you start to think about backups and redundancy it could be a nightmare. Many MSSPs have addressed issues with large or what some people call big data, they have addressed it by adding costs to service. What I mean is that some MSSPs require that you send your logs to their central logging facility. This is how they perform correlation, aggregation, and eventually ticketing security issues to alert you on. Normally this should not be a problem, but if that log data can potentially carry protected information such as payment card transaction information, personal identifiable information, controlled unclassified information, or other intellectual property then you start to have an even larger mess on your hands. Further, most MSSPs will have multiple processing centers and multiple data storage and back-up facilities. This can cause problems if those locations are not in a country that meets your regulatory or government requirements for the protection of that information. To resolve this some MSSPs may be able to control the location of your data but it will come at a premium price. Further you should be aware that most if not all MSSPs will not store all your data indefinitely for free. Instead they will only store your data for a short period of time before its purged unless of course you pay extra for longer storage. Also, be careful of data size limits, an MSSP may charge you for the amount of data you send them as well.

This leads us into a quick discussion on what the costs of working with an MSSP could be.

## COSTS

It is very difficult for me to give you any kind of real cost numbers associated with working with an MSSP. These numbers can change greatly depending on what you are looking to purchase, the terms of the contract and your relationship with the vendor. They will most always work with you to size and scope the service and try to give you the best deal they can based on your needs, the devices you want monitored/managed and the levels of service you are looking for. In some cases, an MSSP may charge you per device, this is great if you are small and have only one firewall but bad if you are large and have several thousand firewalls. There may be Internet bandwidth charges for you to send them logs, so not only do you have to pay for the bandwidth leaving your network but you may also have to pay bandwidth charges for logs entering your provider's networks. Bandwidth charges may be good if there are no device charges, this way if you have many IDS but they are fairly quite and properly tuned and do not produce many alarms then this may be cheaper for you. Then there is the data storage charge like we spoke about above. Depending on if you need 1 month of logs available online and a year off-line or a 1 year online and 10 years off-line or online forever, I am sure there is a pricing model just for you.

Threat intelligence is much of the same way, there are multiple flavors, versions, and services that you can choose from. Depending on what you need or what you want to add onto your MSSP contract may also greatly affect your price. You can almost certainly choose between vulnerability feeds that give you instant notification when a vendor you are interested in publicly announces patch or security flaw. Then there are threat feeds and advisory feeds that help keep you informed on the latest trends or potential threats to your system. Further an MSSP may charge you to participate in live monthly webinars that discuss vulnerabilities, current risks and emerging trends. Then there are vertical threat intelligence services that you can leverage from your industry partners or equipment providers through the MSSP. All of these can be very valuable services but they can come at a cost that may make you think twice about signing up with an MSSP especially if cost was what made you look at outsourcing to begin with instead of doing a SOC in-house.

## QUALITY OF WORK AND STAFFING

When building any security operations center you want to make it as effective and as efficient as possible. Therefore you are going to make decisions that prevent SOC personnel from performing needless functions and allow them to focus on core tasks that give the organization the best bang for the buck. This is all well and good if you own an internal SOC, but at an MSSP, it is a bit of a different story. The MSSP is going to squelch and tune customer logs and sensors so that they get what they believe is the sweet spot of signal to noise ratio. They understand very well that there is going to be a certain percentage of false positive tickets generated but they will work very hard to reduce that as much as possible. They do this so that they can perform more work for more customers and make more profit. What this means to you is that they may tune or turn off completely an IDS alert, log entry or other indicator of attack that they deem to be no threat, low threat or otherwise a waste of their time. Typically an MSSP will do this across all their customers or with sections of customers depending on how their back end infrastructure is built. This matters because you are trusting them to make the right decision for your business based on what is ultimately more profit for them. This is in no way malicious, it is just economies of scale for the business. To help combat these types of issues you need to engage with the MSSP and see if there is are ways you can be part of the change tree that gets notified about these types of things or if there is a technical customer advisory board that you can participate with that discusses these types of technical issues.

Quality of work may also suffer if the MSSP is struggling to manage their workload and is starved for resources. In this case, you may find tickets that have quality issues like missing information, wrong information, and so on. Some of this is fine as you cannot expect everyone to be perfect all the time but it can be cyclical in a MSSP. If there are significant changes in an MSSP SOC environment such as personnel churn over, infrastructure maintenance issues or just generally being short staffed for any one of many reasons.

Just like in any business a MSSP may have waves of employee turnover. Since security is a fairly active job market, anyone getting good quality training at an MSSP does have a fair number of job options out there. An MSSP has to work hard to retain their people, keep them happy and keep them engaged. Even if they are able to keep their people retained it still may impact customers. Because people get promoted or move on to other roles you can see a drop in work quality, mishandled ticket escalations, or any number of other quality issues.

### Questions you need to ask a potential MSS provider

Although we just discussed pros and cons of working with an MSS provider, let us assume you decide to move forward and want to outsource. You have to make sure you are going to work with the right company. This is not simply signing up, hand-shaking and away you go. There is a significant level of trust you need to have in the MSSP you are going to partner with and you need to make sure they are going to be able to get the job done or that you can hold them accountable for when they do not. Also, you need to be aware that even if you have a long-standing relationship with a company for other reasons and you are beginning to look at their MSSP service offerings, it does not mean that it will have the same level of quality or capabilities of their other businesses, this is due to the heavy mergers and acquisitions that go on in the Information Technology area and especially in Cyber security. In some cases where an MSSP was acquired, it may take several years for that business to be fully integrated with the larger parent. They may have different management, billing systems and a laundry list of other differences. Regardless, there are a number of questions or topics of conversation you should have with any potential MSSP to get a better idea on how they handle specific issues that may work with your requirements, culture, infrastructure, and philosophy of security.

So, you want to outsource? What are the questions you need to ask?

Where do you begin? There always seems to be a growing number of companies willing to provide security services. Then it seems that there are always a number of organizations being purchased by larger organizations, and then there are also organizations providing security services that may go out of business. This raises a lot of fears and a lot of questions that need to be answered, ultimately you need to find and select an organization that is going to partner with you and be there for you when an incident occurs. There are a lot of questions that come up that you need to have answered, these are questions that come from the business or may come from your IT department or may come from anywhere in the organization that may have concerns, issues, or just general questions regarding the hiring of a company to perform such a critical service. Understanding some of the more high-level questions you need to ask and filtering the answers in order to be able to reduce the number of potential outsource organizations to select from is a major task to be performed.

## HOW THE SERVICES WILL BE DELIVERED

The first question you may want to ask is how they are going to provide the service you are contracting for. For example, are they going to provide any hardware or do you have to make additional purchases per their specifications. You need to know how they are going to access your network or the resources they need in order to get the information they require to perform the proper service. You may need special firewall rules or need to understand the protocols they are going to use to connect to your devices. You may even have to restrict your network and not allow them to access the devices, in that case you need to figure out how they will get the data they need to perform the services you want them to. These are important issues that need to be well understood so that the MSSP can securely and successfully do their job and that there are no hidden infrastructure costs that you were not aware of. Also, you should find out if you will be assigned a dedicated engineer that will work with you to provision the services and any equipment needed. They should act as a project manager for you and help make sure that you have a smooth on boarding process. When you on board to an MSSP it should not just be a network connection and you start getting alerts. You need to engage with them fairly closely to make sure that any new equipment gets provisioned correctly or that any changes to existing equipment are fully vetted and well understood and that all changes are properly documented and approved by your change management board if you have one. You also need to ensure that your information properly gets loaded into any ticket or database systems the MSSP may have. This could include an asset database and a contact database or even an intelligence database. You need to also work with the SOC up front to ensure that they know who you are, what your IP address schemes are and what they need to do when there is an issue. Most MSSPs will have this process pretty nailed down and will load you up with all kinds of forms to fill out. Just be aware of who you have to deal with, what the processes are or any other odd things that you will need to do in order for them to provide you the best possible service.

## PEOPLE

Next you want to make sure that the MSSP is using people above and beyond your standards to service your account. What I mean there is that you want to ensure that the company you are contracting with is using the same if not better standards to employ people than you do. This could include security clearances, background checks, credit checks or any other research that may be needed. Although difficult to protect against you want to ensure (to the best ability that you can) that there are not going to be any public leaks of information that may be seen on your network by the MSSP. Therefore you need to know about the hiring practices of the MSSP, do they require drug tests, do they only use citizens of the country you are contracting in, do they hold country government or military clearances and so on. Do not forget to find out if there are any suppliers, partners or resellers involved in either your relationship with the MSSP or in how the MSSP provides the service as the personnel in those organizations may need to comply with your requirements or regulations as well. Anyone involved in the processes of providing MSS who may touch, see or interact with your data needs to be understood from all these perspectives to ensure you are working within the confines of your organizations requirements or even your customer's requirements and commitments. As we discussed before, there may be a lot of moving around and turnover at an MSSP so you need to make sure they have and only bring in the highest caliber of people possible and that they will meet your requirements.

Then you need to ensure that once they have found those great people that they are all properly trained and kept current. In a previous chapter, we spent a considerable amount of time discussing what it takes to train a SOC. When it comes to an MSSP, we should expect that the training of the staff to far exceed what we could ever hope to do in our own private SOCs. Do not be afraid to ask what kind of training they provide their staff on a regular basis and to see a list of credentials that their SOC members currently hold. Because all of the people that work in the SOC are in the security field, you should expect their certifications to be an overwhelming list. But do not just stop at certifications, ask about other training like PCI or data handling processes, even ask about their new employee training. You should not expect issues and errors to happen just because there is a new employee or junior person on the job. Get a full view of what their knowledge level is in their SOC and what they do to keep everyone learning, make sure that there is ongoing education at your potential providers that will also include threat trends, new and emerging security research and that it is performed at a rate that is frequent enough to stay current.

## SIZE VERSUS EXPERIENCE

Once you feel comfortable that they have adequate or even incredibly worthy people providing the service you want, the next thing you need to know is if you will have access to those people. You will need to know about how many customers and what the MSSP does to provide all their services to those customers. What you want to look for is that the MSSP is adequately staffed with enough fully trained and experienced people to handle your needs. To ensure they have enough people they need to make sure that they can keep their customer to staff member ratio in balance and that they do not incur too much churn over in staff. As mentioned before, high turnover of quality staff members are not going to win any MSSP security awards in service delivery.

## SERVICE EXECUTION

Once you understand how your service is actually going to be delivered and who is delivering it you need to know what is actually being delivered and how they are going to execute on the service commitments. For example, you need to know how communication is going to work and what communication you should expect.

When there is an incident that needs to be addressed, what is the outsourced organization providing your security services expected to do? Who are they supposed to call and what is the urgency of the call? These are all things that you need to understand yourself and then ensure your outsourced security organization can meet your needs of who is to be notified when there is such an incident that needs to be addressed. You need to make sure that the outsourced organization can call the right people at the right time and solicit the right response to ensure that your organization gets the needed information quickly and efficiently in order to be able to address any security issues. You cannot expect an outsourced organization to be successful if you do not provide them the right communication methods for your organization and your staff. If you provide your outsourced security company with a method of communicating to you, then you need to make sure that you meet them halfway and respond to those communications. Communication is key between the two organizations, everyone must do their part to ensure that there is a successful partnership between the two companies so that the organization is able to stay safe.

## TOOLS

There are many tools that may be provided by the MSSP to help you protect your organization or allow you to get needed information when you want it. One of these tools may be a self-service portal, this is a website that you can go to in order to see any activity that the outsourcer is performing on your behalf or to make changes, open trouble tickets or event create new incidents for the outsourcer to investigate. Self-service portals are a great way to communicate with your outsourcer and have been an invaluable resource for outsources to provide information to their customers. Many outsource security providers use their portals as a place for the customer to be able to retrieve compliance reports, metrics, or even disseminate information regarding new vulnerabilities and exploits that are being detected in the wild. Some of these portals can be so advanced that your internal SOC may use it as its primary security tool and real-time interface with the MSSP.

Depending on what you need from your security outsourcer the self-service portal may be a fully functional system for you to utilize as a cornerstone of your internal security operation center in partnership with your outsourcer all the way to a minimalistic system that allows you to just retrieve basic information regarding escalated of events. Some outsourced organizations may even have Mobile applications that IT or security managers can utilize to address or acknowledge security events wherever they are. These mobile apps maybe fully functioning security portals or just simply notification mechanisms. Depending on your internal level of security these mobile device applications may or may not be something that you can utilize but you should at least be aware that as technology progresses outsourced organizations will continually adopt new technology to better provide their services, or look for a new ways to charge for their services and they will leverage technology as a differentiator of their services in the market.

When selecting an MSSP these are many features and functions that you have to take into consideration as part of service execution and understand that there may be added costs or efficiency gains that coincide with these features and functions.

## SMALLER VERSUS LARGER MSSP

If you are looking at a larger enterprise organization to outsource to then many questions about how long they have been in business or if they are financially stable are not really applicable. But if you are looking at a smaller organization than those are absolutely appropriate questions and smaller managed security services provider should be able to help make you feel comfortable with the appropriate answers to those questions.

With a larger MSSP you get the comfort of knowing their backed by a giant organization is most likely financially stable that has been around for many years. These larger organizations have typically been very successful in providing IT related services to organizations around the world for many years and their ability to provide your organization security services would certainly be no different than their ability to provide services to other companies like yours or ones much larger. One of the major drawbacks of working with one of these larger organizations it they are typically not agile or flexible enough to meet some of your more demanding or special needs. Larger based organizations are not well suited to handle one-off scenarios or special situations for each and every one of their customers, they are able to profit by providing standard solutions that they can sell to multiple companies over and over and over. Although this is a sound business model and it works well as they are capable of providing unparalleled operational services they may not meet your specific needs if you are too far outside of their standard box. This does not mean that they are going to be completely inflexible but there is only so much they will be able to customize. Additionally if there is a crisis situation that affects multiple customers, organizations much larger than yours may get better service because they can command better attention or have paid for better attention from the provider. But with these larger outsourcers they do have deep pockets and wells of resources that they can throw at problems if needed. This helps them win up new services and develop new markets much faster than their smaller counterparts. One thing to keep in mind as was mentioned before, with the larger more established providers is they may have gone through several acquisitions and internal restructuring that has fractured the organization. They may not have been able to fully integrate their services with the rest of their company. So although they may be able to provide excellence security operations if for example, their billing and finance services are not fully integrated you still may not be able to get the right level of service that you need from these larger organizations.

On the other hand with the smaller security providers you may be able to be a bigger fish in a small pond. This may help you get better service and a more flexible service commitment from the organization your outsourcing to. Of course you will now have concerns on the stability of the organization, the financial wellbeing of the organization, and its potential of being acquired by another larger company. All too often I have heard stories about an organization being very happy with a managed security service providers quality of products and services but when after another larger company acquired it, those same services failed to meet the customer's expectations.

I have also heard of a companies who left a large outsourcer because they were too large and went to a smaller outsourcer and was very happy, only to have that smaller outsourcer be acquired by the very same larger outsourcer that they had just left. This may sound funny or even very familiar but ultimately it is extremely disruptive to in organization that is focused on securing their infrastructure. It takes away from the core focus of managing and monitoring an organizations internal network to managing and monitoring your outsourced provider of these very same services.

When looking at smaller organizations to outsource to versus larger organizations there are challenges on both sides and both sides all come with their own problems that you need to address. If you thought making the decision to outsource your security was going to be a very difficult decision to make hopefully you are realizing now that it is not your only difficult decision you need to make. Ensuring that you are going to partner with the right outsourced organization that you are going to be successful with whatever organization you choose is not an easy task.

It is always good to get some honest feedback from counterparts in your industry. If you are in a group of industry professionals I am sure you have a forum in which to ask other organizations if they outsource, who they use and what their experiences have been. It is also a good idea to ask the outsourcer for references inside your industry or for references from companies that are the same size as yours or maybe even in the same local area. All too often I have seen organizations that ask for these references but would never follow up on or never make the phone calls and never speak to people on the reference list. Make sure that you are not one of those organizations. At a minimum get on the phone and speak to somebody who has used the security outsourcer services so that you can get a first-hand account of what it is like working with this potential outsourcer.

Diving deeper into the MSSP selection process there are a lot of other questions you may need to ask, a lot more technical, organizational, management, and service-related questions you need to ask.

Although security services are fairly similar across all organizations not all organizations are the same. As your organization looks to outsource, you are going to have several issues, needs, and requirements that may be very specific to your organization. You should ask a potential managed security services provider if they offer any additional services and if so what are the charges for those services. For example if there are services that you need in order to make the necessary changes in your infrastructure to allow the managed security services provider to get the information they need or access devices they need to, is there a charge for these type services and if so at what rate. You need to make sure that you understand all the services you are going to be getting from your outsourced provider and what if any additional charges there would be for services considered out of scope of services you purchased. Additionally you need to understand any charges and fees you may incur during your contract period. For example your contract may cover the monitoring of 10 security devices but if you decommission one of those 10 and then bring up a new security device onto your network there may be a charge to swap monitoring from one device to another. That is just a simple example, I am sure there are hundreds of much more complex examples, ultimately your situation will be different and you need to have a lengthy conversation with your provider regarding the complexities of your infrastructure and what it would take for them to provide the services you need and at what cost.

You should be aware of any contingency-based services or emergency services that you may need to take advantage of in the future. For example, if you are in a situation where you have detected a potential breach what are the additional costs associated with having your managed security service provider assist you with breach containment activities or incident response. Maybe your provider might not have those services available or they might not be able to even provide forensic services. That does not mean you should not work with that company but it is good to know upfront that it is not available or if it is available and at what the associated costs are.

## SECURITY

This seems kind of a silly topic but even though you are thinking about purchasing security services it does not give you license to forget about how to securely employ these services. An MSSP is a third party provider of these services and your organization might have (should have) strict guidance on how third party providers are handled and managed. This can include administrative items like contracts and legal requirements but also how they will technically connect to your network. Not only how will they connect but how will they protect those connections and who will be accessing resource on your network. This is a great topic of conversation to have with any provider but especially with your managed security services company. You need to know how they are going to manage access to your network and your devices and what is going to stop them from accessing devices that they do not manage while on your network, what audits are available and what kind of access reports will you be able to receive. You may think that you have this all covered with what is in place today but if the MSSP takes over management of your devices you may not be able to log into them to poke around and see what is going on.

Many providers have a policy of not allowing co-management of security equipment. This policy is there to protect the MSSP from things going wrong due to issues or changes they did not initiate, so what this means is that you may not be granted any kind of access to security devices on your network while the contract is in place. There are many ways around this if you have a hard time with it. For one, you could choose to mirror data to another system that they do not have access to. This sometimes works great in the IDS world where you can replicate events to multiple places. One main server sends data to the MSSP and sends data to you that you collect somewhere else. This kind of split or stacked solution can be costly depending on the types of devices and number of technologies you want to do it with but it will allow you to continue to have some visibility.

You cannot blame a provider for wanting complete control over your security devices because this is the best way and sometimes the only way for them to be able to provide the best and most reliable service. Additionally they may implement special controls and protection or signatures in your devices that are proprietary to the provider. These special configurations could be for a number of reasons such as for testing and alerting on the health of the environment or could even be special intelligence based events that they are using. Either way, they may configure your devices to alert on events that are meaningful for them and not you but if you saw them you would not understand them and may even raise unneeded concerns.

As stated before, you should feel completely comfortable with the level of access logs and change reporting that they provide you and if not, then work with them to fix the reporting so that you are completely satisfied and your regulatory requirements are also satisfied.

Last but not least you should be able to get a fully understanding of what the MSSP has done to protect their own network. This should be from not only a technical safeguard but also a physical perspective. The last thing you want is to have a breach or some kind of unauthorized access from your own security provider. Make sure you understand what controls are in place and that they are using world class processes, procedures, and technology to protect their own network.

From a technical perspective, how are they going to handle your data. You may provide them with tons of internal documentation from policies to network maps and device configurations. All of this information must be properly handled but also your real time threat data, vulnerability status and any ongoing or active attacks need to be protected as confidential. Having an analyst tell one company that they have seen this type of attack before at company XYZ is not very good. All employees of an MSSP need to be properly trained on how to handle data and information and the MSSP's network and processes must be enabled to technically safeguard data from intentional or inadvertent disclosure.

*Key point*: Your MSSP's security should be a model of what a secure environment should look like, and be well beyond the level of security you could hope for, so if it is not then maybe you should move on to another provider.

## DR

There are two main things you want to think about when it comes to DR as it relates to outsourcing your security. The first is obviously what devices you want to have protected during a DR situation but secondly what are the charges for monitoring DR or failover devices. These are two very different topics as it relates to DR and should be thought about in separate contexts in order to ensure you make the right decisions and get the most cost-effective solution.

When you think of your entire security infrastructure you hopefully have installed some level of failover and DR infrastructure to support your efforts when a problem does arise. In larger organizations, this could be entire data centers just sitting there getting replicated data from the primary data center. In these situations, you have to decide on if you are going to just outsource security for your primary network or backup infrastructure as well. You may have a different mix of devices in your DR network, with very different controls, access, and support staff. In some organizations it may be completely the same and fully replicated in real-time. What is it that you need to protect during a DR and what level of protection is desired. In one example of a DR outsourced agreement I have seen the company asked that the IDS and firewalls be fully monitored and managed but no threat intelligence or managed SIEM. This is because during a DR (that was not security induced) they wanted to have some level of protections but did not want the full expense of a fully managed environment. The company felt that in a DR situation only the basics were necessary to keep their eyes on security while they were able to focus attention and support into normal business recovery operations. Call this silly or call it smart, the reduction of services and security controls for them were proportional to their overall DR strategies. In your case, you will have to decide not only what security equipment you want protecting your DR environment but what level of support and services you will need during that critical time.

The second topic relates to the failover devices and the costs associated by your MSSP in managing those. In a simple scenario where you have two firewalls, one as the active and the other as a standby, if your MSSP was monitoring and managing those devices, do they charge you for 2 or 1. Maybe they have a partial charge for the standby since there may be ongoing configuration and maintenance that needs to take place on those standby devices to ensure they will properly failover when needed. As for your DR facility, network or data center, will your security devices be responsible for protecting that network all the time, so they are live and active devices or are they just devices that function when there is a failover. You will need to think about how you employ DR designated devices against how the MSSP will charge you for services on those devices.

Once you think you have all these items figured out make sure you talk to your MSSP about being involved in any DR tests. Also make sure you fully communicate to them what your expectations are for a DR environment and understand the proper way to involve and engage your MSSP when those DR scenarios do occur.

## EXIT STRATEGY

This is not something we want to think about but sometimes in a relationship we just have to call it quits. For whatever reason, be it poor service, a change in direction, costs or looking to try out another provider you have to have a plan to cut the cord and move on. When you have a company managing security for you this may not be as simple of a process as you may think. Tons of things can get broken as you disconnect or remove services, there has to be a well thought out, documented and defined change process that you need to go through so that you do not impact your operations and you maintain security throughout the transition.

You need to make sure that the provider removes any configurations that are specific to their needs and access but will not affect your security or performance. Additionally you need to make sure you have all the administrative credentials to all the systems that were managed and that all of the MSSP's accounts will be removed.

## MSSP SELECTION

After you have reviewed all the important elements you are looking for in a provider and you have developed your comprehensive request for proposal, send it out to the companies you think will work the best. Then after you get back all your responses try to quickly narrow it down to only three providers. Once you think you have the three best, start your detailed questioning, review, site visits, and negotiations.

Once you enter the negotiation phase is when you can develop your contract and select the best service agreement possible. See what contract modifications you can make to best fit your needs and ensure the MSSP's operating procedures are acceptable to you. Do not be afraid to continue to ask questions and also interview current or past customers. Additionally you can ask an MSSP for third party audits and reviews. It should go without saying, but your legal counsel should review all the contracts. When you are asking a third party to play a role in managing your risk, it is very important to know where your liabilities are and what recourse you have as well as what the limits on damages are when something goes wrong.

Make sure you are fully satisfied with the terms of the service as you are going to have to live with it.

## PROVIDING THE SERVICE

There are many questions that need to be asked regarding how an MSSP is going to provide services, what their SLAs are and what recourse a customer has for mistakes and issues. There is an almost exhaustive list that can be asked of a provider, some questions will pertain to you and some will not and I am sure I missed some, but what is below is just an attempt to rapid fire a bunch of questions that may help spark thoughts and debate for you without having to go into deep discussion as to why it may need to be asked.

Rapid-fire questions for you to develop for your discussions with a potential MSSP or to put into a request for proposal if you are looking to do an initial bid for services:

General service delivery
1. How do I interface with the service, web portal, email, phone?
2. If I want to speak to a security analyst or engineer is there a time charge or is it part of the service?
3. Service is expected $24 \times 7 \times 365$, what if any expected down time is there?
4. What is the uptime guarantee?
5. How do service interruptions get discounted?
6. Can an organization try before they buy? Trial services?
7. What are the bandwidth requirements for the service to operate?
8. What services are available?
9. What is their prevention strategy opposed to the detection strategy?
10. What are the professional certifications held by the MSSP staff?
11. What is the training regimen for the MSSP staff?

12. Can the MSSP help create exercises to train and test staff?
13. What services does the MSSP have that differentiate them from other providers?

Incidents
14. What happens once an incident occurs?
15. How is a company notified and what is the notification SLA?
16. What actions and countermeasures will be taken prior to notification or are there options once notification is made?
17. Does the MSSP have flexible responses, actions and countermeasures to meet your needs?
18. How will the MSSP identify legitimate traffic from malicious traffic?
19. What are the service level SLAs that can be expected for different types of events?
20. How does the MSSP handle what they see as a successful attack versus an attack with an unknown result?

Reporting
21. Does and organization receive regular reports?
22. Are customized reports available if needed?
23. How detailed are the reports and what if I need more information?
24. How often will an organization receive reports?
25. Can reports be generated through a portal or can they be provided immediately upon request?
26. How are reports securely delivered?
27. Will you be able to call the MSSP to review reports?
28. Will you provide onsite Incident Response and if so, at what cost?
29. What support will the MSSP give me if there is legitimate traffic being blocked by a managed device?
30. What do I do if I am unhappy with the service or a specific incident?
31. What contractual penalties are there for an MSSP not fulfilling their obligations in relation to an SLA?
32. What key performance indicators (KPI) can I expect and at what frequency?
33. How will the MSSP protect all the data they collect from my organization and my network?
34. What technology is the MSSP using to protect their customers?
35. Can there be visits to the MSSP to review services and see how they deliver security through their SOC?
36. Did the MSSP read this book and find better ways to do things?
37. What MSSP provided equipment will need to be installed and where?
38. How will the MSSP's service affect current security devices?
39. How is the MSSP staffed?
40. Does the MSSP use the follow the sun method to support its SOC?
41. Does the MSSP use any third party services or vendors?
42. What is the growth capacity of the MSSP when a customer is looking to scale up its services?

43. How fast can the MSSP react to change requests?
44. What are the priority levels of alerts and the SLAs against them?
45. What are the specific SLAs around notification of an intrusion or attempted intrusion?
46. What happens in the case of a hardware failure? Does the MSSP work on behalf of the customer under the vendors support agreement for replacement or is it up to the customer?
47. Are backups of customers device taken and if so, at what frequency?

Implementation
48. How long does it take to implement the service?
49. Will there be dedicated implementation or service provisioning engineers assigned?
50. Is there a specific implementation plan that will be followed?
51. What problems have been encountered before when turning on new services and how will the MSSP work to avoid those issues?
52. How can we exit the relationship and how long will it take to part ways?

Costs
53. What are the costs for service?
54. What extra costs could be incurred during service?
55. Are their different pricing levels for different types of devices being managed?
56. Are there discounts for inactive for failover DR equipment?
57. Are there and costs savings for longer-term contracts?
58. Are there any bundled services that can reduce overall costs?
59. Is the MSSP capable of providing short-term professional services and what are the associated costs?

Security
60. What are the physical security controls that protect the MSSP's SOC?
61. Who has access to the SOC?
62. What is the process for the MSSP to grant its users access to your devices?
63. What is the authentication mechanism used to access your devices?
64. Are there different levels of access for users at the MSSP to your devices?
65. What is the process for removing user access?
66. Is there role based access to your devices, different users for different services?
67. What are the security controls that protect and safeguard customer's data at the MSSP?
68. Where is your data stored and is it in compliance with any regulations you are required to adhere to?
69. What is the MSSP's business continuity or DR plan and how are they tested?
70. What intelligence networks does the MSSP use?
71. What kind of intelligence does the MSSP create?

Exit strategy
72. How do we regain control over our security devices if we decide to terminate services?
73. Can we use a "Break the glass" procedure for device control?
74. What costs are associated with early termination of our contracts?

## TESTING YOUR MSSP

A very good practice that you must perform is a test against your MSSP. Similar to how we spoke about exercising security staff in the training chapter we need to think about training or testing our MSSP. Performing a simple penetration test or short scan that looks like a type of attack or even just taking a security device off line can do this. The test should be to see the entire process and the length of time it takes them to execute their processes. During several tests I did at one company to test an MSSP I kept triggering IDS events or simulated denial of service events, I even attacked a server using commercial penetration tools while spoofing my IP address. None of my efforts were escalated by the MSSP and there was not even an email that was sent to tell us something was going on. I further attempted to exploit the network and attacked from the outside, I began getting louder and louder meaning sending more bad data and finally after a week of penetration testing and even exploiting several system vulnerabilities I was able to get the MSSP to issue a low value alert to suspicious activity.

After meeting with the MSSP and reviewing my tests with them we discovered several really interesting things. First, some of the events I generated were events that they do not look at because they were not "interesting" to them. They felt that the number of alerts they get are too high so they tune down the events so their SOC does not get inundated. Wow, so I was able to find out that the MSSP was making decisions not based on security but pure efficiency, I guess they were not able to correlate events so that they could get the notifications of malicious activity in a more efficient manner without overwhelming their SOC. To their defense the events were indicators of potentially bad activity not a smoking gun but still, there should be more analysis going on. Next we found that some specific activity I performed was not seen by the MSSP at all, it turns out that there were gaps in the MSSPs visibility of the organizations network. In this case, there was no fault of the MSSP but some very quick corrective actions could be made to resolve these issues on our end.

That is just a quick example of many issues that can be found and there are many others. You need to test to make sure they see something and then escalate the issues properly and in a timely manner that meets your expectations. Then once complete talk to your MSSP, tell them you tested them and how they did even if they did well. Also, do not be afraid to include your MSSP in your tests, you do not always have to keep it a secret from them although from time to time you should. This type of testing can be good for both of you, to ensure services are being provided accurately and to see where there are areas for improvement.

## SUMMARY

There are many different reasons an organization may build a SOC in-house or out-source to an MSSP. If you decide that an MSSP is right for you, make sure you go into the relationship with a clear understanding of your goals and objectives. This will make it much easier for you to contract the proper services at the right price but it will also help the MSSP ensure they can sell you the services you really want and need. I would recommend that initially you focus on outsourcing basic consistent functions and aspects of your security. Once you feel comfortable that things are working well make sure you implement a testing program. This should be something you do that you feel should trigger a response from your MSSP. Make sure they are seeing the right traffic, getting the right logs, and responding the way you expect. If this is all working right consistently and you see no issues then you should feel comfortable to move forward and re-engage with our MSSP reps to look for other functions you may want to outsource. Keep in mind that you can never fully out-source security to the point where you have no control or worries. Security is always your problem and when working with an MSSP you have to treat the relationship as a partnership and a good MSSP will always meet you half way. They will work with you in that partnership to ensure they are providing the best quality of service they can, and although at times it may not seem that way, they do care and want to do their part to protect your organization.

Although the information is quite dated, much if it is still relevant, additional and in-depth information on this topic can be found here:

http://www.cert.org/archive/pdf/omss.pdf.

# Do not forget why you are here

11

In my travels, the many SOCs I have visited, seen, and worked in, I have yet to find a single individual that did not care about security, the mission of protection, or have a passion to learn. Being in the security field, we are all surrounded by a passion to guard and defend the network, we are all monitoring and looking to develop new ways to do so. It is an amazing feeling to be surrounded by that kind of focus and energy and just walking into a SOC and listening to the general conversations or arguments that may fill the air can detect that spirit. It is also that passion that can derail an operation and cause it to stray from its intended purpose while creating a riff in an organizations cultural eco-system.

Running a SOC is a careful balance between what an organization believes it needs to reduce risks and the threats the SOC sees it needs to protect the organization from. Everyone in the SOC needs to remember why they are here, to protect the organization and its users the best way they know how with the best tools and capabilities they can get a hold of.

No matter what type of SOC or what your focus is, make sure you are making good on your core responsibilities and you are taking care of not only the people you protect but also the people who are doing the protecting. The SOC has an amazing list of tasks to accomplish and it's an ever-growing list. Make sure that you properly define that list of tasks, generate all the detailed requirements, and get the proper authority to take on those responsibilities. Your SOC needs to know who the customers are and why the SOC is here doing its job. Once you lose sight of the fact that it is a services organization that must meet the demands of its customers and users then the SOC has failed in its mission regardless of how smart it is or how technically able it is to defend against threats. Customers can be anyone, it is not the servers and networks it monitors but rather the different departments, groups, teams, or external third parties that an organization works with. Sit down with your customers and go over the services the SOC has and its areas of responsibilities so that each and every customer has a good idea of why the SOC is here and what it can do for them. Engage with the customers, keep them up to date, and build use cases with them to make them part of the solution. Do not forget about meeting the expectations of the SOC, ensure that you constantly drive toward making improvements, and listening to your customers on how you can improve and ultimately protect the organization better.

It is not cheap to build a SOC and all the hardware, software, and equipment needed to protect an organization can be mind-blowing when you add up all the costs. Make sure you start small and focus on key areas. Do not take on more than you can handle, start with small key successes, and build over time. Look for key capital purchase such as SIEM systems that help you organize and prepare for future expansion and give you tomorrow's capabilities inside of today's tool sets. Make sure you track your events and incidents so that you can gain valuable insight into trends and review key analysis. Ensure that your tracking and documentation processes of analysis are not harder than the analysis itself. Customize your internal tracking system when you can and simplify your processes at every opportunity. Build yourself a knowledge base, do not leave anything up to anyone to remember. Make sure that your key documentation is always available, easily accessible, and easy to read and understand.

There is nothing wrong with building your own tools opposed to going out and buying commercially available tools. In fact, some of the very best commercial systems being used to monitor and defend networks today were once a home-grown system. Ensure that if you do decide to build your own system, no matter what its used for or its intended purpose, that you are not spending more time developing and supporting that tool then actually using the tool for its designed value and purpose. When you make a strategic decision to purchase a commercial tool, it is not just an investment in a capability, it is an investment in the vendor and a vote of confidence in the product line. Work closely with your vendors, make sure you hold them accountable for the features and functionalities that they said you can get from their products. Building positive relationships with your vendors will aid in getting appropriate support, training and ultimately satisfying your requirements that led you to purchase in the first place. Looks for ways to reduce costs, if you do not need 100% of your organization covered by licenses today then see if you can get a volume discount that can be phased in over time. This gives you the ability to save money while you go through the long process of implementing new systems and technology. Additionally, do not pay for functions that you do not think you will be able to take advantage of right away. Negotiate pricing up front but hold off on any add-ons or features that you will not need right away if possible. There are many things that your SOC is going to need and it is not feasible that they will be able to take full advantage of every feature or capability of every product right out of the box from the start. Make sure that your purchases are cost effective for your organization and that you get only what you need. You will find that this practice will help you negotiate better terms with your vendors but also help contribute to internal budgets and potential cash flow constraints.

Build a SOC organization that makes sense for your needs, add the required layers of management only when necessary to stay operationally focused in ensuring your meeting expectations. Split up your teams in focus areas that make sense either to the technology they are using, or the areas that they are monitoring. The structure of the team should make the SOC more efficient and quicker to act. Reporting lines for the SOC is important but not as important as the overall mission. If the mission is impacted by the SOC management or senior leaders then look to fix those issues through effective communication, proper metrics, and market the successes. Make sure that you have a fully vetted and supported charter that sets the tone for the overall SOC mission. Ensure that the organization takes the mission of the SOC seriously by empowering the SOC's responsibilities and authority through policy. Do not wait for someone to intervene or an incident to occur in order to build a relationship. Work closely with all the different departments in your organization to help establish proper roles and responsibilities, then authority will not matter because everyone with work together in achieving common goals.

Your people are your most important asset and well training security people are difficult or expensive to obtain. Clearly define the roles in your SOC for everyone to see and for everyone to know and understand how they fit into the overall big picture. Analysts come in many different shapes and sizes and although they are typically looked at as some of the most junior of people in the SOC they are characteristically your most important. Having analysts that can spot issues before they become problems is worth a lot. The ability to triage an issue and make the right calls during the incident response process is paramount to the overall success of the SOC in protecting the organization. Engineers need to work hard to stay on top of the equipment and infrastructure that they manage and maintain for the SOC. One bad configuration can flood the SOC and effectively blind the organization. Engineers being some of the most technical resources in your SOC need to be held accountable. They need to make sure that they can help move the SOC forward but not at the expense of others. They need to lead by example for others in the SOC and continually strive to learn their craft to continually increase the security posture of the organization. All the while, engineers need to be monitoring and adjusting in order to defend against the ever increasing skill and stealth tradecraft of the attackers.

Managers and supervisors need to know their people, they need to know their organization and know security. They need to be able to translate all that knowledge into action and execution while ensuring transparent communication throughout the entire organization.

Build your people and build your team, promote from within and grow. Find the right people who have an aptitude for technology, a passion for security and a personality that fits. Train them and provide them with the skills and knowledge to be successful. Give them opportunities to advance and keep them going with positive reinforcement, acknowledgement of achievement and increased responsibility. Work does not have to be boring, have fun, and come up with creative programs that keep people engaged and focused. Allow people to take a break from the norm to work on special teams or special projects and not always suffer with the routine daily grind.

Your SOC has a mission, make sure that you can carry out that mission appropriately for your organization. Weather you need to run a business hours only SOC in one location or a follow the Sun model across many international SOCs ensure that you have the right processes in place to address critical operational needs. Communication is key to ensuring that nothing gets missed and that key tasks and problems do not get dropped. Communicate from shift to shift and SOC to SOC, put important processes in place for people to get help when needed and ensure that management can address issues before they become bigger problems. Performing incident response can be stressful, make sure that you have well thought-out checklists available to ensure that in the heat of the battle all required items are properly covered. Create exercises that test people under real conditions and evaluate responses. Get everyone from the organization involved, security is a team sport.

Train each person in the SOC how to do their job and the required functions of each role. Make sure that training is conducted on the job along with more senior people so evaluation of proficiency and support can be provided. Vendor training and third party certification training reinforces needed job skills and gives organizations good measures to help evaluate training needs of the individual. Make sure that all training is not technical, ensure that everyone understands who the customers are and how to best serve the customers. The SOC must be customer focused and everyone must have the soft skills to ensure they are providing the best possible service. The best security teams and SOCs will go un-noticed, un-funded, and undervalued if the proper attitudes and customer service is lacking or non-existent.

Make sure you build a continuous improvement program for as many areas of the SOC as possible. Ensure you are providing the right training for the right services and in the right areas.

Measure as many of the areas of the SOC as you possibly can, if you cannot measure it then you cannot improve it. The metrics and data that are generated should be geared for the specific user who will review the reports and associated information. Do not just build charts and graphs because they look good or that they are the ones everyone makes. Ensure that you are getting the right metrics to improve your programs, spot trouble areas or to track efficiency. Think about metrics that support the efforts to secure the organization and how different metrics can be leverage to make real-time decisions and course correction. Good actionable metrics should be displayed for everyone to see and should help guild work efforts or indicate problems. Put key metrics and performance indicators out on a reliable time schedule for all to see and look at. Use the metrics as fact-based justifications for change and for a service impact to show all the value of your SOC to the customer.

Building intelligence is one of the primary methods of a mature SOC to stay one step ahead of threats and be proactive in its approach. Ensuring that complete analysis details are wrapped back into the SOC tools sets to ensure the detection of additional activity is critical. Sharing information and participating in external intelligence-driven communities not only helps your organization but others as well. Participation in intelligence networks can provide the SOC an invaluable information source that can help detect activity never previously known about or that would have taken several months to figure out. Combine malware analysis, forensic analysis, and key event analysis along with external intelligence information to better arm your SOC with specific signatures and rules that are custom tailored to your environment and that is designed to defend against key threat actors.

All of these tasks and activities are vital the successful defending of an organizations computing assets. Building, designing, and executing on all of this is too much for many organizations to handle. Instead look for key business relationships that can be leveraged and outsource the specific items that are modular enough for an external entity to be successful with. Ensure that the partner you choose is capable of meeting your demands but at the same time make sure that you are asking for something that is reasonable. Metrics and SLAs are there to guide you and keep you and your outsourced partner on track. If your expectations are not being met then put in tests to find out why, work with your outsourcer to resolve the issues before they become unmanageable problems.

The SOC is a fun and rewarding place to be, work and live. It is the epicenter of security and can be magical when everything goes right and can be a dungeon when everything goes wrong. There are new SOCs being built every day and many existing SOCs looking to make things better. Use the tactics, techniques, and procedures in this book to build your SOC or make it a better place but most of all I hope that this book will help give you the ideas, motivation, and direction that will ultimately help you protect your organization.

# Appendix A

Threats and attacks

Threat vectors:
> An entry point or media that an attacker can use to carry out an attack.

802.11 Wireless
CD ROM/DVD ROM
Bluetooth
Cloud computing
Email
Files
Instant messaging
Internet connectivity
Malicious proxy
NFC scanning
Onion routing networks
P2P
QR scanning
Remote access
Rogue tunnels
Social engineering
Social networking sites
Terminal services
USB storage devices
Voice over IP
Web browser
Web page

Attack types:
> Names given to common methods of disrupting, degrading, destroying, or denying access to a system or resource. Can also be the name of a method that is used to collect data and information.

Backdoors
Botnets
Buffer overflow
Cache poisoning
Cross site scripting
DDOS
DNS reflection
DOS
Eavesdropping/sniffing
Exploits
Key logging
Man in the middle
Password cracking
Pharming
Phishing
Physical theft
Rootkits
Spear phishing
Spoofing
Spyware
SQL injection
Statistical anomaly
Suspicious activity
Trojan horse
Virus
Whaling

# Appendix B

Security devices:

Types of security-relevant devices and systems that can be used to protect an organization and/or feed into a central logging server or SIEM system.

Active directory
Antivirus
Anything that can send SNMP alerts and is security relevant
Anything that can send syslog and is security relevant
Application logs
Asset management system
Authentication logs
Change management system
Database application logs
Data loss prevention
DHCP server
DNS server
DNS servers
Email filtering
Email logs
Evidence collector
Firewall (host/network)
File transfer monitor
Forensic analysis systems
Honeypots
Key management system
Network- and host-based intrusion detection/prevention systems
Intelligence tools
Netflow
Network access controls
Network switches, routers
Operating system logs
Packet sniffer
Proxy server
Routers
SIEM
Two factor systems
VPN system
Vulnerability scanner
Web server
Web proxies
Wireless AP

# Appendix C

Types of functions and services that can be performed in a SOC.
Each service can be provided in one or more of five categories:

- Network
- Host
- Application
- Data
- Intelligence

Application security
Application whitelisting
Audit data distribution
Authentication management
Behavioral monitoring
Binary whitelisting
Blackhole routing
Business liaison
Business continuity
Call center activities
Communicate with executives or outside law enforcement
Content creation, management, and auditing
Database monitoring
DDOS mitigation
Disaster recovery
Device monitoring and management
eDiscovery
Emergency announcements and communications
Emerging threat research
Encryption/certificate services management
Endpoint identity
Endpoint management
Forensic analysis
Forensic artifact collection
Fraud detection

File integrity monitoring
File whitelist management
Host hardening/configuration monitoring
Host intrusion monitoring
Incident analysis, coordination, and response
Insider threat case support
Insider threat modeling
Internet misuse
Intelligence collection and analysis
Log management
Mobile device management/ monitoring
Mobile device recovery
Malware analysis, reverse engineering
Malware impact analysis
Metrics and reporting
Netflow analysis
Network mapping
Patch management
Penetration testing
Phishing detection
Policy and compliance
Product assessment
Real-time monitoring
Remote incident response
Risk evaluation
Rouge device detection

Rouge wireless device detection

Rule creation

Scripting and automation

Security device tuning

Security tool engineering and development

Security training and awareness programs

Signature creation

Situational wareness

SPAM policy management

Strategic security advice and guidance

Surveillance

Third party security

Threat and vulnerability management

Tradecraft analysis

Triage

Unknown binary analysis

User administration/identity management

Unauthorized access

Vulnerability scanning

VPN management

Web application malware monitoring

Web proxy policy management

Wireless monitoring/management

# Glossary

| | |
|---|---|
| AV | antivirus software |
| APT | advanced persistent threat |
| BC | business continuity |
| C&C | command and control |
| C2 | command and control |
| CISO | chief information security officer |
| DNSBL | Domain name system blacklist |
| DR | disaster recovery |
| EOC | emergency operations center |
| ePHI | electronic protected health information |
| GRC | governance, risk, and compliance |
| HIPPA | health insurance portability & accountability act |
| IR | incident response |
| IT | information technology |
| ITIL | information technology infrastructure library |
| KPI | key performance indicators |
| MOC | mission operations center |
| MSL | master station log |
| MTA | mail transfer agent |
| NAT | network address translation |
| NOC | network operations center |
| OSINT | open source intelligence |
| OT | operational technology |
| OJT | on-the-job training |
| P2P | peer-to-peer |
| PCI | payment card industry |
| PCI-DSS | payment card industry-data security standards |
| PHI | protected health information |
| PII | personal identified information |
| POC | proof of concept |
| RFI | request for information |
| RFP | request for proposal |
| SCADA | supervisory control and data acquisition |
| SDLC | system development life cycle |
| SLA | service level agreement |
| SLO | service level objectives |
| SMS | short message service |
| SOC | security operations center |

| | |
|---|---|
| SOP | standard operating procedure |
| SOX | Sarbanes–Oxley act |
| TOC | threat operations center |
| TOR | the onion routing |
| TTP | tactics, techniques, and procedures |
| URI | universal resource identifier |
| US-CERT | United States computer emergency response team |
| VPN | virtual private network |

# Index

Printed in the United States
By Bookmasters